BLACK TUESDAY OVER NAMSI

A True History of the Epic Air Battle of the Korean War

Earl J. McGill
Lt. Col. USAF (Ret.)

EAGLE EDITIONS
2008

EAGLE EDITIONS
AN IMPRINT OF HERITAGE BOOKS, INC.

Books, CDs, and more—Worldwide

For our listing of thousands of titles see our website
at
www.HeritageBooks.com

Published 2008 by
HERITAGE BOOKS, INC.
Publishing Division
100 Railroad Ave. #104
Westminster, Maryland 21157

International Standard Book Number: 978-0-7884-4619-1

Dedicated to all B-29 flight and ground personnel who served in the Forgotten War

Of an event that too many refer to as "The Forgotten War:" Find here remembered a story of great and common men, of bounty and sacrifice, of life and death, of America, Korea and a freedom so costly won. Find here a story to tell to your children so that they too may know and understand how high to carry the torch.

John N. Duquette, Lt. Col. USA (ret)
Every Man a Tiger Web Site

History is opaque. You see what comes out, not the script that produces events . . . There is a fundamental incompleteness in your grasp of such events, since you do not see what's inside the box, how the mechanisms work . . . the generator of historical events is different from the events themselves, much as the minds of the gods cannot be read just by witnessing their deeds.

Nassim Nicholas Taleb
The Black Swan

Table of Contents

LIST OF ILLUSTRATIONS

Back Cover: B-29, serial #44-86295, Baker Lead, commanded by Lt. William Reeter on Black Tuesday. (Photo was taken on an earlier daylight combat mission.) *Courtesy of Alan Reeter*

FOREWORD

Black Tuesday over Namsi chronicles the calamitous B-29 daylight-bombing mission flown by the 307th Bombardment Wing on 23 October 1951 against Namsi Airfield. What many experts consider the epic air battle of the Korean War and perhaps the greatest jet engagement in the history of aerial warfare has largely become another forgotten battle in a forgotten war. The few accounts that exist have been reconstructed, for the most part, from disorganized and sometimes inaccurate US and Russian government records. Most are from the fighter pilot's perspective and do not provide the information or insights into the 307th's vital and tragic role on the mission that forever ended massed-formation precision daylight bombing.

Astonishingly, virtually nothing has been published about this event. Official Air Force historical records mention it only in passing. Literature of the period too often emphasizes the gung ho aspect of Hollywood-type action movies rather than the grim reality of war. Most of what is written is, in fact, rife with exaggeration, myth, and downright lies. Some of this is most certainly the result of the way the war was reported; mostly by young, inexperienced airmen who thought this was the proper way to impress their commanding officers. A more serious hindrance to sorting out events that took place half a century ago is simply finding the records. Much of the Korean War paperwork was sent to the National Archives (NARA) in cardboard boxes, unsorted, and in no particular order.

In an effort to find an accurate account of the great air battle of the "forgotten war," I employed several methods, but mostly a tool that was not available until recently, the Internet search engine. My Internet searches have yielded numerous informative pieces from combatants on both sides of the Korean War. Unfortunately, very few touched on the Black Tuesday mission. One short piece detailed events after the mission and the only other references contained errors that have little to do with what actually happened. As for written material (except for John R. Bruning's, *Crimson Sky, The Air Battle for Korea*), none of the published material, historical or otherwise, acknowledged the sacrifices of the airmen involved or showed appreciation for what they experienced.

This book is the result of several fortuitous occurrences. After viewing my "B-29s in the Korean War" web site, Rolland Miller, left gunner on the crew of the Able Flight lead B-29 on the Black Tuesday mission, emailed me. Rolland provided a great deal of information about the mission, including the email addresses of the navigator, Fred Meier, and Nick "The Greek" Kourafas, the bombardier. Together, we were able to assemble a series of Black Tuesday web pages. Then, on the occasion of the 50th anniversary of the Korean War, Rolland suggested I write and submit an article to *VFW Magazine*. The editor, Richard Kolb, accepted and published the article, which also appeared again as part of the VFW anthology, *Battles of the Korean War*.

Research for the short version of "Black Tuesday Over Namsi," published in the October 2001 issue of *VFW Magazine*, and subsequent contacts provided a treasure chest of previously unrecorded facts about the mission. Following publication, e-mail, phone calls, and letters began pouring in from other crew members that had flown the mission and from the children and grandchildren of those combatants who are no longer with us. Old scrapbooks, photographs and personal correspondence were opened for my inspection, some of them not shared in a lifetime. I felt privileged to be so honored. I also felt a growing sense of duty to write the full story of Black Tuesday with all of its ramifications, its historical significance, and especially because I felt, in no small way, that I owed my life to those who flew, fought, and were lost.

My contacts include experts on the Korean Air War, from both the Allied and the Soviet perspectives. Together, both Americans and Russians have supplied never before published photographs of the mission and its aftermath, including the aerial photo of the Namsi Airfield that was used to plan the mission. This book also records, from verifiable historical documents, the broader events and conditions that led up to confrontation, plus the first-hand accounts of aircrew members and ground personnel who were there. The facts and circumstances of the event are further verified by reconstructing the mission from first briefing to final landing. With help from others who were actually there, I've assembled what I believe is a true and accurate account of that historically important but forgotten air battle, the story of a Korean War bombing mission on a day marked forever in the minds of Allied airmen who flew and fought in the Korean War as Black Tuesday.

ACKNOWLEDGMENTS

Without the following eyewitness contributors, this project could not have lifted off the runway (listed alphabetically):

Fred L. Beissner, Jr: Copilot on Baker Two.
C. J. Christ: Copilot, Oct. 22 1951 mission.
Ray Coia: Radio Operator at Able SHORAN (Ground) Site.
Archibald Cummings: Flight Engineer on Baker Three.
Paul Dickerson (D): Right Gunner on Baker Three.
R. W. Gray: Commander, 15th TRS at Kimpo AFB, S. Korea.
Jim Higgins: Radar Operator on Charlie Two.
Stan Kavrik: Copilot, Oct. 24 1951 mission.
Nick Kourafas: Bombardier on Able Lead.
Francis Kroboth: Flight Engineer on Charlie Two.
Fred Meier: Navigator on Able Lead.
Rolland L. Miller: Left Gunner on Able Lead.
Edward Moore: Radio Operator on Charlie Two.
Max Nelson: Radar Operator, Oct. 24 1951 mission.
Walter H. Polk: Crew Chief on Baker Lead.
Dewell Turner: Left Gunner on Baker Three.
John Wagenhalls: Bombardier on Charlie Three.
Lloyd Wentworth: Navigator on Baker Two.

I owe special thanks to Fred Meier, Rolland Miller, and Nick "the Greek" Kourafas, the aircrew members on Able One who launched this project by providing first hand accounts, documents, and personal insights into the Black Tuesday mission; to John Duquette who provided much of the material and most of the incentive for me to get into this project; to Alan Reeter, Jack Shields, and George Pyfrom, whose fathers flew the mission and are no longer with us; to Stephen "Cookie" Sewell, whose translations and interpretations provided the core of Soviet involvement chronicled; to Ralph Livengood (who passed away while this book was in progress) for *B-29 Navigator, Korean War 1951*; to Bud Farrell for his unwavering support and invaluable source of Korean War B-29 material in his book, *No Sweat*; to Diego Zampini for his unstinting assistance in providing firsthand accounts and impressions from the Russian perspective: and to Richard Kolb, editor of *VFW Magazine*, for his assistance in publishing the original article that inspired this book.

I must also thank Clyde Durham for his expertise and sharp eye for picking out mistakes in the manuscript. Clyde's newspaper experience, combined with service as a B-29 gunner on twenty-six Korean War combat missions in the same unit I flew with, provided a unique and invaluable perspective that I was indeed fortunate to have available when needed.

*   *   *

The material contained in this book is the end result of seven years of research into a core event that lasted fifteen minutes. In spite of having taken place in a mere snippet of time, the air battle over Namsi has been clouded by misinterpretations and contradictions. In sorting through the many inconsistencies, I have endeavored to reach a consensus of "truth" by weighing the evidence and writing what I believe is closest to the truth. I apologize to those whose views may differ, acknowledging that any errors contained herein are mine and mine alone. EJM

INTRODUCTION

An hour and a half before sunup on Tuesday, October 23, 1951, nine B-29s of the 307th Bombardment Wing lifted off from Kadena Air Force Base, Okinawa on a bombing mission against Namsi, a North Korean airfield under construction in the heart of MiG Alley. Five and a half hours later they would engage in an air battle that would forever change the conduct of strategic aerial bombardment. Six of the nine would not return, the highest percentage of United States bombers ever lost on a major mission.

*   *   *

Following the mission briefing the evening before, Able Flight lead navigator, First Lieutenant Fred Meier, had scribbled in his diary, "Supposed to go on R & R but briefed for MiG Alley mission. Namsi Airfield." In a letter to his wife, Libbie, he instructed her to cancel the Buick order, concluding, "I don't think you would have liked it anyhow."

The last bomber to take off replaced a B-29 grounded by engine trouble. The nine proceeded over the East China Sea to the assembly point where the formation divided itself into three flights of three aircraft. Due to lower cloud cover over the target, the formation would employ an electronic system, called SHORAN, recently developed so precision bombing could be conducted without actually seeing the target.

As the World War II heavy bombers lumbered toward Namsi, they passed through a maelstrom of radar-directed anti-aircraft flak. Two of the nine were severely damaged. Moments before bombs away, a swarm of MiG-15s, the newest, fastest jets in the Soviet arsenal, attacked the bomber force. Three B-29s were shot down over the target area and three more were so severely damaged they were forced to make emergency landings at a forward base. Only one of the remaining three escaped major battle damage. In the bloodiest air battle of the Korean War, six bombers and twenty-seven lives were lost. Twenty crew members were wounded and eight taken prisoner. In percentages, "Black Tuesday" marked the greatest loss on any major bombing mission in any war the United States has ever engaged in, and the ensuing battle in a chunk of sky called "MiG Alley" still ranks as perhaps the greatest jet air battle of all time.

North Korean and Chinese pilots supposedly flew the MiGs. Factually, the pilots who attacked the B-29s were members of the elite 64th Fighter Aviation Group, a crack, battle-seasoned unit from the Soviet Union.

Years of speculation have led to varying theories as to why, on that fateful October morning in 1951, the B-29s were sent to Namsi. The official reason was, of course, to bomb the airfield in such a manner that it would be rendered useless as a MiG base. Although this undoubtedly was the primary objective, those who argue the incongruities of the mission, correctly point out that the objective could have been accomplished under cover of darkness, employing the same SHORAN bombing techniques that were used when the bombers were most vulnerable to visual attack. By its very nature, SHORAN bombing in broad daylight subjected the aircraft and crews to the greatest risks. Throughout the bomb run, when the danger of attack was greatest, the pilots were required to fly a continuous arc that precluded evasive maneuvers. Because of the added risk of mid-air collision, one ship was dropped from the usual diamond formation, leaving three instead of four. The remaining three had to be spread out, denying the bomber force its most effective and potent protection, concentrated defensive firepower.

This is the story of the Americans and Russians who clashed in the skies above Namsi, the events leading up to it, Black Tuesday's historical impact on aerial warfare, and, for the first time, fresh conclusions based on a careful analysis of the specific factors that went into the execution of this and other bombing missions.

*   *   *

A few days after Black Tuesday I was seated in the copilot's seat of a B-29, waiting for the takeoff order that would send the 19th Bombardment Group deep into MiG Alley. Parked just down the Kadena ramp from the 307th on Okinawa, we had witnessed, first hand, the aftermath of what had happened to our sister unit. We were going back, many of us felt, to our certain destruction--until a last minute reprieve returned us to quarters. Because of the bloody results of Black Tuesday, daylight B-29 missions into MiG Alley, we were told, had come to an end. Those minutes before the reprieve taught me the meaning of fear, which I have never experienced since, not even now as life grows short. So it is with gratitude that cannot be adequately expressed that I will attempt, like another old soldier, Bernal Diaz, who marched and fought with Cortez during the conquest of Mexico and wanted, before he died, to set the record straight. In Bernal's words, my wish is to tell the story "with God's help ...without twisting the facts in any way." EJM

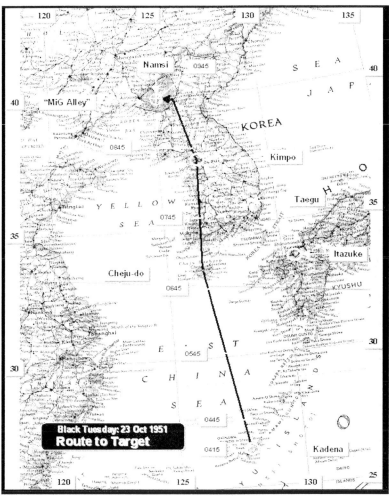

Courtesy of John Duquette

1: The Mission

My crew and I were crouched around a fifty-caliber ammunition crate, playing poker in our hut overlooking the Kadena flight line. We were trying to push the war out of our minds. Autumn, which had started out as a milk run, had turned sour. On the second of October we'd survived crashing *The Outlaw* on takeoff. Ten days later, Typhoon Ruth provoked a full-scale evacuation of our Okinawa-based B-29s to Japan, and knocked our tin hut off its foundation. To take a leak in the elevated toilet we had to stand on a chair--the least of our worries. The day before, up north, MiG-15s had jumped our group's twelve-ship formation and shot down one B-29. Now we were sweating out news of our sister unit, the 307th Bombardment Wing. Rumor was they'd run into big trouble. When word came they were inbound, we folded our hands, piled into a Jeep, and headed for the flight line. Minutes later, we saw a lone bomber silhouetted against the tranquil Pacific sky. One B-29 out of nine--with a hole in the tail fin we could see sky through.

*   *   *

For the 307th crews, the mission had begun with a 1900 briefing the night before. Lt. Nick Kourafas, lead bombardier, and his navigator, Lt. Fred Meier, had worked all afternoon, planning and making computations. Namsi Airfield was less than fifty miles southeast of Antung and its politically protected jet fighter bases in China. The nine aircraft formation would be attacking a target within easy range of more than a hundred MiG-15s stationed there. As a veteran of 44 missions, Nick knew what that could mean.

On May third, Kourafas and Meier had received spot promotions to first lieutenant. They would fly their entire tour together and lose their promotions when their tour ended in November 1951. Meier remembers that the crew's first radio operator, a Texan, found religion while flying the B-29 and always read The Bible on their way to the target. They also had a different Central Fire Controller (CFC) who was tall, lanky, and older than Fred Spivey, their new CFC. Their left gunner, Rolland Miller, had flown his first combat mission when he was 18. This mission to Namsi would be his 45th and make him a seasoned combat veteran at 19. Meier called their crew aircraft commander, Captain Clarence Fogler, "the lucky one." 'Fog' had survived the brutal low-level Ploesti raids of WW II. He'd also brought his crew home from the deadly April 12 mission against the bridges at Sinuiju. With luck he would also bring them home from Namsi.

Meier wrote in his diary, "I hope I'm wrong but I think the MiGs will be in the area."

Major William Griner, acting squadron operations officer for the 372nd, took over as commander on aircraft #44-86295, substituting for Capt. Brisey who was unable to fly because he'd sprained his wrist.

Wake up was at 0100; take off at 0415.

At 0230, Airman Second Class Dewell Turner, on loan from the 301st Bomb Wing and assigned TDY as a spare gunner with the 307th, was awakened by the charge of quarters and told he would be flying with Major Griner in place of a gunner who'd been grounded. Turner's late assignment precluded him being in on the pre-flight duties, except for the last minute prior to boarding. He noted in retrospect that the short notice was probably a good thing because it didn't give him time to contemplate the gravity of the mission. Major Griner and his CFC interviewed Turner briefly before take off and placed him in the left gunner's seat.

Another 301st substitute gunner who had accompanied Turner from Barksdale, Paul Stainbrook, was picked to fly with Captain Shields on aircraft #44-70151. Stainbrook hoped to be permanently assigned to Shields' crew.

For reasons that are not fully understood, a ranking officer was assigned to fly as an observer on each of the three flight lead aircraft. Colonel Henry Ledbetter joined Fogler's crew; Colonel John Carroll would fly with Reeter, and Lieutenant Colonel Julius O'Neal, slated to be the new 370th squadron commander, climbed aboard Shields' ill-fated B-29. For most of the mission, all three observers would perch on the forward compartment "aisle stand," a box with a seat belt that was situated between and slightly

Nick Kourafas, Bombardier on Able Lead. *Rolland Miller*

Rolland Miller, Left Gunner on Able Lead. *Rolland Miller*

behind the pilots. In spite of the potential for heavy flak and MiG attack, all but one of the nine aircraft would have extra personnel aboard.

Capt. James "Archie" Foulks and his crew would be flying their 44th mission. For his copilot (officially listed as "pilot" on a B-29 crew), 1st Lt. Fred Beissner Jr. and several others on the crew, Archie Foulks would be their third aircraft commander. Before Foulks took over, they'd flown with their squadron operations officer, a West Pointer, and another pilot, Major Martin L. Jones.

Flying only his second combat mission, Sgt. Edward Moore was assigned to fly as Major Field's radio operator in place of Dick Chamness, who'd managed a job swap that put him on a crew that would soon rotate back to the states. Moore, who had joined the Marine Reserves when he was sixteen, had already flown with the crew, once as a sub on the Typhoon Ruth evacuation to Yokota and again on a combat mission that was inserted into their return to Kadena.

Preflight inspections were carried out with the aid of flashlights, and it was still dark when the ten B-29s started their engines, pulled out of their revetments, taxied, and lined up for takeoff. Although four 370th squadron aircraft were scheduled to take off, one of them had an excessive rpm drop during engine run-up, and the spare took its place. Rolland Miller's gunnery school chum, Gene Woods, was on a 370th aircraft that aborted and later, the gunners who flew the mission kidded Gene about putting straight pins in the spark plug leads during the engine pressure check to cause the excessive rpm drop.

Griner's aircraft was number six in line with Shields directly behind. Although only nine aircraft would bomb Namsi, it was standard procedure on missions involving several aircraft to have a spare B-29 ready to launch. On Black Tuesday, the spare, commanded by Major Don Field, himself a volunteer, filled-in for the aircraft that aborted because of engine trouble.

The huge Box Y on its vertical stabilizer identified a B-29 as belonging to the 307th Bombardment Group, and the foot-wide color band at the tip designated which squadron it was assigned to. Green identified a 370th B-29, yellow the 371st, and the 372nd was painted red. Like all B-29 aircraft, each bomb symbol on the nose denoted a combat mission. Unlike other units, the 307th had no nose art.

In turn, each bomber lined up on the runway, throttling all four engines for a full power check before brake release and the agonizingly slow acceleration that would often gobble up the entire available runway before lift off. With landing gear and flaps coming up, the B-29 was flown level and often appeared, to the ground observer, to be settling back to earth as it gathered speed, usually to 190 mph, calibrated airspeed, before resuming its climb to 5000 - 9000 feet.

After leveling off, the bomber crews were in for a boring two and a half hour grind over the open East China Sea that gave them way too much time to think about what lay ahead. Cpl. Rolland Miller and his crewmates on Able Lead occupied some of their time by having an in-flight lunch, "C" or "K" rations packed inside a 2"x 6"x 8" brown cardboard box with the contents printed on the outside. The several choices included small cans of pork and applesauce or beef stew, packages of crackers, cans of peaches or fruit cocktail and chocolate bars. There was also a napkin, which could be used for toilet paper, and a tiny folding "P-38" can opener, which almost everyone who had anything to do with rations attached to his dog tag chain. Crew members in the aft compartment heated cans of meat on the Aldis signal lamps or the radar operator's equipment inverter. Some rations contained meat in double-walled cans. Holes could be punched in the top of the outer can and water added. Chemical reaction heated the inner can. Miller remembers the meal "because it was always the same," adding, "We usually tried to eat before formation assembly so in case something happened and we went down we would have a partially filled stomach."

Fred Meier recalls, "The flight lunches were WW II vintage leftovers, sometimes rotten and inedible."

Toward the end of their flight over the East China Sea, the bombers climbed to their formation altitude. "I couldn't believe they sent us with no altitude equipment," Meier recollects. A drop of water on the deck turned to ice instantly, and he was forced to sit on his feet to keep them from freezing.

First light streaked the horizon fifteen minutes before they reached the assembly point, but sunup was still twelve minutes away, at 6:57 local time. Headwinds had been stronger than

Lt. Reeter (l.), Baker Lead A/C, briefs his crew before take-off.

Capt. Lewis (kneeling, l.) and crew of Able Two,
Black Tuesday mission.

predicted, necessitating the aircraft speed up in order to arrive at the assembly and fighter rendezvous points on time. This required more power; therefore more fuel. The climb to 19-21,000 feet was begun to arrive at altitude over the orbit/assembly point, Cheju-do, a volcanic island in the southwest sea of the Korean peninsula.

Cheju-do is large and oval-shaped, with Halla, an extinct volcano, situated almost dead center. The 6,400' cone presented a perfect radar return, therefore an ideal coast-in point for northbound B-29s. To the people in the region, Cheju-do has always been a place of mystery, and the constant parade of bombers circling and massing far overhead could have only added to that mystery.

Time limited the orbit to one big circle before proceeding north as three separate three-ship formations. In Able Flight, Capt. James Lewis flew Fogler's right wing, while Capt. Robert Krumm held position on the left. Behind them Lt. William Reeter, accompanied by the 372nd Squadron C. O, headed up Baker Flight with Capt. James Foulks on the right and Major William Griner flying left wing. Capt. Thomas Shields led Charlie Flight. Major Donald Field flew on his right and Lt. Peter Dempsey on the left.

At 0745 the nine bombers passed near Kwanju on the southern Korean Peninsula. An hour later the formation crossed the front lines into North Korean airspace, but there was no need to go on the defensive just yet. For the next fifty-five minutes they would be flying through skies ruled by American and British fighters. At 0940 that would change.

Farther up the peninsula, their fighter escorts, straight wing F-84s, joined the nine B-29s. Another formation of more advanced sweptwing F-86s flew high cover ahead of them.

On the north side of the Yalu, Soviet communications monitoring systems detected the heavy radio traffic, indicating a major air attack was brewing--confirmed a short time later, at 0910, on their radar screens. The size and direction of the inbound bombers indicated a major attack and the decision was made to launch all of the fighters they could get airborne. Thirty-eight of the most advanced fighters in the Soviet arsenal, Mikoyan-Gurevich MiG-15s, commanded by Lt. Col. Aleksandr Pavlovich Smorchkov, were the first to take off.

Because the forecast layer of lower clouds prevented bombardiers from seeing the target, a newly developed electronic bombing system called "SHORAN" was to be used. Although the system enabled crew radar/SHORAN operators to pinpoint small targets with great accuracy, the procedure required keeping the aircraft centered on an electronically generated arc. Signals from the operator controlled an instrument on the pilot's panel that was little more than a needle with calibrations. Keeping the needle centered at twelve o'clock kept the aircraft on the arc, but flying in a continuous banking maneuver made close formation impossible--even dangerous. It also precluded concentrating the B-29s' firepower. The massed concentration of firepower that a large, tight formation afforded was their greatest source of protection against enemy fighters. Instead, the formation would be divided into Able, Baker and Charlie, three-ship flights, strung out in a manner that subjected them to defensive blind spots and made them extremely vulnerable to attack.

Shortly after passing over the initial point on the arc for the bomb run, nearing Taechon, North Korea, the bombers came under heavy and accurate anti-aircraft (AAA) fire. Reeter and Shields took direct hits.

Fogler's left gunner, Rolland Miller, watched as the puffs of deadly flak faded. He aimed his personal camera at Krumm's B-29 to catch the moment of bombs away. Just as the shutter snapped, he heard the dreaded word, "MiGs!"

Smorchkov and his MiG-15s attacked high from the right side of Charlie Flight. He lined up behind Shield's lead bomber and fired his cannons. His first burst missed, but the second set the B-29 wing on fire. At the same time, one of his wingmen, Nikolay L. Korniyenkom, hit Dempsey's B-29.

Meanwhile, Major Dmitriy Pavlovich Os'kin and his five wingmen were attacking Able and Baker Flights. Os'kin caught Krumm in his sights before moving back to Foulks in the Baker two slot. Stepan Antonovich Bakhayev shot out engine #3 and pierced the fuel tanks in the right wing of Krumm's aircraft. Georgiy Dyachenko's attack inflicted heavy damage on Reeter's aircraft.

The enemy fighters had overflown the F-86s and barreled right through the outclassed F-84s. With 182 aircraft swirling in the sky above Namsi, the largest single air battle of the Korean War had broken out over MiG Alley.

Foulks' B-29 was fatally wounded on Os'kin's first pass. With his left wing burning, and losing power, he fell out of formation and bailed out his crew. More MiGs, piloted by Captain Stepan Bakhayev, Lieutenant Georgiy Dyachenko and Captain Sergey Bychkov attacked head on. Krumm was taken out next.

Fred Meier would record four nose, four pursuit, and 37 tail attacks. Two MiGs buzzed by his window at near supersonic speeds with F-84s on their tails. The crew's Central Fire Controller, Fred Spivey, poured fire into the MiGs. One pulled up and to the left and Nick Kourafas, the bombardier, got off hundreds of rounds, which appeared to find their mark as the jet shuddered and seemed to hang in the air not a hundred yards away.

Miller spotted another about a half mile out, closing rapidly from eight o'clock. Puffs of smoke were coming from the nose cannons as Miller framed him in his gun sight and fired. Pieces of metal peeled off the fighter's wing as he rolled and passed under the tail.

With Foulks shot down, Baker Flight was in disarray. Reeter and Griner had wounded and dying aboard. A 37mm cannon shell had blown up inside Reeter's plane. A shell gutted Griner's rear fuselage. Another group of MiG's had finished off Shields.

The actual battle lasted fifteen minutes.

Fogler, Reeter, and Griner turned for the nearest friendly landing strip, Kimpo Airbase near Seoul, South Korea. Observers by the Kimpo runway watched the three battle-damaged B-29s limp in with wounded aboard. Griner landed with an engine burning and his left main tires shot out. He bounced and another tire exploded as he swerved to the left and went into a sideways skid in a line directly aimed at the scattering spectators, and came to rest in a thunderous cloud of dust.

Fogler's crew landed safely, parked their plane, and surveyed their damage. Flak had riddled the bomb bay doors and tail section. They counted over 500 holes. Later they would find an unexploded shell in a fuel tank. Fog's luck had held.

Minutes after the greatest air battle of the Korean War became history, Lieutenant Norman "Duke" Duquette flew his RF-80 Shooting Star over Namsi on a bomb damage assessment run. He recalls the sky as "suddenly and eerily vacant."

Fred Meier's final entry into his diary for October 23, 1951 reads, "I never want to go there again."

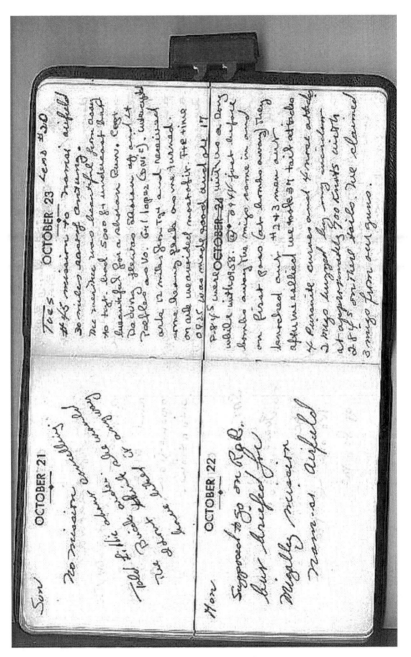

(1) Fred Meier's Diary, 21-23 October 1951. *Courtesy of Fred Meier*

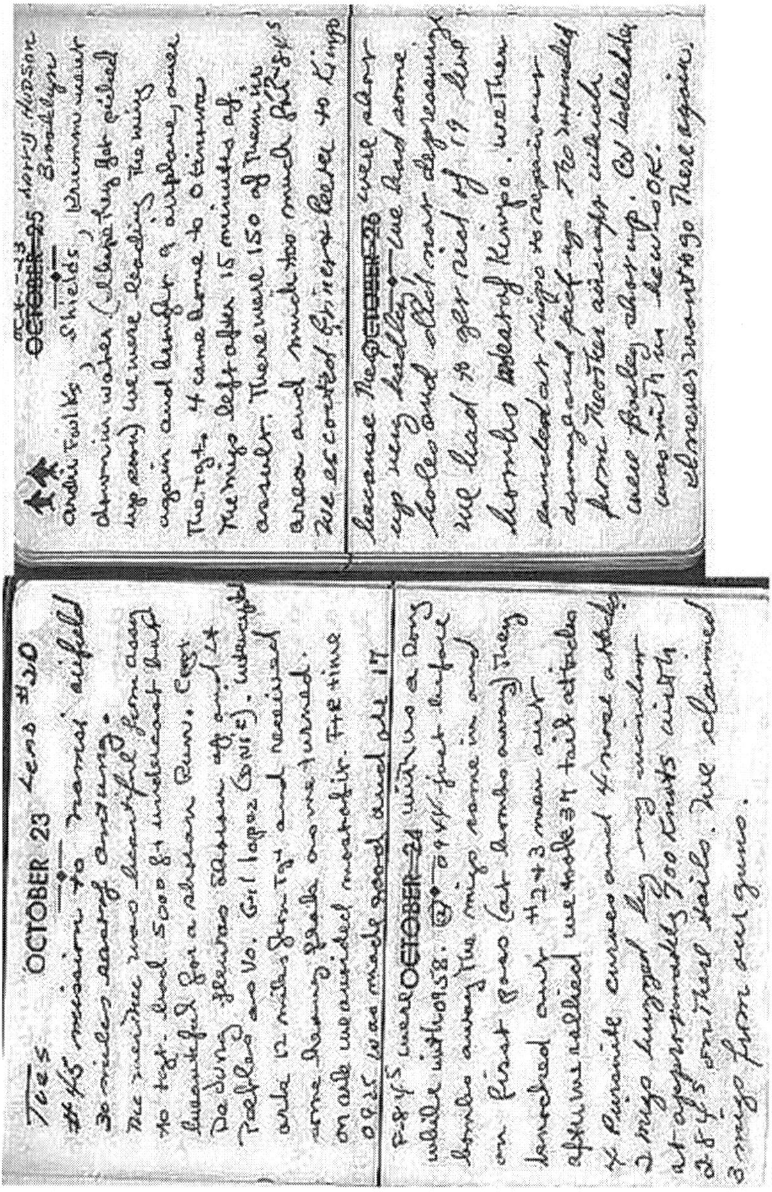

(2) Fred Meier's Diary, 23 October 1951. *Courtesy of Fred Meier*

(3) Fred Meier's Diary, 23 –27 October 1951. *Courtesy of Fred Meier*

2: The Korean Air War

Whether combat is waged on the ground, sea, or in the air, the complexities of any armed engagement confound simple analysis. Much of what a person believed took place depends to a large degree on how that person viewed the battle. The attacker sees the battle from a different perspective than the one being attacked. Perceptions can and do diverge, even from the same vantage point. This is especially true when a battle takes place in an arena as vast as the sky. Analysis of the air battle that became known as Black Tuesday has been made even more exceptional because of the bizarre rules under which it was fought.

Throughout the conflict, UN airmen complained of being "handcuffed" by political constraints that kept them from attacking the enemy where he is most vulnerable, at his home bases. Likewise, Soviet pilots stationed in Manchuria were hobbled by rules that restricted them to flying within the boundaries of a specified area over the North Korean landmass. Frustrated that they were prohibited from flying over the ocean, they complained to their superiors that when the US fighters, fighter-bombers and bombers saw that their MiG-15s were winning a battle, they always escaped towards the Yellow Sea. On the UN side, F-86 Sabre pilots complained that when the MiGs were in trouble they ran across the Yalu, knowing the Americans were prohibited from pursuing them into Manchuria. The Allies could not bomb the MiG airbases in Manchuria and Soviet pilots could not attack UN forces or pursue crippled bombers over the ocean. However, there reportedly was no such prohibition on MiG pilots if they took off from airstrips in North Korea. To take advantage of this peculiar loophole, the Communists decided to repair damaged airstrips in North Korea.

The rationale behind the seemingly inexplicable Allied rule was that the United States did not want to risk Soviet involvement, thus a wider war, by bombing targets beyond Korean borders. The Soviets, however, were already heavily involved and there is every indication that the Allies knew they were. Furthermore, on at least one occasion, (this writer's first mission, to Rashin) bombs not only impacted outside of Korean borders, they reportedly fell on Soviet soil. On the opposite side, Soviet politicos did not want their pilots captured, which would confirm the "secret" that they were truly involved. In retrospect, both sides seemed either overly paranoid or deeply delusional.

Black Tuesday was further complicated by a series of mistakes (mostly American), and although it can be stated without reservation that mistakes were made, the same could be said of any battle where there is a discernable winner. To understand what really happened that Tuesday over Namsi, it helps to examine both sides of the equation, regardless of how much their observations differ. However, to reach a degree of understanding compatible with varying, and sometimes conflicting views, we first need to place the Black Tuesday mission within the context of the Korean War in general.

Korea's history has been marked by invasion and armed conflict, particularly with Russia, China, and Japan. Eventually, in 1910, Japan defeated its competitors, annexed Korea, and remained in control until the end of World War II. At Yalta, the Allied leaders agreed that Japanese troops surrender to US forces south of the 38th parallel and to Soviet forces north of that line. As a result of this agreement, the Republic of Korea emerged in the south and the Democratic People's Republic of Korea in the north. Syngman Rhee became the Republic of Korea's first president and the Democratic People's Republic of Korea (D.P.R.K.) was established under Kim Il-sung. The country had been divided roughly in half, with Communists above the 38 degrees north latitude and pro-Westerners below. Although it continued to provide modest military aid to the South, the US withdrew its occupation forces, leaving behind a 500-man Military Advisory Group.

The West's belief that the Soviet Union masterminded the invasion of South Korea and China's intervention was largely unfounded. Still reeling from the ravages of WW II, the Soviet Union had too many of its own unsolved problems to be taking on someone else's. This did not stop them, however, from supplying their Communist allies. Feeling confident that South Korea would be a pushover, Soviet leaders began to move stockpiles of arms to the North Korean Army. With the massive amount of weapons supplied by the Soviet Union and Chinese Communist Party, North Korea launched guerrilla warfare against the South.

Fighting in the south, as well as clashes between southern and northern forces along the 38th parallel, intensified during 1948-50. Over ten thousand North Korean youths were taken to the Soviet Union for military training. A draft was instituted, and two divisions of the former Korean Volunteer Army in China that had trained under the Chinese Communists returned to North Korea.

At the same time, conditions in the South deteriorated. A major rebellion on Cheju-do Island in April 1948 claimed tens of thousands of lives. South Korea's military forces were plagued by mutinies and defections while a Communist-led revolt of army regiments, known as the Yosu-Sunch'on rebellion, monopolized the army's dwindling resources. In reaction to the rebellion, a law passed in December 1949 made communism a crime.

When it became clear that guerrilla warfare could not defeat the South, North Korea massed between 150,000 and 200,000 troops along the 38th parallel. The attacking force was organized into ten infantry divisions, one tank division, and one air force division, with 210 fighter planes and 280 tanks. Soviet equipment included automatic weapons, T-34 tanks, and Yak fighter planes. The opposing South Korean army numbered fewer than 100,000 men. It lacked tanks, heavy artillery, and combat aircraft.

Most historians agree that the Truman Administration originally did not expect a major military conflict, and believed that the next war would be similar to the Second World War, with nuclear weapons put into use early on. The North Koreans took encouragement from the US policy--which also left Korea outside the US "defense line" in Asia, and the probability of American intervention. The inadvertent exclusion of South Korea from this "line" probably had as much to do with its geographical location as any other factor. The Korean Peninsula extends southward from the Asian mainland like a tongue protruding from China's mouth. It is located west of the Japanese Islands, across the Sea of Japan. To its west, on the other side of the Yellow Sea, the belly of China bulges and curves a thousand miles farther south. The entire Korean Peninsula is about 600 miles from tip to tip, varying in width from 105 to 215 miles. Except for a tiny portion in the northeast corner that touches Russia, North Korea borders China. The northern-most point of the peninsula is about on the same latitude as Boston. The 38th parallel lies four degrees to the south. The total land area for South Korea is about 61,000 sq mi, or somewhat smaller than Florida. Seasonal monsoon winds affect Korea's weather throughout the year. The southerly summer monsoon brings hot, humid weather, while the northerly winter monsoon has the opposite effect. Weather would play a vital role throughout the Korean War, especially in planning the invasion.

North Korea invaded South Korea for the same reasons all countries wage war--because they believed they could get away with it--but it is also widely accepted that the invasion was a direct result of a colossal miscalculation. A speech given by then Secretary of State Dean Acheson had mistakenly omitted South Korea as a country the United States would defend against communism.

Acheson had served as Franklin Roosevelt's Under Secretary of the Treasury before becoming Secretary of State under Truman in 1949. He believed that the best way to halt the spread of communism was by working with progressive forces in those countries threatened by internal upheaval. Acheson and George Marshall, Secretary of Defense, came under increasing attack from right-wing politicians who considered the two men to be soft on communism. Senator Joe McCarthy called for Acheson to be impeached, describing him as "the heart of the octopus." Later, Acheson would further upset the right wing when he took the side of Harry S. Truman in his dispute with General Douglas MacArthur. Acheson and Truman wanted to limit the conflict to Korea, whereas, they felt, MacArthur wanted to extend the war to China.

In a Washington, DC speech, given on 12 January 1950, Acheson told the National Press Club that the American "defensive perimeter" in the Pacific stretched from Alaska, through the Japanese archipelago and Okinawa to the Philippines. Because of this diplomatic oversight, North Korea incorrectly assumed that the United States would not defend South Korea. The Secretary of State's omission made the divided country ripe for plucking.

Emboldened by the exclusion of South Korea from the American defense line in the Pacific, Kim Il-sung decided to invade the South. He almost succeeded.

The South was ill prepared and poorly equipped to resist invasion. Before dawn on Sunday 25 June 1950, the North Korean army, spearheaded by tanks and self-propelled guns, stormed across the 38th parallel at several points and plunged southward into the Republic of Korea. At the same time, North Korean troops made an amphibious landing at Kangnung, on the east coast, and North Korean fighter aircraft attacked airfields, destroying one USAF C-54 on the ground at Kimpo. Caught unprepared, the South Korean army of Gen. Chae Byong Duk reeled back from the 200-mile border.

On the same day, the United Nations Security Council held an emergency meeting and called, in accord with its Charter, for intervention. They established a sixteen member United Nations Command (UNC) led by the United States, which included Australia, Belgium, Canada, Colombia, Ethiopia, France, Greece, Luxembourg, the Netherlands, New Zealand, the Philippines, Thailand, Turkey, and The Union of South Africa. Medical support was also provided by Denmark, India, Norway, Sweden, and Italy.

The three-year "police action" had begun.

Eight hours after the UN commitment, the USAF's 5th Air Force entered combat. Early the next morning, 682 US citizens boarded the Norwegian merchant ship *Reinholte*, which, along with other freighters, was bound for Japan. USAF SB-17 aircraft provided rescue cover, and F-82G Twin Mustang fighters provided air cover for the ships. The 374th Troop Carrier Wing (TCW) used C-54s, C-47s, and C-46s to evacuate an additional 748 persons. To protect evacuation and ROK forces, Fifth Air Force embarked on a mission to establish air superiority over South Korea. Major James W. Little fired the first shot in the first air battle of the war. Lt. William G. Hudson, flying an F-82, Twin Mustang, with Lieutenant Carl Fraser as his radar observer, scored the first aerial victory. That same evening B-26s, flying from Ashiya Air Base (AB), Japan, attacked enemy targets in South Korea, but bad weather made the raids ineffective.

Prior to the North Korean invasion of South Korea on 25 June, Air Force aircraft assets in the area consisted of F and RF-80s, F-82s, B-26s, C-54s, RB-29s, RB and SB-17s, and one B-29 Bombardment Group, the 19th stationed on Guam. When war broke, the Far East Air Forces (FEAF), commanded by Lieutenant General George E. Stratemeyer, controlled the largest USAF inventory of combat aircraft located outside the continental United States. Although FEAF had been organized for air defense, it would be used for tactical air support. All of the units, including those assigned to SAC and the RAAF were made available to General MacArthur, as Supreme Commander.

Between wars, the Convair B-36 entered the USAF inventory. Weighing in at more than twice the B-29's weight caused the WW II Boeing to be re-classified as a medium bomber. At the start of the Korean War there were 22 operational B-29s assigned to the Far East Air Force's 19th Bombardment Group, as well as six RB-29s for photoreconnaissance and four SB-29s for air-sea rescue.

By the 28th of June, the North Koreans were advancing into Seoul, the capital of South Korea. Early that morning, an RF-80 piloted by First Lieutenant Bryce Poe II, of the 8th Tactical Reconnaissance Squadron (TRS) took off from Itazuke Air Base, across the Korea Straight near Fukuoka in northern Kyushu, Japan, and flew over the Korean Peninsula. This, the first jet combat reconnaissance mission and those that followed, paved the way for FEAF to successfully launch bomber and fighter-bomber missions against the invading North Koreans. Flying from Kadena AB, Okinawa, the 19th Bombardment Group, carried out the first B-29 medium bomber strikes against a railroad bridge and tanks, trucks, and supply columns along North Korean invasion routes. USAF aircraft also bombarded other North Korean air bases, effectively achieving air superiority in a single day's strike. USAF bombings notwithstanding, the invaders quickly overran South Korea's capital, Seoul, the port of Inchon, and captured Kimpo Airfield.

A day later, the capital fell. Eight B-29s of the 19th BG attacked enemy-held Kimpo Airfield and the Seoul railroad station. As the bombers turned toward Kadena, NKA aircraft attacked the formation and one was reportedly shot down. MacArthur ordered weapons and ammunition shipped to South Korea and prepared to send in US ground troops. At the same time, Truman ordered US naval units to enforce a blockade of North Korea.

By the end of July 1950, the NKA had conquered the entire Korean peninsula except the area southeast of Hamch'ang bordered by the Nakton River. The USAF moved two additional B-29 groups, the 22nd BG and the 92nd BG to the Far East to join the 19th BG. Gen. Hoyt S. Vandenberg, Air Force Chief of Staff, met in Tokyo with General MacArthur to discuss the most efficient use of the B-29. MacArthur allowed the Air Force to employ some Superfortresses in a campaign against strategic and deep interdiction targets, such as chemical plants, oil refineries, and marshalling yards, but insisted that the bulk of US air power be used against the advancing enemy troops.

The first strategic air attacks of the war took place on July 6 when nine B-29s bombed the Rising Sun oil refinery at Wonsan and a chemical plant at Hungnam in North Korea. Shortly after the bombing, Far East Air Forces organized a provisional bomber command at Yokota, under Maj. Gen. Emmett O'Donnell, Jr. On July 12, North Korean fighters shot down their first B-29. A day later forty-nine B-29s from the 22nd and 92nd bombed the Wonsan marshalling yards and oil refinery. At the same time, the 3rd. Air Rescue Squadron (ARS) began flying SB-17 aircraft off the Korean coast to drop rescue boats to downed B-29 crews.

Fearful of negative Communist propaganda that might result from fire attacks on North Korea and, consequently, civilian casualties, Washington prohibited the indiscriminate use of incendiaries. High-explosive raids would necessitate additional sorties, but radar-bombing techniques had proved that weather was not the problem FEAF planners had expected. Between 13 July and 31 October, each of the eighty-assigned B-29's averaged 8.9 eight to eleven hour missions per month.

During August, the Superfortresses continued bombing marshalling yards, industrial targets, port facilities, and bridges. They also conducted one major carpet-bombing raid near the front. The addition of the 98th and 307th Bomb Groups from the States brought the total number of B-29 units in the theater to five. The 98th flew its first mission on August 7 and the 307th the following day. On August 12, more than forty B-29s attacked the port of Rashin in northeastern Korea near the Soviet Union border. In the largest employment of airpower in direct support of ground forces since the Normandy invasion of World War II, ninety-eight B-29s dropped more than 800 tons of 500-pound bombs on suspected NKA troop concentrations northwest of Taegu. Unfortunately, the troops had already left the area. August ended with seventy-four B-29s bombing Chinnampo, the largest strategic mission of the month. Among the targets were aluminum and magnesium plants.

In spite of massive air superiority throughout the summer of 1950, the North Korean advance pushed Republic of Korea and US ground forces into an ever-decreasing space. Near summer's end, UN Forces were crammed into the southeastern corner of the peninsula, in a battle area that came to be known as the Pusan Perimeter. Truman's hasty commitment had been made with pitifully poor resources that had quickly disintegrated, and, although the Marines hung on tenaciously, another Dunkirk loomed.

While the United States armed forces faced what threatened to become the greatest defeat in its history of armed conflict, Truman repeatedly referred to what had become a full-scale war as a "police action." This official view from the top would eventually make the disastrous events of Black Tuesday possible, even predictable.

September, which began with the North Korean Army on the verge of total victory, ended in full retreat across the 38th parallel.

Just when it appeared that North Korea had won, on 15 September, MacArthur landed his forces half way up the west side of the Korean Peninsula at Inchon, a Yellow Sea port twenty-five miles west of Seoul. The landing, timed to coincide with the breakout of the Pusan Perimeter, cut road and rail line supply routes and shattered the backbone of the North Korean war machine. Having pursued its strategic bombing campaign to conclusion, Bomber Command directed its attention to close air support for the UN offensive.

By late September, US Marines had driven NVA forces from Seoul and taken control of the capital building. The Joint Chiefs of Staff ordered MacArthur to cross the 38th parallel and destroy the NKA. As ROK troops advanced into North Korea for the first time, MacArthur officially restored Seoul to ROK President Syngman Rhee.

On October 8, two F-80s accidentally strafed a Soviet airfield near Vladivostok, USSR, on the coast northeast of the Korea border. Stratemeyer removed the group commander and ordered a court martial of the two pilots, further emphasizing the restriction against bombing outside of North Korea--an order that would later endanger all UN bombers that flew within range of the new Soviet jet fighter that would soon be operating out of politically-protected Manchurian bases.

Throughout the Allied advance, all of the important industrial areas of North Korea were targeted for aerial bombardment: Pyongyang, the capital and a key choke point on the main west coast railway; Chongjin, the center of North Korean iron and steel production; Wonsan, one of the best harbors on the east coast as well as a petroleum refining and possessing center; and the large chemical center, Hungnam.

UN forces pushed steadily North, taking Pyongyang, the capital, and Wonsan. In hopes of ending operations before the onset of winter, MacArthur ordered an advance to the northern Korean border with China. With victory apparently at hand, by the end of October, ROK troops arrived on the banks of the Yalu River separating North Korea from China.

The Korean War might have been quick and "easy" if the People's Volunteer Army of China had kept to the north bank of the Yalu. However, on October 8, 1950, Mao Tse Tung, Chairman of the People's Republic of China, issued the order for the "Chinese People's Volunteer Army to fight "American imperialism."

Fearing that the Allies would continue across the Yalu River and attempt to overthrow communism in Mainland China, Mao ordered the deployment of 850,000 "volunteer troops" of the Chinese People's Liberation Army north of the Yalu River. Mao also feared US forces would seize control of all of Korea and control Southern Manchuria's power supply, which was generated in North Korea. He believed that if the Western forces prevailed they would blockade the China coast all the way from Korea to Vietnam. It would be far easier, he believed, to beat the Americans on the narrow Korean Peninsula than on a front that stretched over a thousand miles around China's perimeter. The Chinese Armies swarmed across the Yalu, driving the UN back south, and although the cost in lives was astronomical, Mao was right.

During a mid-October meeting with President Truman on Wake Island, MacArthur predicted that China would not intervene and the war would be over by Christmas; however, just three days later an RB-29 reconnaissance crew spotted more than seventy-five fighters at Antung's airfield in China, just across the Yalu River from North Korea, strongly suggesting that Communist China might indeed enter the war. A few days later, Chinese soldiers moving into Korea attacked the ROK 6th Infantry Division near the Yalu River.

During the same period, FEAF Bomber Command temporarily quit flying combat missions for lack of B-29 targets. After destroying most of the strategic targets in North Korea, two of the B-29 groups, the 22nd and 92nd, returned to the US during October and November 1950. For the rest of the Korean War the core of the Far East Air Force's Bomber Command embraced three medium bombardment groups--the 19th, 98th, and 307th, each with an authorized strength of thirty-three B-29s.

B-29 strikes on enemy ports and bridges over the Yalu River failed to stop the Chinese forces crossing into North Korea. Where fixed bridges were damaged, they used pontoon bridges and, by the end of the month, thick ice that covered sections of the river. Prohibited from overflying Manchuria, B-29s attacked the bridges by following the course of the river. Fighter escorts could only fly on the Korean side of the bombers, which left the B-29s wide open to Communist fighters and antiaircraft guns based in China. Although so far in the war, the B-29s were equipped to handle whatever the Communists threw at them, all of that would change in November when MiG-15 jets piloted by Soviet Air Force fliers appeared for the first time in the skies over Korea.

On the first day of November, the 1st Cavalry Division exchanged fire with Chinese forces, the first such encounter between US and Chinese forces. Elsewhere, a formation of six Mig-15s fired on a propeller-driven T-6 and a flight of F-51 Mustangs. Soviet-built MiG-15 swept-wing jet fighters, faster than any USAF aircraft in the theater, had entered the war. To counter the MiG threat, the United States hustled to ship F-84 and F-86 fighters to the Far East by sea, but by the end of November none had entered combat.

Eight days after the first MiG encounter, a 91st SRS RB-29 flying out of Johnson AFB, Japan, was jumped by MiG-15s while taking pictures of Yalu River bridges. Although the jet fighters shot out both left engines, the aircraft managed to limp back to Johnson. Bill Welsh, a 91st SRS RB-29 crew member, recalled watching the crippled plane circle the field at low altitude as it prepared to land. "The two left engines had feathered props, and a huge V shaped chunk was torn out of the trailing edge of the left wing." Bill wondered how they got the airplane back with two

92BG-325BS in loose formation after bombing N. Korean target. The 92BG and 22BG returned to the U.S. during Oct.-Nov. 1950 due to a lack of B-29 targets. *Courtesy of Carl Thomas*

307th BW B-29 at "bombs away," snow-capped N. Korean mountains in background. Note how the bomber pitches up after releasing its load of 500 pound bombs. *Courtesy of John Wagenhalls*

engines out on one side and thought the crew would surely bail out. "But then they made an approach and lowered the gear and flaps. As they neared the runway on final approach, I heard someone yell, 'Damn! They're gonna make it!' No sooner had he said it, than the airplane seemed to stagger and fall off on the left wing. In what seemed like slow motion, it rolled about ninety degrees and hit the ground just off the end of the runway. A huge cloud of smoke erupted as crash crews raced to put out the fire. The entire front of the plane was rolled up in a ball, but the aft section of the fuselage had broken off just behind the wing and ridden up over the wreckage. They had made it all the way back to Johnson on two engines, but on final approach, the left wing stalled and it went in. Everyone in the forward compartment was killed, except Cpl. Harry Lavene who had been up front for the expected crash landing!"

MiG pilots began to exact their toll. On November 10, MiG-15s shot down a 307th B-29, the first of many to follow. Four days later, fifteen MiGs attacked and damaged two B-29s bombing the bridges at Sinuiju. On December 1, in the first prolonged MiG attack of the war, six MiG-15s engaged three B-29s for six minutes, damaging them considerably in spite of their F-80 escorts.

On the ground, winter had become one of the coldest on record. Spawned in Siberia, howling winds swept across the peninsula and plunged temperatures to well below zero. American commanders issued a warning that their troops were not equipped for the bitter cold in the mountains of North Korea and "were spreading themselves too far, too fast."

By Thanksgiving, UN forces had pushed northward in two columns, separated by a spine of mountains that splits North Korea. The Chinese, numbering several hundred thousand, hid in the mountains until the UN troops were enveloped before attacking. They wore quilted brown uniforms, yelling, screaming, and blowing bugles as they charged. For many Allied soldiers there seemed no end to them. The Chinese Army cut down Americans and their allies by the thousands, but lost even more of their own. Under the withering fire, bodies piled high and many others froze to death. Nonetheless, sheer numbers won the day. The drive to the Yalu had cost the UN 13,000 dead, wounded, captured or missing, and thousands more suffered severe frostbite.

As 1950 came to a close, Chinese forces crossed the 38th parallel into South Korea and most of North Korea was back in Communist hands.

The New Year was marked by seesaw battles that found the UN and Communist ground forces repeatedly fighting over the same turf. At the same time, tensions between Truman and MacArthur were headed toward confrontation. Although MacArthur's Inchon landing had been called a brilliant success, his advance to the Yalu had backfired. To recover from the calamity, MacArthur asked to unleash the United States' allies in Formosa, to bomb Chinese bases in Manchuria, and for more US troops to attack the Chinese.

Truman and his advisers wanted no part of a wider war, especially one that might bring in the Soviet Union with its superior conventional forces and its new atomic capability. Instead, they sought a negotiated end to the war. MacArthur would have none of it. In press interviews, conversations, and letters, he ridiculed the notion of a negotiated peace and complained of the "restrictions" and "inhibitions" being placed on him from Washington.

Near the end of January 1951, UN forces had launched a counter-offensive, forcing the enemy northward toward Seoul. FEAF Bomber Command continued their raids on marshalling yards, airfields, and supply centers, dropping more than 6,700 tons of bombs. B-29 crews also struck bridges with radio-guided bombs but largely avoided an area that became known as MiG Alley.

Although described as an "alley" by USAF pilots, the area of operations more closely resembled the shape of a trapezoid. Geographically, MiG Alley occupied the extreme northwest sector of North Korea, limited on the north and west by political decree and to the south and east by the jet engine's fuel consumption. American combat flyers were forbidden to cross the Yalu River boundary with Manchuria and Russian regulations prohibited their MiG pilots from flying over non-Communist-controlled territory, which included the UN-controlled Yellow Sea. MiG Alley, therefore, became the arena for all but a handful of jet air-to-air skirmishes during the Korean War and the birthplace of jet fighter combat.

With a total force of ninety-nine B-29s, FEAF Bomber Command launched an average of twenty-four daily, rotating missions among the 19th, 98th, and 307th bombardment units. By March, F-86 fighters flying out of Taegu and Suwon were able to escort B-29s on their renewed interdiction campaign in northwest Korea. Air-to-air combat increased, especially in the Sinuiju and Sinanju areas. On March 1, twenty-two F-80s sent to escort eighteen B-29s arrived ahead of the Superfortresses and returned to base because they were running low on fuel. MiGs attacked the unescorted B-29s, damaging ten, three of which had to land in South Korea.

In mid-March, UN forces re-entered Seoul, the fourth and last time the capital changed hands since the war began.

As spring approached, Fifth Air Force light bombers and fighters, which had handled interdiction during the winter, could not destroy the larger Yalu bridges, so when the river thawed, B-29s returned--this time with fighter escorts. The Communists were also busy constructing new airfields and repairing damaged ones. Considering this increased activity as possible evidence of a planned enemy air-ground offensive, Stratemeyer directed the bulk of B-29 raids against these targets.

By then, the front had stabilized along the Han River north of Seoul. Although there would be offensives and counteroffensives, the geography of North and South Korea was virtually as it had been on the day the war began, a peninsula split in two by the 38th parallel, and it would stay that way until the ceasefire. Nearly all historians of that period credit the UN's ability to stop the overwhelming numbers of the CPV and KPA in their tracks to the absolute air superiority achieved by FEAF.

In an article that appeared in *Mir Aviatsiya_* (Russia, Feb. '99), titled, "The Black Week for Bomber Command," Leonid Krylov and Yuriy Tepsurkayev wrote that "The aerial terror along the roads in North Korea never ceased for an hour, and only slackened at night. It was impossible to use the roads in daylight even with single trucks, to say nothing of truck convoys. The Korean-Chinese forces, literally cut off from their own rear area units, suffered from terrible shortages at the front in the most critical of needs-- reinforcements, weapons, ammunition, provisions, medicines." The authors point out that it was impossible for the Soviet 64th IAK to cover all of the lines of communication in

North Korea because of " ... significant numerical superiority of the enemy aviation," lack of Chinese and Korean aviation support, and shortage of combat-ready MiG-15 pilots and operating airfields.

While the United States Secretary of State was hinting at a willingness to talk with the Chinese, General MacArthur insisted that the Chinese military force was overrated and demanded that the commander of the Chinese Army meet with him personally or risk a wider war. Finally, in early April, Republican Congressman Joseph Martin read a letter from MacArthur on the House floor, which criticized the president's decision not to use forces from Formosa against the Communist Chinese.

In an address to the nation on April 11th, 1951, Truman explained why he was removing MacArthur from command--which boiled down to preventing a third world war. Opinion about the firing was split down the middle, mostly along political lines. The uproar would eventually die down, although MacArthur's words to a joint session of congress would resonate in the minds of B-29 crew members in the months to follow. "Once war is forced upon us," MacArthur said, "there is no other alternative than to apply every available means to bring it to a swift end. War's very object is victory, not prolonged indecision."

On April 12, the largest force of B-29s ever to attack a single bridge complex encountered intense MiG opposition. The ensuing encounter resulted in the largest jet air battle so far in the war. Escorted by a hundred fighters, forty-six B-29s, attacking the Yalu River Bridge at Sinuiju were intercepted by MiGs launched from their sanctuary in Manchuria. Three bombers were shot down and seven damaged. B-29 gunners and F-86 pilots claimed the highest daily MiG tally to date. Although numerous bombs hit the bridge, it remained standing.

At President Truman's direction, Lt. Gen. Matthew B. Ridgway, replaced General MacArthur. At the same time, General Stratemeyer suffered a severe heart attack and was replaced by Lieutenant General Otto Paul Weyland.

FEAF Bomber Command flew a daily average of ten B-29 sorties against Pyongyang, Kangdong, Yonpo, and other North Korean airfields. At night, over the western sector, a B-29 close air support strike against enemy troops forming for an attack on the US Army IX Corps broke up the assault. The first indication of enemy radar-controlled antiaircraft guns came with the loss of three F-51s making an air-to-ground attack against a target at Sinmak. During May, B-29s initially bombed rail and highway bridges, airfields, and supply and troop centers in North Korea. Later in the month, when the Communists initiated their offensive, FEAF shifted the B-29 effort to close air support. In psychological operations, B-29s dropped millions of leaflets and flew ninety-four sorties against enemy ground forces, far more close air support missions than in any previous similar period.

On June 1, a flight of F-86s from the 336th FIS escorting B-29s engaged eighteen MiG-15s, destroying two. In another engagement near Sonchon, twenty-two MiGs jumped B-29s of the 343rd BS. One B-29 was destroyed and another damaged. General Weyland directed FEAF Bomber Command to keep the thirteen most important North Korean airfields out of service. On June 23 the Soviet Ambassador to the United Nations called for an armistice based upon the separation of the armies along the 38th parallel. The recapture of Seoul and completion of repairs to Kimpo's short runway permitted the 8th FBG to move and resume combat operations.

The mushrooming numbers of MiG-15s in the theater made the B-29 increasingly vulnerable during daylight visual raids, so in June 1951, B-29 units began experimenting with SHORAN, an electronic navigation/bombing system that allowed crews to drop bombs accurately on targets obscured by weather or darkness. If bombardiers could see the target below, the bomber had to be in the clear, which also gave MiG pilots the ideal situation for aiming at their target. SHORAN development would ultimately allow the bombers to operate almost exclusively at night.

Even at night, B-29 aircrews were directed to use extreme caution to avoid bombing in the vicinity of reported POW camps.

By the middle of 1951, after a series of attacks and counterattacks, the front lines stabilized near where the war had begun a year earlier. Ceasefire negotiations were initiated, but would take two more years while the contending forces fought on. Commanders on both sides centered on armistice negotiations by altering military strategy to affect favorable outcomes in these negotiations. Accordingly, FEAF increased the tempo of fighter and light-bomber activities, particularly against vehicular movements and targets of known troops, supplies, or installations.

It was during this period of negotiations, when either side could have made concessions to end the bloodshed that so many bombing missions, including the one against Namsi, were flown and so many lives were lost.

The dramatic increase in the numbers of MiG-15s and the growing experience and competence of pilots led the Communists to seek air superiority as far south as Pyongyang. Avoiding formidable jet fighter formations escorting B-29s, the MiGs instead attacked vulnerable fighter-bomber and reconnaissance aircraft operating north of Pyongyang. Because of attrition and increased numbers of aircraft out of commission FEAF was suddenly faced with a shortages of combat aircraft.

When negotiations broke down scarcely a month after the first meeting at Kaesong began, FEAF launched a rail interdiction campaign to prevent a Communist buildup of supplies needed for a sustained offensive or effective counteroffensive. The fighter-bomber campaign against North Korean railroads was stepped up and B-29s were sent on nightly SHORAN bombing attacks on enemy marshaling yards. While Bomber Command knocked down key railroad bridges, Fifth Air Force and the Navy fighter-bombers cut the rail lines. Meanwhile, B-26's were shifted from daytime interdiction to nighttime truck hunting.

On August 17, Typhoon Ruth interrupted B-29 operations out of Okinawa.

Although one-quarter of the oil supplying the North Korean war machine was being transported through Rashin, the strategic North Korean rail hub for importing supplies from the Soviet port of Vladivostok hadn't undergone a large scale bombing attack in over a year. Acheson worried that striking a target only seventeen miles from the Soviet border might provoke Soviet intervention. Nevertheless, in a meeting with Truman and Acheson, Chairman of the Joint Chiefs, General Omar Bradley and Defense Secretary Louis Johnson requested the President authorize another bombing, citing FEAF's belief that two medium groups could destroy the complex in thirty days. Truman agreed, stipulating the raid must be conducted in daylight and that bombardiers visually identify the target to be sure they were dropping on the correct target and not on the wrong side of the border.

On August 25, thirty-five B-29s, escorted by USN fighters, dropped 300 tons of bombs on the marshaling yards at Rashin.

Cloud cover over the target was scattered and the bombs were observed to impact within the confines of the rail complex. Although flak was intense and fairly accurate, no MiGs made contact and no bombers were lost   (This was the author's first mission.).

Although there was 9/10th cloud cover, eight B-29s from the 19th BG used SHORAN to knock out the center span of the Sunchon rail bridge (author's seventh mission.) on Sept. 23. A week later Brig. Gen. Joe W. Kelly assumed command of FEAF Bomber Command.

Following a two-month suspension, armistice talks resumed at Kaesong in late October. FEAF Bomber Command continued daylight B-29 strikes against airfields, rail bridges, and marshaling yards, dedicating a few night sorties to close air support, leaflet drops, and reconnaissance. B-29s flew thirty-one day and night sorties, the high for the month, including attacks against rail bridges, marshaling yards, and the Samchang airfield, plus leaflet drop and reconnaissance sorties. On October 22, two SA-16s, 3d ARS, rescued the twelve-man crew of a downed B-29. In the last ten days of October, large numbers of aggressive MiG-15 attacks, particularly on Black Tuesday, resulted in mounting B-29 losses and forced FEAF to end daylight B-29 operations in MiG Alley.

As B-29s night operations mounted, to counter increasingly effective searchlight illumination, Bomber Command camouflaged all B-29s with black gloss lacquer on their undersides. Contrails, however, were often lines in the sky that pointed directly to a bomber.

Nighttime attacks on key rail facilities and jet airfields at Saamcham, Taechon, and Namsi continued. In addition, B-29s flew nightly close air support missions, dropping 500-pound air fragmentation bombs over enemy troop concentrations. Communist jet fighters operated from an airbase at Uiju on the south bank of the Yalu for a short time, but heavy attacks soon rendered it unusable. As the war dragged on, ground defenses were greatly improved.   More powerful, radar-directed searchlights tracked UN bombers in conjunction with radar-controlled AAA and MiG attacks. Newly installed antiaircraft guns could hit B-29s above 20,000 feet. During a June raid by the 19BG on the rail bridge at Kwaksan, North Korea, MiGs, operating in conjunction with radar-controlled searchlights and flak, destroyed two B-29s and badly damaged a third. This development in the enemy's air defense system sent FEAF scrambling for new electronic countermeasures (ECM) to jam and confuse enemy radar.

In a change of tactics, FEAF shifted to targets that had been previously banned. Over 1,200 sorties were flown against hydroelectric facilities, cutting off ninety percent of North Korea's and twenty-five percent of Manchuria's electric power potential. In spite of the destruction raining down on them, the Communists failed to move toward an armistice. The war's largest air raid came on 29 August 1952, when FEAF and carrier planes bombed Pyongyang in a 1,403-sortie assault.

On September 19, 1952, the first daylight B-29 raid in eleven months, thirty-two B-29s with F-86 escorts attacked an enemy barracks and two supply areas southwest of Hamhung. A four engine jet bomber, the RB-45, preceded the B-29 formation, and orbited in the assembly area, providing weather information.

Having campaigned on a promise to seek an end to the Korean War, Dwight D. Eisenhower was elected President of the United States on November 4, 1952.

In mid-November, six 98th BW B-29s attacked the Sonchon supply center, thirty-five miles from the Manchurian border. Weather in the target area was clear, and enemy interceptors dropped flares to help searchlights lock onto the bombers. One B-29 riddled by four fighters forced the crew to abandon ship over Cho-do Island.

A maximum effort mission on November 28/29 directed all three medium bomber units to hit at Sinuiju and Uiju at forty-five-minute intervals. Ninety-four radar-controlled heavy guns and forty searchlights defended the targets. Preceding the attacks, five B-26s bombed and strafed suspected gun and searchlight emplacements. Fourteen B-29s bombed Sinuiju Airfield; six struck the Sinuiju locomotive repair facilities; ten hit the Uiju Airfield; and four attacked the Uiju communications center. In spite of clear weather, by using ECM and chaff, the B-29s escaped losses.

By January 1953, darkness no longer afforded protection for the B-29s. Using a combination of ground radar controllers, moonlight, contrails, searchlights, and flares, night interceptors shot down four B-29s during the month. On January 28/29,

Communist fighters apparently silhouetted a 19th BG B-29 against a full moon and shot it down over the target southwest of Sariwon. This was the last B-29 combat loss of the Korean War. Thereafter, Bomber Command compressed bomber streams and scheduled B-29 attacks against heavily defended targets irregularly during the dark of the moon, avoiding contrail-forming altitudes. On the bombing run, B-29s varied altitude and employed electronic countermeasures. The compressed bomber stream provided a much greater concentration of chaff and electronic jamming power in the critical target area. USMC Skynight jet aircraft escorted the bombers and one Skynight was credited with downing the first MiG to be destroyed at night by a radar-equipped jet fighter.

After a six-month suspension, armistice negotiations between Communist and UN forces reconvened on April 26.

On July 21/22, eighteen B-29s bombed Uiju Airfield, the final mission for FEAF Bomber Command. Capt. Ralph S. Parr, Jr. became a double ace with the last air-to-air victory of the war by shooting down an IL-12 transport. In the final hours before the ceasefire, Fifth Air Force fighter-bombers hammered North Korean airfields. Flying a 91st SRS RB-29, Lt. Denver S. Cook piloted the last FEAF Bomber Command sortie, dropping leaflets over North Korea. An 8th Bomb Squadron B-26 dropped the last bombs of the Korean War in a night, radar-directed close support mission, and an RB-26 of the 67th TRW made the last combat sortie of the war over North Korea.

At 1000 hours on July 27, 1953, Lt. Gen. William K. Harrison, Jr., USA, senior UN delegate and Gen. Nam Il, the senior delegate for the Korean Peoples Army and the Chinese Peoples Volunteers, signed the armistice agreement to produce a ceasefire in the Korean War. As the Korean War formally ended, by 10:01 p.m. all of FEAF's aircraft were located either south of the front line or more than three miles from North Korea's coast. In accordance with the Armistice Agreement, in August, prisoners of war were exchanged in Operation Big Switch--77,000 Communists for 12,700 UN men, 3,597 of them Americans.

Cold statistics show that FEAF units flew 720,980 sorties and dropped 476,000 tons of bombs that killed nearly 150,000 North Korean and Chinese troops and claimed the destruction of more than 975 aircraft, 800 bridges, 1,100 tanks, 800 locomotives, 9,000 railroad cars, 70,000 motor vehicles, and 80,000 buildings. The B-

29s had flown 10,125 day and 10,323 night sorties, and dropped 168,368 tons of bombs. NKA losses are estimated at more than half a million troops and by the time the armistice was signed, almost no modern buildings were left standing in North Korea.

Referred to as "America's Forgotten War" may be a sobriquet well deserved. Statistically, among major wars, up to and including Vietnam, percentage of population under arms was smaller only in two other conflicts, the Mexican and Spanish-American Wars. Korea was on par with The War of 1812, at 3.8%. World War II, by comparison, had over three times as many citizens inducted or enlisted in the Armed Forces. Although other sources cite higher figures, in numbers of American casualties, the Korean War is officially listed as having had 33,651 killed and 103,284 wounded. Conspicuous by its absence, however, is an official toll of "other" deaths. Korea is the only war since 1812 missing this number. Unintentional or by design, it should be noted that many casualties occurred that were officially labeled "Non-operational" or accidental. This was particularly true with Air Force losses that were oftentimes a direct result of damage incurred in combat but were not manifested until later--for example, crash landings that were chalked up as accidents. (The author was involved in the crash of *The Outlaw*, on a test flight flown to check damage repairs from a previous combat mission. *The Outlaw* was not listed as a "loss" in the Korean War.) Using WW II percentages of "combat" to "other" would approximate the Korean War's "other" figure at 13,258, bringing the total killed to 46,909.

In actual per capita costs, Korea was the third costliest American war.

3: The Combatants

As in no other air war in recent history, the Korean War was fought by opposing combatants who no stake whatsoever in the territory in dispute. When the North invaded the South, Americans entered the battle openly and with heavy commitment. The Soviets elected to go undercover with limited aid in material and especially in manpower. For whatever reason, neither side expressed a specific goal or objective, other than to fight one another and to hopefully bring the whole sad affair to an end. Unfortunately, the war never officially ended. In spite of over a half century of negotiation, neither side has surrendered or agreed on a formal truce to end the armed conflict. Instead, both sides signed a tenuous ceasefire agreement and technically the combatants remain at a state-of-war.

Secret Soviet Involvement

By the end of October 1950, the Korean and Chinese aviation assets had been combined into a single Unified Air Army (OVA) to protect a limited number of rear area resources. Short of equipment and lacking combat experience, they were unable to overcome UN air superiority and fulfill even this limited role. It soon became clear that unless the Soviet Union became involved, the Americans and their Allies would dominate the skies over Korea.

In November 1950, Lt. Colonel Alexandr Pavlovich Smorchkov was flying a MiG-15 when the commander of the Moscow Air Defense, General Colonel K. Moscalenko, informed him that he was to initiate "Polikarpov Po-2 in Flight," a top-secret deployment. Without delay, Smorchkov's regiment boarded a secret night train to travel to the Far East to fight in the Korean War. Days later, the Soviet 64th IAK (*Istrebitel'niy Aviatsionniy Korpus* or Independent Fighter Aviation Corps), arrived at their destination, greeted by tropical downpours so heavy that ducks were swimming on their airfield.

The regiment first operated from the airbase at Mukden. A few days later they transferred to Antung Airbase where they joined other regiments. The primary mission of Smorchkov's regiment was to protect the bridges across the Yalu River and the Antung power station, which supplied electrical power to North Korea.

In his Autobiography, *In the Skies of Two Wars*, Sergey Makarovich Kramarenko details his experiences as a MiG commander in the 176th Regiment from March 1951 until early February 1952. The Soviet involvement, he wrote, came as a complete package that included not only fighter units but also anti-aircraft artillery, air traffic control, communications, and support. In December 1950 the 28th IAD (*Istrebitel'naya Aviatsionnaya Diviziya* or Fighter Aviation Division) was relocated to Xingdao to train Chinese and Korean jet fighter pilots. The Russians implemented rigid training in air-to-air and air-to-ground combat. They also increased the number of radar and visual observation posts in the air defense network. While part of the OVA went out to destroy UN bombers before they reached their targets, reserve units were assigned to repulse surprise attacks and cover the landing of their own aircraft. Aircraft were dispersed and concealed, and organized for quick turn around and takeoff.

Given the magnitude of their mission, one would assume that the logistics of supporting a brand new jet fighter in a combat environment at so great a distance from the source of supplies would be insurmountable. Although various reports written at the time suggests that the Soviets periodically ran out of fuel, ammunition, and most of the other materials necessary to conduct a successful combat operation, when queried, the pilots of the 64th IAK could not recall ever having to cancel a combat sortie because they lacked airplanes, spare parts, ammo, or fuel. The only materiel shortage mentioned in Russian archives was a lack of drop tanks in November 1950. This forced Soviet fliers to retain them except when under attack, and limited maneuverability when they were attacking UN bombers. The problem became more critical as the distance to the combat zones over Uiju, Sinuiju, and Sonchon increased. When Soviets moved their aircraft forward to Antung, wing tanks ceased to be a major problem because of the decreased distance to the combat zone, as well as improved logistics.

Although materiel support is not generally acknowledged to have been a serious problem, between November 1951 and January 1952 the 303rd and 324th IAD ran short of an even more important commodity, pilots. This was due in part to combat attrition and in part to illnesses. To make matters worse, the replacement pilots that arrived in early November were, in Kramarenko's words, "rookies." While most of Kramarenko's pilots were WW II veterans with over three hundred hours piloting jet aircraft, the replacements had only 50-60 hours in jets and little combat experience.

Feelings among the older pilots of the both Soviet combat divisions were that General Yevgeny I. Savitskiy, Commander of Fighter Aviation and Anti-Aircraft Defense (and one of Stalin's favorites), felt envious of their successes in the Korean theater. Much like their U. S. counterparts, who glorified competition between the Army and Navy, and more recently the Air Force, the Soviet military thrived on competition between the VVS and the PVO. By sending rookie replacements to the elite 303rd and 324th IAD, their success rate was sure to suffer and provide General Savitskiy with a valid argument to replace them with divisions of his own forces, the 97th and 190th IAD. Whether this was fact or rumor has never been ascertained.

In his book, *Neizvestnaya Voyna* (*The Unknown War*, translated by Stephen "Cookie" Sewell) veteran 196th IAP MiG pilot Captain Boris Stepanovich Abakumov describes what everyday life was like for the Soviets in far-off Manchuria:

"We ate at a mess hall. For the first few days we only had Chinese cooking to eat. Their dinner consisted of 7-8 courses, but all of them were simple. They made them very tasty, and we had many different dishes on the table but their portions were very small, and after dinner we were still somewhat hungry and wanted just a bit more to snack upon. For example, the course portion of roast potatoes amounted to five large spoonfuls of potatoes and that was it. That was the way with every course--well prepared and tasty but skimpy. Chicken was dark gray, since we only got it several days after we requested it for our table, but we could see that it was cured and then even the legs were cut into several pieces. The same sort of thing happened with veal medallions.

Veal was cut up and cured by medallions. This habit was odd to us (and) was why the chicken had such a strange color--curing was no different than the same method the Chinese used to cure pork. Frequently we could hear the "squeals" of pigs from the village near our garrison. These were not pleasant to hear. We asked ourselves, 'What's the matter?' It turned out that this method was the way that they drove the 'evil spirits' out of the pigs . . . The command, noting our insufficient provisions, moved to have food prepared by our cooks . . . The Chinese cooks were stunned to see the size of our portions, which we freely devoured. They began to shake their heads and click their tongues. Of course, none of them had to fly jet aircraft (in) combat. We needed high calorie chow, or we would not be able to handle the stress.

"We had two 'mustachios' in our regiment, that is, two men with large mustaches. They were Volodya Alfeyev and Lev Ivanov. Each of them had a personal score of ten victories . . . and they had been recommended for the title of Hero of the Soviet Union ... I also had a mustache up until I could not get it to fit under my oxygen mask in flight, and as a result I had to trim it back. But these boys would not shave theirs off until our combat tour was over . . . (and) brought great delight to the local residents, who could seldom get them to "sprout" on their faces. Their admirers attempted several times to grow a mustache, which brought about lots of exclamations and head bobbing in some kind of clattering language. On occasion one of them would begin to sprout a mustache and the 'attention' would fall on them, and they, completely satisfied, would begin to move with outthrust jaws, supposing that they now had a sting in their arms. This would bring out gales of laughter . . . We had our own ringleaders, as one has in any collective. Lev Ivanov was one such ringleader, as he was an outgoing, sympathetic comrade. He had a lot of different facetious sayings, which he was perfect at choosing the time and place to say them . . . It was no accident that he loved to play chess, too . . . the games often took on a merry nature, if one of the participants was Aleksey Ivanovich Mitusov, who . . . played chess in every free moment that he was not in the air, and frequently bantered with his partners . . .

"We occasionally got movies at the airfield, which we would play when we went down into the bomb shelter. The greatest hunter we had--Vasya Fukin--would do his best between flights to bag ducks with a shotgun. This is how we kept up our normal routine. The pilots were enterprising and cheerful people. During the rains, when the airfield flooded with water from the 'opening of the heavens' and the pumps were not able to get it over the berms, the fishermen among us would then carry out their skills. Using just their hands they would catch rather large fish, like you see in the cowboy movies, but it was unknown how they got into the deep basins that fed the pumping stations.

"We received a 30% bonus, which we dubbed 'field money' as it was paid in local currency, and which we could use to purchase various items in a specialty store in the village. We attempted to turn our mess hall into a local hall with everything there. Ivan Nikitovich Kozhedub (CO of the 324th IAD, top allied WW2 ace with 62 aerial victories) and his assistants also ate here in this hall.

"Once Ivan Nikitovich was walking among the tables in the mess hall when he spotted Sasha Litvinyuk sitting rather sadly. Kozhedub went up to him and asked, as he placed his hand on Sasha's shoulder, what was bothering him and what he could do to make things better. During the conversation, which we recall to this day, Sasha will always recall the warmth of the conversation with him.

"Eight men sat around our round table. We ate here in the mess hall twice a day, (first, breakfast) in the mornings long before dawn, when there was no hint of sunlight. We would pour down cups of coffee or cocoa, eat bread covered in pear butter and cookies or chunks of chocolate bars. Before dawn we just had no appetite for any other food. ... In the evenings, after our missions, we could safely eat hearty meals: up to two portions of meat and two portions of vegetable, and then after some great warm Siberian dumplings, of course, we would receive 100-150 grams of spirits. At the mess hall we each received a bottle of beer, and also a bottle of cognac or port wine. But, as we held ourselves to account, nobody ever exceeded his limit. We still held this though: at home we kept full bottles, but here they would remain in the mess hall. And functionally everyone knew that tomorrow the combat missions with their great stress on the body were coming, and nobody wanted to fail to make correct reactions in a complicated aerial situation.

"Korean and Chinese pilots frequently ate with us, so that they got to eat our food, and not just rice. They knew to fight well in combat; their rations just would not support them. On occasion we would also invite them to eat our hearty meals as well as to share our cognac. After lights out the flight personnel went to sleep, but the technicians and service personnel went to watch movies.

"About 0900 hours we would have breakfast at our airfield. After breakfast almost nobody was relaxed. The same happened with dinner. Before a mission you just lost your appetite. The Americans specially organized their raids to coincide with our meal times (assumption probably not true--author). They knew that carrying out high stress maneuvers with a full stomach created a very large weight on the body, and subsequently shifted the center of gravity, and that had a negative effect on health and self-awareness; therefore, we consumed the majority of the calories we needed at supper, and got the 'combat ration' of one hundred grams to settle our nervous system down. This helped us quickly fall asleep. On occasion we would go over and pick up some vodka from the store and just before supper drink it with a small group of comrades. This was a forbidden situation, as they say, which we did on the run like swiping apples from a tree. But I have no idea why this was accepted, as we kept the bottles quite openly on our tables, free for all who shared the same spirit. Of course, even after such a procedure at your table in the mess everyone remained pretty close to sober. No one demanded you stay close to the norms. It was more a fact of strict self-control. Perhaps there was some sort of psychologically thicker side to the required amount of spirits you could intake with a narrow circle of comrades."

Abakumov recalled that the area around the air bases at Antung, Myaogou and Dapu in China contained numerous fruit orchards. At the right time of year the pilots would find baskets full of fruit at their tables and during their free time between flights, some pilots picked fruit for themselves.

Boris Abakumo piloted a MiG-15 in the battle on 12 April 1951, and probably shared the shootdown of the B-29A # 44-62252 with his buddy Boris Obratsov. Later, on 21 July 1951, he also downed the F9F-2 of Lt. Richard W. Bell and damaged Kenneth H. Rapp's F-86A on 27 September 1951.

Although one might assume that Chinese rations would be insufficient for the Russian appetite, the pilots say they always got enough food and considered their rations more than adequate--even though they believed that the poor initial performance of their Chinese counterparts was due, in large, to inadequate nourishment. Sergey Kramarenko, who instructed Chinese pilots, recalls, "The main difficulty for us was the unimpressive physical condition of the students. After a flight in the zone they were completely fatigued and could just barely crawl out of the aircraft. It came to pass that a great deal of serious attention was paid to the rations of Chinese pilots, who were being fed a low-calories diet (of) three bowls of rice a day and a small bowl of soup made of cabbage. After several weeks of increased rations at Soviet jet pilot norms, the Chinese were able hold their own in flights in the zone with our pilots."

Initially, Soviet combat formations were made up of 24 MiG-15s in three groups of eight aircraft. For reasons of secrecy, all aircraft carried Chinese insignia. Soviet pilots dressed in Chinese uniforms and were even assigned Chinese pseudonyms. They were instructed to speak Chinese or Korean over the air and personal conversations were forbidden. The Soviets believed that if UN listening posts picked up Russian spoken on combat frequencies it would have alerted the UN to their presence.

G. K. Kormilkin, a Soviet MiG pilot, recalled classes for memorizing basic commands in Chinese. Because most Russian pilots had to use Korean dictionaries for even simple phrases, the order was soon abolished. In fact, from the first encounter, most American airmen were convinced that veteran pilots from the Soviet Union flew the MiGs. It is also widely accepted that the United States was engaged in a cat and mouse game and refused to admit how good its communications intelligence was, presumably for the same reasons that the best US bombers were kept in reserve, to monitor and prevent a much more serious nuclear war. A number of American-employed Russian linguists monitored MiG transmissions and, although the Russians were supposed to speak Chinese, they soon learned that it was not an easily assimilated language or suitable for an air-to-air battle command and control.

Radio chatter, the Soviet planners also believed, denied regimental commanders the ability to control the air battle. Only group leaders had the right to transmit over the air, either the regimental commander or, and if the squadrons were operating independently, the squadron commander.

Eventually, the basic Soviet formation in Korea became an element of two aircraft. Two elements made up a flight, two or three flights a squadron. There were three squadrons in a regiment and two to three regiments in a Division. At the top of the organizational ladder was the Corps, made up of two or more Divisions. This particular organization was unique to Soviet forces in Korea. A division would often consist of as few as 48 aircraft rather than the 108 found elsewhere in the Soviet organizational structure.

Although radar simplified the search for the enemy, especially when operating at great altitude or in the soup, the placement of pairs of fighters along the front at different depths and altitudes produced the best results when searching for UN bombers. Opposing enemies in air combat generally saw each other at about the same time. This made the most important factor, the Soviets understood, the fighter pilot's ability to think. In this respect, Soviet and American fighter pilots shared the same belief.

In a post-glasnost, Russian newspaper interview, Lt. Colonel Smorchkov told the reporter, "Our attitudes towards the American pilots were complicated. During the Second World War, we had been allies against Hitler. Therefore, in Korea, we did not view the Americans as enemies, but only as opponents. Our motto in the air was 'Competition--with whomever.'"

Before long, the regiment was up against North American-built F-86 Sabres. Their first aerial victory was scored by a Soviet pilot named Akatow, who shot down an F-86 but died of wounds received in combat after only one aerial victory. A short time later, Smorchkov said, his friend, Valentin Filimonow, was shot down by two F-86s.

Other Soviet pilots, including his friends Vladimir Voistinnykh and Pete Chourkin, shared Smorchkov's opinion that the American pilots were very good. He ranked the F-80 Shooting Star as not very good, the F-84 Thunderjet, average, but the F-86 Sabre, he conceded, was very good. He thought the Soviet MiG-15 was the better aircraft, admitting, however, it had one big problem. The engine would sometimes stop abruptly during a sharp turn.

"One day we attacked a group of Australian Gloster Meteors. They were big, easy targets for us. My friend Os'kin and I destroyed five Meteors during this one fight," Smorchkov continued. "One night we intercepted B-29 Superfortresses. I was listening to my radio and heard, 'Group of B-29s in front of you!' I dove my MiG-15 with my heart pounding. Soon I saw the B-29s with many protecting fighters. I attacked and destroyed two B-29s and one of the escorting Sabres. Over my radio came the question, 'Alexandr! How are you getting on?' I answered with a furious, 'Victory! It's O.K!' That night our regiment destroyed five B-29s." Smorchkov's newspaper interview concluded: "Before my last flight of the War, my division commander ordered that we were to attack Sabres and then fly back to the USSR. On this flight, I was wounded in the leg. Back in the USSR, I learned that an American pilot with the Russian name, Makhonin, had been captured along with his brand new F-86. It was interesting to study his aircraft up close. Thus, the war was finished for us. However, many of my good friends had perished in Korea and were buried at Port Arthur."

Smorchkov finished the Korean War credited with twelve victories, five B-29s, two F-86s, and five Meteors.

Most Soviet pilots were veterans of World War II. Some were aces. One of the regiment commanders, Ivan Kozhedub, three-time "Hero of the Soviet Union with three Gold Stars," had 62 German kills to his credit. During the Korean War, his pilots would claim 258 victories out of a total of 1,300 UN aircraft of all types the Soviets claimed they shot down, while losing 345 of their own. Sixteen Soviet MiG-15 pilots would make ace and claim they outscored the American F-86 pilots by 2:1. On the other hand, some reports indicate that the Americans knocked down MiGs in the hands of North Korean and Chinese pilots at a rate of 13:1. There are no recognized Chinese or Korean aces.

The number of aircraft shot down or destroyed in any particular series of engagements depends on whose report is cited. Both the UN and the Communists probably inflated their victories and deflated their losses.

In October 1951, for example, the Soviet's 64th IAK claimed to have shot down 103 UN aircraft, which included 45 F-86s, 26 F-84s, 16 B-29s, nine F-80s, four Meteors, two B-26s and one F6F. They reported their losses as eight MiG-15bis and nine MiG-15s flown by the Chinese. The USAF claimed to have destroyed 34 MiG-15s, 24 by the Sabres, nine by the B-29 gunners and one by an F-84 while admitting to fifteen losses from MiG-15 fire: six B-29s, five F-86s, three F-84s, and one RF-80. Curiously, both sides appear to have inflated their claims by about the same figure, 50%. Omitted from the UN's loss figures are five B-29s that made it back to South Korea, Japan and Okinawa but never flew again. Crediting questionable losses to AAA instead of MiG cannon, and not listing losses partially due to accidents (including one I was involved in), lowered the UN totals considerably. Other records show that during the month of October, 1951 Soviet MiG-15 and La-11 fliers shot down or damaged beyond repair 41 UN aircraft: eight F-86A/Es, nine F-84Es, eleven B-29As, five F-80Cs, two RF-80As, two F2H-2s, one B-26B, one F7F-3N, one F4U-4 and one F9F-2B. They also damaged four F-86Es, three B-29As and one Meteor F.8.

The disparity in the numbers of kills reported by the two sides can be partially explained by the method each used to tally their totals. For the most part, Americans counted an aircraft a loss only if the American plane went down over the combat area. The US Air Force usually did not count aircraft damaged beyond repair or forced to land elsewhere as "shot down," even if they were never flown again. The Soviets counted these damaged aircraft, so their kill totals are higher than Allied loss totals.

It is also probable that a portion of the inflated totals can also be attributed to the "reward bonus" of 1500 rubles ($53) paid to some Soviet pilots for each confirmed kill. According to Sergey Markarovich Kramarenko, MiG flight commander in the 176th GIAP, no rewards were paid from April 1951 until January 1952, although in January, Nikolay V. Sutyagin of the 17th IAP/303rd IA received a monetary bonus for being the first pilot credited with twenty victories. The 1500 rubles reward, Kramarenko recalls, was implemented later by the 97th and 190th IAD, the units that replaced the elite 303rd and 324th IAD. The replacements from the Soviet Defense Force had been trained to intercept bombers, but not to dogfight. During the period, February-August 1952, both replacement units suffered heavy losses, became demoralized, and were reluctant to engage the F-86s. As motivation, a 1500 rubles reward bonus was tendered for each confirmed kill.

To further motivate their pilots a rumor was started that American Sabre pilots were shooting at MiG pilots in their parachutes after they ejected. This apparent barbarism was further supported by eyewitness accounts. As it turned out, the American fighter pilots were not firing at the parachutist but off at an angle because F-86 gun cameras were activated by the trigger and the only way to confirm some "kills" was to get a picture of a parachuting MiG pilot--although the poor guy in the parachute would have no way of knowing that.

Diego Zampini, author of several articles on Korean War aces, has thoroughly researched the topic and interviewed numerous Soviet as well as Allied combatants. Zampini believes that no less than 50% of the 1,300 Soviet claims are unsubstantiated and that 15% of the remaining half were aircraft that were heavily damaged and thought to have been shot down, but somehow limped back to their bases in South Korea. This leaves, in Zampini's estimation, 35% that were genuine aerial victories.

Further complicating the tally was a tendency to view the figures in reports from different units as separate entities when they may all have been based on the same engagement viewed from different perspectives. An extreme example occurred on Black Tuesday. One Soviet report placed the total number of attacking B-29s at 27, when, in fact, there were only nine. Such an error can best be explained by figuring that there were three separate reported sightings of nine B-29s (9 + 9 + 9 = 27) that did not take into account that all three were seeing the same formation. Likewise, the Russians claimed they shot down ten B-29s, which included those that had "ditched at sea or crashed in South Korea due to damage."

Although many American pilots were veterans of World War II, virtually all of the Soviet pilots were combat seasoned. Whatever the controversy, it cannot be argued that eventually the Soviet pilots were the primary reason the US switched B-29 combat operations from day to night bombing in areas that were not off-limits to MiG pilots.

Pilots on both sides of the conflict were prohibited from crossing certain lines. For the UN pilots, it was the Yalu River. For the Soviets it was an imaginary line drawn between Pyongyang and Wonsan--the southern limit of an area that became known as MiG Alley. Soviet pilots were also prohibited from flying over the sea. It was assumed that if they were shot down, an American ship would pick them up and their secret involvement would be out of the bag. This observer, however, has wondered all these years why the pilots themselves did not take the initiative, especially in cases where bombers were severely crippled. When asked for the most likely explanation, Stephen Sewell (Korean Air War Historian) said that a Soviet Air Force officer either got ahead or got his head handed to him. In other words, for the same reason that we did not cross the Yalu and bomb the Manchurian MiG bases.

The Soviets were also severely restricted by the shortage of suitable landing strips. Until early 1951, Antung at the mouth of the Yalu was the only airbase available for combat operations. On the South side of the Yalu, North Korea's 34 airfields were bombed before they could be used. Namsi Airfield, the 307th target on Black Tuesday, was being built not only to move the MiGs closer to the front lines but to provide a launch base that the Soviets, for whatever reason, believed could be used to conduct operations outside of MiG Alley.

In October 1951, the 303rd Fighter Aviation Division, headed up by General-Major A. Kumanichkin, consisted of two Fighter Aviation Regiments and one Guards Fighter Regiment assigned 36 MiGs each. Also available for combat was the 324th Fighter Aviation Division commanded by Colonel I. N. Kozhedub. The 324th had 72 MiGs assigned, split between two Fighter Regiments.

When the MiG pilots went up after a bomber formation, they usually divided into two groups, the attacking or strike group and the covering group. When attacking, the first priority of the strike group was to knock down as many bombers as possible in their initial attack. B-29s were usually attacked from the rear, the MiGs opening up their cannon fire from long range while flying at high speed. After the first pass, the squadrons broke into individual pairs and flights, continuing the attack from various directions until fuel dictated they must return to their home base. During the battle, strike and covering groups would often change places.

Before picking a fight with the B-29 fighter escorts, which sometimes numbered close to a hundred F-80, F-84, F-86, or British Meteors, the MiG pilots would seek a performance advantage. In many cases after attacking the opponents head-on, the MiG pilots would pull a high speed breakaway, climbing for altitude and a subsequent turn towards their safe haven across the Yalu. When UN aircraft tried to intercept MiGs returning to their protected airfield on the north side of the Yalu, they would be met by fighters assigned to protect returning squadrons. When American naval fighters came in from the Gulf of Korea to intercept the returning MiGs, Communist jets from a neighboring airfield would be launched to support landing operations at the blockaded airfield. Whatever the circumstances, the OVA covered the landings in the air, with additional fighters on ground alert, ready for take-off if the intervention continued.

The basic combat flight maneuvers used by MiG-15 pilots included the combat turn, tightening spiral, zoom climb, and split S. The MiG's altitude advantage made the split S a particularly effective combat maneuver. Flying well above a UN fighter, the pilot would execute a half-roll and dive on the hapless fighter below. Because the MiG had a nasty habit of stalling without warning, especially when turning away from an attack and losing airspeed, combat maneuvering required the pilot to maintain a healthy speed reserve. The Russians were well aware that these stalls could prove fatal and even when recovered would often place the MiG in an attitude highly vulnerable to attack.

The regimental strike group were usually first to enter the fray. Overhead, a covering squadron would keep an eye on the progress of the battle, entering into it only when UN numerical superiority became overwhelming or to protect fellow pilots when they had to break off and head home. During the initial attack the leading pair in the strike group would maneuver to get behind their opponents and close to the leader's effective cannon range before firing. The wingman would keep the leader informed of the whereabouts of enemy aircraft and engage those who tried to attack. If necessary, aircraft from another pair would attempt to ward off attacking UN fighters.

Only the regimental commander had the authority to break off combat. His decision was based on the situation. Voluntary or free exit took place in those instances when the MiG-15 fighters could leave without interference from the enemy. An essential or forced exit from the battle arena occurred when the situation was leaning in favor of the enemy or when the MiGs were low on fuel.

Returning to their home base, the formation would disperse across a broad front to make them less vulnerable to a surprise attack by UN fighters. To economize on fuel they would approach the field at high altitude, typically between 32,500 and 45,500 feet and descend on cue from the regimental command post, making a diving, straight-in approach, using their air brakes to slow for the final flare and touch down. Approaching the field at treetop level, using the lay of the land for cover, the fighters would land, one at a time, at 10-15 seconds intervals.

On 23 October 1951, the Soviet Order of Battle boiled down to the 64th IAK, which controlled all USSR combat aircraft in Manchuria. Major General Georgiy Ageyevich Lobov, a World War Two veteran who had 19 victories against the Nazi Luftwaffe and four more against American F-80 Shooting Stars in August and September 1951, commanded the unit.

The 64th IAK controlled two divisions, the 324th and the 303rd, commanded by Colonel Ivan Nikitovich Kozhedub and General Major Aleksandr S. Kumanichkin, respectively. As previously noted, Kozhedub had earned the honor of being the greatest Soviet and Allied ace during World War Two. Although divisional commanders usually flew with their subordinates, Kozhedub was prohibited from flying combat missions. As the most famous airman in the USSR, the government felt that if he was shot down and killed his demise would be difficult to hide or to credit to "training" or "operational" duties. Kozhedub had two regiments under his command, the 176th GIAP (*Gvard Istrevitelniy Avia Polk* or Guards Fighter Aviation Regiment), led by Lt. Colonel Sergey Fedoseyevich Vishnyakov, and the 96th GIAP, led by Colonel Yevgeny Georgievich Pepelyayev.

The three regiments of the 303rd IA were the 17th IAP, led by Major Grigoriy Ivanovich Pulov, the 18th GIAP, under Lt. Colonel Aleksandr Yefimovich Belostotsky, and the 523rd IAP, commanded by Lt. Colonel Anatoly N. Karasyev.

Each Soviet regiment had about 30 MiG-15s, and divided them into three squadrons, usually numbered 1st, 2nd and 3rd. Two of the squadron commanders, Smorchkov and Os'kin, were key players in the Black Tuesday air battle. The 64th IAK, the fighter corps defending northern North Korea, launched regiments from both the 303rd and 324th. The 324th, nicknamed the *Paradnaya Divisiya* or Parade Division because it flew most of the exhibitions in Moscow, tangled with the fighter escorts while all three regiments of the crack 303d hit the bombers.

By the time Black Tuesday rolled around, MiG units had developed combat tactics against B-29s that would prove devastating. Aimed at using a squadron of MiG-15s against a group of up to eight B-29s with a covering group of up to twelve F-80s or F-84s, doctrine decreed that the attack be carried out at top speed either simultaneously or sequentially by flights. Such an attack, they surmised, limited the fighter cover's time to prepare against it. Further instructions read, "attacks should be made from behind at a deflection angle of 0 /4 to 2 / 4 using the moving reticle in the sight and aiming at their fuel tanks, engines, and cockpit. Long bursts should be fired from ranges of 800 meters down to 300 meters. When breaking off the firing pass it is best to go beneath the B-29 with a subsequent turn in front of it at an angle of 20-30 degrees. Waiting 1-1.5 minutes, the aircraft should then turn 180 degrees to the opposite side and make a second attack from the front at a deflection angle of 0 /4 to 2 / 4. Firing should be carried out at a range of 1300-1200 meters; the firing run should terminate at 400 meters after which they should break off combat without changing direction."

According to Soviet records, over 19,000 daylight sorties were launched from November 1950 to January 1952. During that time they claimed to have shot down 500 UN aircraft, more than 17% of them bombers. The highest scoring Soviet ace of the Korean War was "Evgeni" Pepelyaev, known as the "Big night boy," with 23 confirmed kills. He was credited with twelve F-86s, six F-80s, four F-84s, and one F-94. Two of these were "shared" kills. Anatoly Karelin's nine claimed victories were all B-29s shot down at night.

When, as a direct result of Black Tuesday, the UN stopped daylight B-29 raids within range of the MiGs parked across the Yalu, bombing in that region was conducted under cover of darkness. Because the MiG-15 was not equipped with radar for search and target acquisition, the fighters were only able to effectively intercept bombers that were illuminated. In other words, the question was no longer "how to shoot them down" but "how to find them." Nonetheless, using an unusual combination of primitive and new technology, fighter pilots would sometimes home in on bonfires that were laid out like points on a grid map and lit by people on the ground. This gave them a ground reference point that they could use to attack the bomber--along with altitude, course, and distance information provided by a ground controller. Without airborne radar and other visual aids, due to blackout conditions on the ground, MiG pilots could be directed to the bombers by the ground radar controllers with reference to the fires. Even when their radar was electronically jammed or cluttered by chaff, Soviet ground controllers could broadcast the position of the bomber in relation to the numbered bonfires to the MiG orbiting closest to that location. The MiG would then come in underneath the bomber's flight altitude looking for the glow from the engine turbo chargers before opening fire. The bonfires were limited to nights when the skies were fairly clear, the moon wasn't out, and the MiGs were prepared to launch. These factors would severely limit the number of occasions for the use of such bonfires, plus terrain would sometimes prevent them from being laid out in the true grid pattern necessary for precise intercepts. Because of the mountains, mobile radar stations likewise had great difficulty in strategically locating themselves for their most effective deployment.

In 1992, the Russians revealed that a total of 26,000 men had been assigned to Soviet air defense and fighter units during the Korean War. With that number of personnel and all the Soviet aerial activity, it is hard to believe that the official intelligence agencies in the United States did not have a clue that the Russians were flying the MiG-15s. It is perhaps easier to believe that the information was being deliberately withheld, on both sides of the Iron Curtain, for political reasons. Whatever the reasons, the crews flying the B-29s during the period leading up to Black Tuesday were well aware that you couldn't stick a foot soldier in a high performance jet fighter and expect him to accomplish much more than to kill himself.

America's "Retreads"

The Americans who crewed B-29s in the Korean War were divided into two distinct groups, those who had chosen active duty and those who hadn't. Although it might be expected the two groups to have had differing attitudes toward the conflict, this observer detected none. Every man who flew combat had two goals. One was to get the job done and the other was to return home alive. There were doubts and anxieties, especially when it came to the first goal. It seemed to many that the politicians really did not want to finish the task. This resulted in minor rebellions that the media inflated beyond their proper proportions, but were really of no consequence.

Those, like myself, who had chosen the Air Force, were mostly men who had enlisted of their own volition for the simple reason that they wanted to be around airplanes. Fred Meier and Lloyd Wentworth, classmates in the navigator class of 12 October 1950, were likewise among the new guys. The other group was made up almost exclusively of recalled veterans. These were the pilots, bombardiers, radar operators, and navigators who had already won the big war. Many had survived the bloody air battles that raged over Europe and Japan. They were the survivors who had gone back to college under the GI Bill, earned their degrees and were happily entrenched in whatever their chosen profession happened to be. Most were married and had children. On the crew I served as pilot (right seat), the other officers had been recalled from such diverse civilian occupations as farmer, minister, engineer, and grocer. Our aircraft commander owned oil wells on his farm in Kansas and shot golf in the high seventies. The navigator was a terrific artist who became an ordained Baptist minister. The radar operator had managed a Safeway, had three kids and a new home in Las Cruces, N.M. The bombardier had just gotten his feet on the postwar ground as a chemical engineer. He loved bass fishing and White Horse scotch. None of them had received pay for having been in the active Air Force Reserve. All had been members of the involuntary reserve, a group of ex-active duty personnel who were required to remain in the reserve for a period of time after their discharge. None of them expected to be recalled--especially to fight in a war against a small, unknown Asian country.

Even in the dark days after Pearl Harbor, those who were called out of the inactive reserve usually served in an administrative or training capacity within the United States. This made sense. They were older, wiser, and more experienced. Many, like Max Nelson, hadn't operated the equipment they would be required to use in the Korean War in six or more years. The Air Force, however, was in a bind. Even though the United States had undergone the most massive build-up in both resources and manpower for the costliest war in U.S. history, after Japan's surrender the armed services were virtually disbanded. This was particularly true of the Air Force. Thousands of airplanes were either stacked and scrapped or placed in "moth balls" on vast, empty tracts of the American West. A few B-29 bomber units were retained for what would eventually evolve into the Strategic Air Command (SAC).

The prevailing belief that SAC would answer the call in any armed conflict that required bombers was never realized in the limited conflicts that became the hallmark of the Cold War. SAC had adopted a policy of nuclear deterrence, which Truman had deemed unsuitable for what he called a "Police Action." Several conventionally armed B-29 units answered the initial call but their officer crew replacements were eventually drawn mostly from the inactive reserves.

The United Sates Air Force needed bomber crews right away, and the inactive reserve was the only source readily available.

Those who had been in the inactive reserves jokingly referred to themselves as "retreads," so-named after the tires that during World War II were returned to service after being recapped. B-29 retreads were routinely "recapped" with a quickie refresher course at Randolph Air Force Base, San Antonio Texas, followed by combat crew training at Forbes Air Force Base, Topeka Kansas. The entire program could transform a man from "prospering civilian" in Chicago to "combat loss" in MiG Alley seven months later.

What was most unpalatable to many combat crew members was the glaring unfairness of not sending SAC's well-trained, professional elite into the fray. Instead, those who had felt their lives settled and secure were yanked away from their families to put their lives on the line under what many saw as an absurd set of rules. Morale dipped even lower when it became apparent that those who had been thrust into harm's way were not receiving the same promotions that SAC's elite crew members were at bases back home. Enlisted personnel attached to a combat unit but assigned to another group could not be promoted at all. Eventually some of the disparity was removed by allotting spot promotions, but these were retracted as soon as the combat tour ended. At one point, not long after the Black Tuesday debacle, replacement flight crews training at Randolph AFB staged a minor revolt that received the usual media coverage but had little overall effect. When threatened with courts-martial, those involved reluctantly joined the fray, a few rebelling in their own way by aborting missions and performing poorly.

On a check ride Fred Meier (lead navigator, Black Tuesday) supervised, his replacement navigator directed the airplane toward a thunderstorm over southwestern Japan instead of Cheju-do Island, the coast-in point for Korea, claiming that on radar he couldn't tell the difference between an island mass and a thunderstorm.

With very few exceptions, as they always had, the men who crewed the B-29s performed with honor.

Traditionally used as a basic and primary training base where fledgling pilots earned their wings, Randolph AFB was best known as the "West Point of the Air." Located just outside the northeastern city limits of San Antonio, Texas, Randolph's most famous and enduring icon, Bldg. 100, is best known among airmen as the "Taj Mahal." The most notable feature of the essentially Southwestern architecture is the 147 feet tall central "bell" tower, which actually contains a 500,000-gallon water tank. This tile and plaster tower, covered with ornamental concrete grill work and topped with a blue and gold mosaic tiled dome, has become an oft-used symbol of United States air power—especially in old Hollywood films. Officially dedicated in October 1931, the building is listed on the National Registry of Historic Places.

In late 1950, the "West Point of the Air" suddenly found its parallel ramps crowded with the heaviest operational bomber of World War II when B-29 combat crew training became the highest Air Force priority. Crews had to be reactivated from the vast pool of Reserve personnel and Randolph AFB was quickly converted from basic T-6 pilot to advanced B-29 aircrew training. At its peak, around eighty B-29's were flying daily in the USAF Air

Training Command pipeline program that provided replacement aircrews for the Far East Air Forces (FEAF).

Most B-29s were manned by eleven aircrew members. Up front and most vulnerable, the bombardier occupied the foremost position in the green house with two pilots seated a few feet behind. Sticking to a tradition that has continued to this day, the pilot in command occupied the left seat with the copilot on his right. The Aircraft Commander was usually referred to as the AC, and the copilot was officially called the pilot. The flight engineer rode backwards in a seat directly behind the pilot. The navigator and radio operator completed the forward compartment complement. In the aft compartment, the blister gunners were called left scanner and right scanner, although they usually preferred being identified as "gunners," while the Central Fire Controller was called "CFC" by everyone, including himself. The CFC sat in an elevated "barber chair" between the scanners and looked out through the top blister. Having the best all-around view, he was the gunner who directed the remote control firing of all the B-29's guns except the tail turret. Curiously, the tail gunner retained his title as "Tail Gunner." The only officer to occupy the rear section of the aircraft aft of the bomb bays was the Radar Operator (R/O), most often addressed as "Radar," as in "Radar, this is Pilot." Radio and Radar operated the meager ECM equipment, which included chaff and very little electronic interference--which seemed to work not-at-all against the big radar tracking guns. Although the normal crew complement was eleven, other personnel were often on board for training or simply as "observers." It was not uncommon to have a "weenie" or "ground pounder" (anyone without wings) along just to earn his combat pay. The egalitarian nature of the military required a person fly in combat in order to draw combat pay.

After completing B-29 flight training at Randolph, the crews transferred to Forbes AFB, Topeka, Kansas for combat crew training before being shipped either to Okinawa or Japan. When my flight engineer and I reported for duty in May 1951 the Topeka hangars were filled with hay and there was only one B-29 on the field. We were told to take additional leave and come back when they were ready--which turned out to be about a month later.

Part of becoming combat ready included a trip to Camp Carson, Colorado for survival training. The concept behind Carson was to teach crews what they should know to survive in case they were shot down behind enemy lines. This included living off the land and finding a way back to friendly lines. Parachutes became tents and survival rations, particularly a brick labeled "pemmican," became missiles that airmen chucked from mountaintops to see how far they could be thrown. Pemmican was the dried fatty meat that was the mainstay of the ration kept in the survival kit. Even though pemmican was not very appealing (fairly disgusting, actually) the apparent reason for its inclusion was that it lasted a long time and had great caloric content for its weight. In fact, most crew members found the fatty meat indigestible, often sickening. Others (like myself) learned that it could be consumed if liberally sprinkled with chili powder.

Another military staple deemed necessary for survival was the .45 Automatic Colt Pistol (ACP) that had been designed for and accepted by the Army in 1911. The large caliber handgun is still famous for its stopping power, both real and imagined--although it was said that just the sight of the .45 ACP in the hands of his victim often stopped an aggressor in his tracks. Notwithstanding, for survival purposes the handgun had more drawbacks than advantages. The bulky automatic was worn in a shoulder holster that could tear loose from the wind forces encountered during bailout. If an airman still had the .45 after he landed in enemy territory, its short range and relative inaccuracy would have been ineffective against an enemy armed with rifles--or (if the shots missed) even pitchforks. Also, the much ballyhooed intimidation factor that the mere size of the Colt ACP was supposed to evoke would probably not work against anyone who'd ever fired the weapon. Beyond room-range, it was notoriously inaccurate in the hands of all but the most experienced shooter. Its inaccuracy coupled with the noise factor made the .45 ACP unacceptable as a survival weapon. Not only would the sound alert all humans and potential meals within hearing to the location of the survivor, the shot would in all likelihood miss its target. To remedy this shortcoming, a .22 Hornet survival rifle was placed inside the survival kit that strapped onto the parachute harness and was sat on like a stadium seat. After a bail out landing, the Hornet had to be unpacked and assembled. The single-shot Hornet was limited to one cartridge and one shot each time it was loaded, and (because of the Geneva Convention) could not be used for self-protection. Because of these limitations, many crew members carried an extra handgun. I carried a small caliber .22 pistol for rabbits and chickens, while counting on the Colt to dissuade angry farmers.

The course also taught airmen how to resist interrogation, a notion that later, in Korean prison camps, would backfire and cause embarrassment to downed crew members and the United States government. Originally, the instructions issued out of Camp Carson allowed and even encouraged prisoners of war (POWs) to go along with their enemy interrogators, to do whatever it took to survive and fight another day. Later, when American POWs actually signed "confessions" they believed were basically absurd, the subsequent propaganda fallout prompted the survival school to recant their earlier instructions.

While many found themselves back flying as unwilling B-29 combat crew members, William Eldon Reeter, Baker flight leader on Black Tuesday, arrived at his position by a somewhat different path. With the rapid demobilization following the WW II, like so many other servicemen, Bill Reeter returned to the farm; however, it did not take long for him to realize that farm life was not for him. In 1948, the newly created Department of the Air Force began recruiting former pilots to fly the Berlin airlift. Bill was one of those pilots who were soon flying C-54's in the airlift. After returning to the US, he transitioned to the left seat of B-29's.

As an aircraft commander, Bill was a natural leader. In photos, he bears a remarkable resemblance to Zack Mosley's handsome and tall WW II cartoon pilot, Smilin' Jack. Like many others of his generation, he took his job to his country seriously. His sense of loyalty was remarkable and his crews returned this loyalty in spades. He was one of those aircraft commanders that crews would do anything for because they knew he would be calm and effective in the most chaotic emergencies. All of these attributes would prove crucial in the aftermath of the MiG attacks on Black Tuesday and earn Bill Reeter the third highest award given for valor in the face of the enemy, the Silver Star.

When I inquired about Bill Reeter's character, his son, Alan, sent the following: "There was one interesting aspect of his character that is undisputed. He never said anything negative about anyone. Even in conversations about the most evil dictators of his time, Bill avoided the invective used by almost everyone else. This demonstrated a rare, and extreme respect for others. His crews, perhaps unconsciously, understood and responded to this."

William Reeter was born on November 27, 1921 on a farm in central Illinois, the older of two bothers and a sister. His grandfather had emigrated from Germany in the 1890's and settled in the Midwest. They were typical of recent German emigrants, Protestant, hard working, loyal to family, and stoic. The family farm was virtually self-sufficient. They raised almost all their own food in a large garden. They had abundant apple and cherry trees. The women canned enough food to last year round. All meat was grown, butchered, and smoked on the farm. While they would buy shoes at a store, they did much of their own shoe and leather repair. Being the oldest child, Bill took on farm chores at an early age. Milking the cows was one of his first duties. While he was still very young, almost all of the family's farm implements were horse drawn. When Bill reached the age of eleven, he was allowed to hitch horses to the plow and work the fields. The very next year, his father purchased their first tractor.

It's interesting to note that Bill began his working life walking behind a horse drawn plow and within 25 years piloted the Convair B-58 Hustler, a mach 2, nuclear-capable bomber that set more world records than any other type of combat aircraft.

Work occupied the center of life, but Sunday was reserved for church and afternoon potlucks shared with their large extended family that lived on neighboring farms within easy traveling distance. Music was also an important family tradition. Everyone was expected to play some instrument, so Bill learned to play the trumpet.

Smoking and drinking were sins. The children never saw adults do either. At the age of 90, Bill's father claimed that a drop of alcohol never passed over his lips, but admitted to taking a single puff of a cigar when he was young. The family took a strict, disciplinarian approach to child rearing. Good behavior and respect for adult authority was strictly enforced. Children were not allowed to speak at the dinner table unless spoken to. Infractions of any kind were not tolerated. Punishment often consisted of a "switching," a formalized punishment for specific infractions. The number of lashings was set to conform to the offense. Tradition dictated that they be delivered out of sight of others, behind the smoke house.

As a student, Bill was well above average. He played basketball, and trumpet in the high school band. One of the things that distinguished him early on was his height, over 6'2"-- exceptionally tall for the times.

In what was to be his junior year at Milliken University in Decatur, Ill., Bill joined the army, was sent to bugle school and became the post bugler. When the Army Air Forces began taking applications for flying cadets, Bill applied and was accepted. After graduating from flight school, he was assigned to fly the Martin B-26, known by some as the "Widow Maker," and eventually instructed in the airplane at Dodge Army Airfield in Kansas. While stationed there he met and married June Ellen Ward, who had also grown up on a farm. When she and Bill met, she had just graduated from nursing school. He never saw combat during World War II—an experience he would more than make up for in the skies over Korea.

Perhaps more typical of those who, like me, were in the Korean War by choice, Stan Kavrik had graduated in Aviation Cadet Class 50E and would find himself in the right seat of a B-29 under attack by MiGs on the day after Black Tuesday.

A native of Little Ferry, New Jersey, Kavrik grew up on the Hackensack River within view of Teterboro Airport. Watching WW I Jenny biplanes flying in and out of the airport when he was a boy made him decide that aviation was the field for him. He went to work for Atlantic Aviation. Roscoe Turner, the famous air race pilot, was one of his boyhood heroes and Stan remembers (with embarrassment) putting gas in Roscoe Turner's oil tank by mistake. Stan also worked as a valet parking attendant and will never forget Frank Sinatra tipping him "a whole quarter." Stan's description of the famous crooner could have served admirably as a topic for nose art. In 1944, when he was seventeen, Stan enlisted in the Army Air Force and flew as a flight engineer on an OA-10, the air force's designation for the PBY Catalina flying boat. Eventually, he was accepted into the Aviation Cadet program and graduated in late 1950.

His first assignment was the 98th Bombardment Wing at Fairchild AFB, Washington. He was sent from there to the 92nd in

Yokota, Japan as an individual copilot replacement. He arrived on 15 July, 1951 and shortly thereafter wound up back in the 98th when that unit transferred to the Far East. He was assigned to Robert S. Calling's crew, where he would remain until they returned to the ZI the day before Christmas, 1951. Calling's crew did not fly on Black Tuesday, the day widely accepted as the last daylight mission flown by B-29s into MiG Alley, but the next day, October 24, 1951. Caught in the machinery of military inevitability, they took off unaware what had happened to the 307th just twenty-four hours earlier and flew headlong into the same determined and lethal opposition that had greeted their sister unit the day before.

Max Nelson, a radar operator on another 98th crew, flew the same mission.

Like Kavrik, Max's stint on a B-29 crew did not follow the usual path of being crewed up in the states before being sent overseas. After finishing radar school two weeks after WWII ended he stayed in the inactive reserve until, in 1950, like most former servicemen in his shoes, he signed on with the active reserve. No sooner had he done so than he was ordered to Castle AFB to fly B-29s with the 93rd Air Refueling Squadron. Max was recalled as a second lieutenant, received a spot to 1st Lt., which was confirmed, then a spot to Captain, which he lost when he returned stateside. When he left active duty, his rank reverted to 2nd Lt because reserve promotions were frozen while on active duty. In his words, "I was so ticked at that point I requested either a restoration of the Captaincy or a discharge. The discharge came almost by return mail. End of military career!"

In April 1951 Max received orders attaching him, temporarily, as an individual replacement with the 98BG, Yokota Japan. Being assigned temporary duty at Yokota, Max remembers, was in many ways fun. The permanent duty officer's wives were always put out at the "bomber boys" for crowding the swimming pool and the Officer's Club. He notes that it was "great in other ways too."

It was never fun or great, we both agreed, to fly combat missions.

After flying an orientation mission, Max and ten other individual replacements were lumped together to make up a crew, and not long after flew their first combat mission. It was the first time any of them had flown together and the first time Max had seen a radar set since 1945. He felt, however, luckier than most. The crew got along well and had a good sense of camaraderie, as well as humor. Whenever they approached touch down for landing, the gunners gathered by the door to the bomb bay, then "ran like hell to the rear to try to get the tail skid to drag so they could get the free case of beer (a B-29 tradition) from the A/C." Max added, "It seldom worked--probably because his aircraft commander had over 3000 hours in B-29s." Max felt that his Navigator and Bombardier were also the best he ever flew with. The combination of experience and skill paid off. The crew soon became a wing lead crew and Max was sent to Iwakuni, Japan in September 1951 for SHORAN training.

By mid-1951, the Korean War had sunk into a rut it would barely budge from. The front lines stabilized near where the war had started and ceasefire talks were begun. Nevertheless, it would take two more years of fighting and dying for the belligerents to reach an agreement that would stop the shooting.

At the same time FEAF Bomber Command began receiving the newly trained replacement crews and B-29 aircraft. These crews were assigned to one of three units stationed in the Far East, the 98BG at Yokota AFB, Japan, or the 19BG and 307BW, both operating out of Kadena AFB, Okinawa. Those who felt themselves unfortunate to have been recalled and assigned to combat duty hoped they would at least be 33 1/3% lucky and wind up in Japan instead of Okinawa, an island that had been nearly pulverized in WW II and had earned the not-so-affectionate nickname, The Rock.

Japan, which had capitulated so completely, was considered the ideal assignment for more than a few reasons. Movies such as *Sayonara* and *The Bridges At Toko-ri* captured the essence of the pleasant cultural jolt that awaited young American servicemen bound for Japan--albeit with the censor's touch. Prior to our arrival on Okinawa, my crew was lucky to spend several days in the Tokyo area after being diverted from our destination by an August typhoon. Among the amenities that awaited us was a round of golf at the Koganei Country Club for a ten-cent caddy fee. (A recent check reveals that the green fee, with caddy is $95) The ridiculously low cost of everything was a result of reparations agreements reached after WW II that totaled one trillion and thirty billion yen. A man earning a GI's low pay could live like a king in Japan. An even bigger attraction for young men raised by ascetic Western standards was the overwhelming availability of women who had not been raised by those standards. WW II had so depleted the male population that women far outnumbered men. Women (many of them still girls) did most jobs, such as the aforementioned caddying. Additionally, the overabundance of the fairer sex was further enhanced (in those pre-PC days) by their relative subservience to the male ego. Among the amenities provided to Japan-based B-29 crew officers were the mansion-like buildings that had once housed ranking Japanese officers and were turned over to the Americans for use by the military. Each officer had his own room and two maids to handle the cleaning, laundry, and other domestic chores. Stan Kavrik recalls that he never had it so good.

All totaled, being stationed with either the 92BG or the 98BG in Japan was far more desirable than being stuck on a bombed-out island inhabited by deadly snakes and people who lived in grass huts, as was the fate of the 19th, 22nd and 307th bombardment units on Okinawa.

By later, 1951, the disparity in assignments was further aggravated by differences in amenities provided to the two groups stationed on Okinawa. Crews in the 19th, sometimes referred to as "an arm of MacArthur's Air Force," were moved from Quonsets to small, relatively private metal huts they called "hooches." At the same time, the 307th, on loan from SAC, was relegated to the tent city set up to accommodate their predecessor, the 22BG. Even though crew replacements from both units were on temporary duty assignments, the apparent thinking was that the SAC units were "visiting" while the 19th was in it for the long haul. As it turned out, primarily because the peace talks dragged on for years, the 307th was also in it for the long haul.

Most commissioned crew members in both the 19th and 307th took their meals at the Officer's Club, while the enlisted personnel had a mess hall. Everyone got their mail from the same small window used for mail call and watched the same movies in a theater where large rats were sometimes seen scouting the rafters.

There was speculation that the Strategic Air Command didn't believe the 307th would entrench itself on Okinawa when it denied its crews one of the small pleasures of flying a combat aircraft with a lot of unadorned aluminum on the nose. Most likely a brass hat up the chain of command decided that the 307th, a SAC outfit, would not lower itself to the standards of the 19th by painting dirty pictures on its airplanes, and those that had pictures, such as *Sit & Git*, were scrubbed clean. Nose art, which had reached its apex on WW II bombers, particularly on B-17s, was stretched to the limits of the double-entendre when applied to the noses of Korean War B-29s. Indeed, most nose art had several layers of meaning. *Memphis Belles* and other named aircraft that evoked nostalgia for loved ones or home were replaced by names like *Miss Minooky* and the enigmatic *FUJIGMO*.

Korean War nose art more often expressed the true sentiments of the crews that flew them. The art not only identified and distinguished individual aircraft, but units as well. Bombers stationed at Yokota reflected a ready access to top-notch Japanese artists, whereas Okinawan nose art was often on the primitive side. In all cases, however, there was a propensity to display the female form sans clothing. Tolerance to nudity fluctuated throughout the conflict but appears to have become less after the peace talks began. This sudden censorship was rumored to have had various sources, from overly sensitive base commander's wives, pious chaplains, and commanders who didn't want to have their bombers with dirty pictures rotated back to the ZI. There was also the general presumption that the naked babes could become propaganda devices for the Communists, along the line of, "depraved Americans drop bombs on innocent women and children from airplanes adorned with whores." There is no evidence that the Communists had a clue as to the underlying satire and sarcasm embodied in nose art.

Officers flying B-29s in the Korean War were a far cry from even themselves in WW II when many of them flew combat missions. They were older, much better educated, successful professionals in other fields. Most had married and saw themselves as husbands and fathers. Most never imagined they would be called up and sent back. So when Harry Truman declared war, and back they went, a common thought floating about was, "They didn't get me the first time so they're sending me back "

This influx of "civilian hats" scuttled traditional military discipline. In its place was something best described as a begrudging professionalism. There was a job to be done and they would do it. C.J. Christ, a copilot in the 19th, recalls some rowdy nights. On one occasion he and other crew members took their dates to dine at the Officer's Club at Naha, the USAF fighter defense base on Okinawa. "They said they couldn't seat us as there wasn't enough room," C.J. remembers. "While waiting in the lounge, we spotted a mouse. We turned over the couches to block the door and tried to kill him with our shoes. I don't remember what happened to the mouse but they threw us out of the club."

A certain amount of discipline was evident in the way crews prepared for a mission. The general mission briefing covered navigation, bombing, radio procedures, ordnance, tactics, and intelligence, which included current escape and invasion information.

C.J. recollects a pep talk from mustachioed Col. Breckenridge, the 19th Bomb Group commander. He'd placed the group on stand-down because they'd missed hitting a bridge. As he angrily paced back and forth on the briefing room stage smoking a Pall Mall inserted into his signature ivory cigarette holder, flicking ashes, he said, "Men, you are jeopardizing my career."

Before long, Breckenridge became affectionately referred to as "Broken-bridge." His likeness mysteriously appeared on the face of a baby, who had replaced a watermelon cradled in the arms of *Dixie Babe*, a bikini-clad lass on the nose of a 93rd Bomb Squadron B-29. The "baby" wore a moustache and was puffing on a cigarette inserted into an ivory cigarette holder.

After final briefings the crew would board a canvas-canopied, six-by Army truck that would take them to their assigned B-29. On their way they would stop off to pick up their parachutes and other flight gear from a building that just about everyone called "the PE (personal equipment) shack." Flight lunches were usually the next stop before finally arriving at their airplane. After unloading themselves and their equipment, each crew member went through his preflight checklist in his specialty area, checking nuts, bolts and data needed to successfully complete the mission. The pilots would walk around the airplane, visually inspecting engines, controls, and the airplane's general condition in much the same manner they had with all the airplanes they'd ever flown, dating back to the Piper Cub.

Glenn Garig, a copilot with the 19th BG, remembers worrying about the gunners checking for fuel leaks while the engineer turned the props.

Crew inspection came just before boarding. The crew lined up to the left of the nose wheel in a specified order beginning with the copilot. Although this inspection was more show than substance, it assembled the crew for one last gathering before boarding. As unlikely as it was that anyone would forget their survival gear, the aircraft commander made sure everyone had an oxygen mask, flashlight, Mae West, and parachute. One of the rituals was to don the parachute, adjust the buckles on the webbed straps to fit, and do a right-face and have the next-in-line check the inspection dates in a little record book that was kept in a pocket on the side of the pack. In the rare event that the chute was past due or accidentally deployed while moving around inside the airplane, extra parachutes were carried.

Equipment shortages were more the rule than the exception. Fred Meier recalls that winter flight clothing was unavailable for 307th combat crewmen--especially boots. He often had to sit on his feet to protect them from frostbite. The planners apparently believed that crews based on sub-tropical Okinawa flying pressurized B-29s had no need for warm gear, forgetting that the B-29 was poorly insulated and spottily heated against temperatures that could register sixty below--much less the possibility of bailout. Ponchos were also in short supply, which made life on Okinawa, where it rained most of the time, even less bearable. Other shortages included footlockers that Meier and his fellow crew members rescued from the dump. To make matters worse, in-flight lunches were too often C-rations left over from WW II. In Meier's words, "they were rotten . . . spoiled (and) inedible."

One of the carry-overs beliefs from peacetime operations was the idea that a busy soldier was a happier soldier. Toward that end, nearly everyone was assigned an extra duty to keep them from mischief when they weren't flying. Mine was 28th Bombardment Squadron PE Officer--a task routinely dumped on shavetails (new second lieutenants). A crew member flying every third day had little spare time to perform any function that might be useful in managing the supplies that he and his fellow crew members would need to fly a mission. Nevertheless, military reasoning dictated, an officer had to be responsible, and who better than the new guy?

My first duty as Squadron PE Officer was to assume responsibility by signing the inventory. Parachutes and the B-4 "Mae West" life preservers comprised most of the PE Shack's usable stock. Supposedly there were also articles of apparel such as warm jackets, gloves and boots needed for emergency survival. When I showed up at the PE Shack, an old master sergeant (the one really in charge) shoved a pile of papers in front of me and said, "Please sign these, Sir." When I asked what I was signing, he said it was the inventory for personal equipment. Most of the items on the sheets were listed as "crates" with vague references to contents. Tons of flight clothing and equipment had been stockpiled for the WW II assault on mainland Japan and transferred to the 19th, presumably for safekeeping. The list contained items we'd never been issued, such as insulated boots and fleece-lined gloves. When I refused to sign without actually seeing the stuff, the M/Sgt. looked at me like I was nuts, and reluctantly drove me to a fenced-in yard stacked with giant, rotting crates. We found a listed boots crate and pried it open. Out tumbled dozens of pairs of fleece-lined flight boots. I tried on a few and my foot went right through the bottoms. In spite of having been sealed in some sort of brown plastic, they'd all rotted. The warm gloves were likewise unusable, but we did stumble upon a crate containing soft doeskin Navy fighter pilot issues. I requisitioned a few for myself and made sure the rest were handed out to crews--although I doubt any made it over to the 307th.

When I stubbornly refused to sign the inventory without actually seeing the items, the M/Sgt. tried to entice me into signing by giving me one of the new blue Air Force jackets. He said there were only three on the island, two issued to the Wing and Squadron commanders and the one he was issuing me. A few days later mine was lifted off the rack at the Officer's Club where I'd hung it while cashing a check because wearing flight clothing inside the club was forbidden. Later, in village of Naha, I spotted an Okinawan on a bike, riding through a crowd, wearing a blue A3 jacket. Unfortunately, he disappeared almost as quickly as he'd appeared.

A few days before their departure from Kadena, C.J. Christ's crew sent their flight jackets into Naha to have their airplane nose art, unit insignias, name, rank, and wings painted on the jackets by an artist. When they went to collect they couldn't find the artist or the jackets. C.J. also remembers seeing the brand new blue jackets showing up on the Naha black market before the crews received them.

When we left Okinawa six months later, I still had not signed the squadron PE inventory.

On Black Tuesday, the inequities in amenities that existed between the three active B-29 units in all likelihood aggravated the unhealthy competitive spirit that contributed to the disaster over Namsi.

4: The Machinery of War

The opposing combatants in the Black Tuesday air battle crewed two very different machines, each designed for a specific task. In short, the United States' Boeing B-29 Superfortress had been engineered to destroy the enemies' ability to wage war, while the Soviet's Mikoyan-Gurevich MiG-15 had been designed to destroy the B-29 Superfortress. The B-29 had achieved its design goal and a place in history in awesome proportions by dropping the first atomic bombs on Hiroshima and Nagasaki, bringing to a close man's bloodiest modern conflict.

The destructive potential of the B-29 made it of paramount importance to the Soviet Union's military planners to develop, fly, and have combat ready, an aircraft that could stop the B-29 from inflicting catastrophic damage on their already battered homeland. In a few short years, the Soviets interposed just such an airplane, the Mikoyan-Gurevich MiG-15, into the Korean air war.

The B-29 had been designed to carry a maximum of 20,000 pounds of high explosives. On most missions in the Korean War this "maximum" translated to forty 500-pound bombs. Although the B-29 was notorious for not wanting to become airborne at maximum design gross weights, the bomb load was seldom reduced to provide an added safety margin. Like highway speed limits, the maximum allowable was considered the norm. Unfortunately, numerous B-29s crashed on or shortly after take off because an engine sputtered or weather conditions weren't quite right, simply because the airplane was overloaded.

Another factor that greatly influenced results and, no doubt, morale, was mission duration. B-29s based on Okinawa faced an average of nine hours in the air on each mission, with occasional jaunts up to eleven hours. During a maximum effort involving all three groups, it could take as long as two additional hours just to form up the attack force and its fighter cover. MiGs, on the other hand, could intercept the B-29s and be back on the ground in 45 minutes.

Behind these two most obvious machines was a technological structure of command and control embraced by both sides. On the UN side, FEAF (Far East Air Forces) Bomber Command selected the targets and directed the missions. Once airborne there was little control other than what had been preplanned, with its prescribed set of rules. If the target was unavailable for various reasons, including weather or lack of fighter support, a secondary target had been predetermined, as well as a target of last resort, usually bombed if a particular B-29 was experiencing mechanical trouble.

The Communists, on the other hand, gave command and control their ongoing top priority. As the war progressed so did the efficiency of the command structure. Once the OVA was organized, command and control of combat operations of the air forces belonged to the command post of the Commanding General of the Unified Air Army (the Soviets). Independent command posts were organized for the Korean and Chinese air; however, their impact on the overall air war was negligible. The OVA also set four auxiliary command posts in the areas of Supungdong, Hichen, Pyongyang, and Anju, as well as a radio and eight visual information posts deployed 250-300 kilometers south of the MiG bases. Communications was via high frequency radio—used by both sides for long distance communications.

Command posts were outfitted with combat control tables and a portable radarscope fed by as many as five radar stations. Based on the previous days' combat reports, regimental commanders would schedule the pilots and group leaders, their call signs, takeoff order, and missions for the day. Once the incoming bombers were spotted the command posts would assess the situation, decide how best to repulse the enemy raid, order the fighters into the air, and guide their intercept.

When repulsing mass air raids during daylight under clear weather conditions, the MiGs would be flown into zones drawn up on a coded map. Prior to making contact, the Soviet group leader would maneuver to give his fighters an edge in speed and altitude. Minutes before actual contact, the MiGs would drop tanks and increase speed to 573-590 mph (930-950 kph).

Radio and Radar

By intercepting UN radio transmissions, the Soviets were able to track almost every phase of Allied combat operations. From listening to these transmissions they would know the size of the strike force, types of aircraft involved, and the nature of their mission. In many cases they were able to follow the UN air forces aircraft from takeoff to landing, including rescue work and post strike reconnaissance aircraft.

The main radio intercept post was dispersed among buildings, bunkers, tents or specially equipped trucks in the immediate proximity of the command post. Its equipment included 10-20 HF and VHF radio receivers, tape recorders, and an air situation map table for plotting radar data. Forward, truck-mounted radio intercept posts were deployed along the front lines to intercept radio messages transmitted from Allied airfields during aircraft preflight and launch stages. Trucks allowed the operators to move quickly to the best position for picking combat related VHF and HF radio signals and send them directly to the OVA fighter aviation formations by landline. The personnel who manned radio intercept posts all spoke English.

Without ground radar stations, the Communists would have been hard pressed to pinpoint the location of UN bombers until it was too late to intercept them. North Korea's mountains were, however, a problem. Radar positioning required a reasonably level surface elevated enough to prevent the search radar antenna from picking up excessive clutter from surrounding obstacles. To overcome the problem, stations were deployed in pairs. One station was used for spotting distant and low-flying aircraft, and the other for acquiring and observing close-in targets--as well as for guiding fighters to the enemy aircraft. Long range and low flying acquisition radar stations were situated on low peaks that permitted 360-degree relatively clutter-free rotation. Close-in sites were usually set up below the crests of the mountains in locations where higher terrain often blocked radar signals and created a large number of blind spots. In most cases, however, the combination of radar stations allowed one to overcome the shortcomings of the other.

The search radar station was normally located between a third and one and a quarter miles (500 to 2000 meters) from the unit command post. To protect the control cabin from bomb and shell fragments, it was usually placed in an excavated pit below ground level. Where it was impossible to dig, sandbags were piled around the cabins and an additional protective layer placed on top of a framework of heavy wooden beams. Generator power units for the radar stations were also dug into the ground. To further conceal radar stations, antennas were hidden among trees or tall bushes. In open terrain, trees were clustered around antenna mast structures and replaced as necessary to retain their natural look. One particular Soviet radar system, the SON-2b, required a minimum flat area radius of fifty meters, which was nearly impossible to find in the mountains of North Korea. Because of this, SON-2b stations were positioned in such unlikely places as rice paddies or sports stadiums.

Antiaircraft weapons guidance stations, sited with regard to gun placement, provided additional radar coverage.

When unidentified aircraft were first spotted on radar, the station duty officer would attempt to identify them by using a radio identification system and radar code settings that were similar to our present-day transponder. Each aviation division and regiment had their own codes so their settings would not be compromised if another unit's aircraft fell into enemy hands.

Although most radar station operators were poorly trained in the early stages of the war, the quality of operations improved as they gained experience in tracking targets under conditions of varying terrain and jamming. A sharp operator could determine the exact number, type, and airspeed of aircraft by the shape of the blip, the nature of its pulse values, and the direction they were flying.

Radar operators were also responsible for determining the precise moment that MiGs interceptors should drop their external wing tanks. By watching where the American fighters dropped their tanks, a radar operator could tell whether the American aircraft were going to bomb ground targets or fly protective cover. This awareness helped commanders decide on the best aerial tactics they should use to repel a raid.

In 1951, the UN began using noise jamming from specially developed transmitters mounted in bombers. On the ground search radar screens, the jamming appeared as illuminated sectors. The width of the sector being jammed changed based upon the distance, and on occasion blotted out the entire screen. By using the side lobes from the antenna to observe in several directions simultaneously while also varying the frequency of their radar transmitters, Soviet radar was able to overcome much of the Allied jamming.

In an effort to passively jam communist radars, UN bombers also dispensed metallic strands called chaff. The metallic ribbons came in sizes long and short. Long chaff ribbons, contained in packets of 10-12, were 75 to 100 feet long. The short ones were two to six inches long. Chaff would appear on radar screens as blips that were similar to a large group of aircraft. The long ribbons would create screen interference lasting 25-30 minutes and short sections sometimes even longer. Operators easily detected the difference between chaff and aircraft returns because of chaff's characteristically slow forward speed. The precise location of target aircraft was more difficult to determine. Large concentrations of ribbon chaff created a bright, solid blip, which made it impossible to track a target, especially at shorter ranges.

Although Allied jamming had proven generally successful against radar-directed defenses, especially on night missions, on Black Tuesday the 307th attacked Namsi when they could be intercepted and shot down simply by being seen--negating the benefits of the various radar countermeasures that would have protected them at night while using the same SHORAN bombing technique.

SHORAN

When it became unmistakably clear that continued use of the Norden bombsight in cloudless daylight conditions would result in unacceptable B-29 losses, engineers scrambled to come up with an accurate bombing system that could be used in clouds or at night. The solution appeared in the form of SHORAN, SHOrt RAnge Navigation, a precision radar beacon navigation/bombing system.

An early SHORAN system had been developed and demonstrated to the 8th Air Force stationed in Europe in 1943. Unfortunately, the engineers and technicians involved in design and development were killed in a plane crash in Newfoundland. The system had to be reconstructed and redesigned from hand written notes and sketches left by the original design crew. Once developed, its short effective range (under three hundred miles) limited its use in WW II to the Italian theater where it proved to be an accurate alternative to visual bombing.

By October 1, 1950 the 1st SHORAN Beacon Unit had set up in South Korea and was broadcasting signals to guide B-26s on night missions. As UN forces moved northward, the unit set up sites at Wonsan and Pyongyang in North Korea, but mountains around Wonsan interfered with signals. Shortly thereafter, the Chinese offensive forced evacuation of both sites. Two new beacon sites set up in South Korea in December did little more than prove equipment inadequacies. SHORAN was, at best, used experimentally with junk equipment from WW II mostly for navigation of B-26s hitting small towns and bridges. By the end of the 1950, the continued advance of enemy troops had forced the unit to move back to Japan. After recalibrating and repairing its equipment, the unit returned to South Korea in early 1951 and set up at four sites, two on islands off the coast and two atop mountains just south of the 38th parallel. Able site on Tok-Chok-Kun-Do and Charlie at Taechang-do, islands in the Yellow sea, were paired with Baker, a central site on Usan-bong, a 4,430-foot mountain fifteen miles north of Taejon. SHORAN sites were located on mountaintops because the system was limited to line-of-sight. The First SHORAN also trained crews in Japan and Okinawa how to operate the airborne SHORAN equipment.

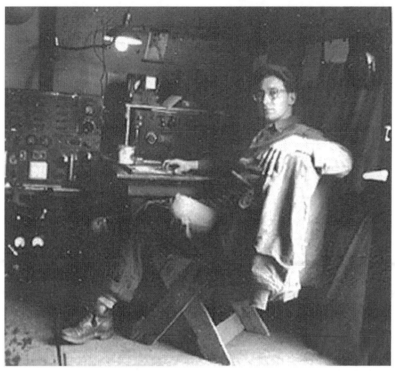

Ray Coia, SHORAN Operator at his work station on Tok-Cho-Do.
Courtesy of Ray Coia

SHORAN Beacon Unit on Tok-Cho-Do Island. Quonset huts resemble discarded 55 gallon drums. *Courtesy of Ray Coia*

Beginning in 1951, the 3903rd RBS squadron operated three sites that controlled aircraft dropping bombs, usually at night and during bad weather. S/Sgt. Ray Coia was stationed on Tok-Chok, twenty miles off the Inchon coastline. Although words like SHORAN and radar conjure images of dark rooms filled with radar screens and hi-tech equipment, such was not the case with the First Beacon Squadron. The operator's chairs were little more than crate slats fashioned to sit on and the equipment looked like leftovers from a ham operator's yard sale. Dungarees were the uniforms-of-the-day in a setting that was shabby even by M*A*S*H standards. Viewed from above, the site looked more like a dump than a radar site, the Quonsets more closely resembling discarded 55-gallon drums than living and operating quarters. It was from these cold, colorless, dark, and dismal places that the bombers received signals that guided them to their targets in the worst weather and on the darkest nights.

According to one operator, "We had pretty good accuracy, but lousy range, so we were mostly 'assigned' to an Army group for protection and moved up and down the peninsula with the front lines so that we could cover as much enemy territory as possible. Got downright exciting. Under direct orders from 5th AF HQ, we used an unfamiliar type of radar/computer system and controlled a B-29 to release their bomb load on ourselves."

The SHORAN system required an airborne transmitter, receiver, operator's console, and bombing computer tied electronically to a pair of ground stations. The bomber's transmitter alternately sent electronic pulses to each of the ground stations and computed distance by measuring the elapsed time between the transmitted and returned signals. Knowing the exact location of the ground stations and the target permitted the bomber to be flown along an arc formed by the intersection of the two distance signals to a predetermined bomb-release point that would place the bombs on the target.

In addition to the three hundred mile limitation, SHORAN could not be used by more than twenty bombers at a time. SHORAN'S Achilles' heel, however, proved to be its predictability. In order for the system to perform as designed, true air speed (TAS) and bombing altitudes had to be calculated before take off and adhered to during the bomb run. Also, because of angle limitations and other factors, there were only four possible approaches to any one target. All of these factors came into play on Black Tuesday.

In all liklihood, Soviet electronic intelligence had acquired high-frequency direction finding equipment in WW II that enabled them to fix the precise location of the "drift" and "rate" SHORAN stations. If so, it would have been a simple process for them to have swung arcs from those locations to potential targets and used these plots for positioning AAA and aerial interception--which appears to have been the case on Black Tuesday.

In the B-29, the SHORAN equipment was positioned in the rear pressurized compartment on a rack just behind and within easy reach of the Radar Operator. On a typical mission, the SHORAN operator directed the Pilot to the Initial point (IP), usually located on the arc approximately 55 miles from the target.

Max Nelson, a B-29 Radar and SHORAN operator who became the 98th Bombardment Wing SHORAN Officer after his 24 October mission, tells of starting bomb runs on SHORAN and switching to visual if the target cleared. The procedure didn't work well unless the transition was made early on the bomb run. On September 22, 1951, while flying squadron lead on a run against a bridge at Pyongyang, Max used SHORAN to stay on course while his bombardier, Chuck Hudson, took the rate visually. The combination worked so well that the bombs impacted with a circular error (CE) only 39 feet from the bridge. Two other flights that went full visual, Max recalled, missed the target.

B-29 SHORAN bombing also required close coordination between the operator and the pilots. Airspeed and altitude had to be exactly as planned while maintaining position on the arc, which was accomplished by the pilots keeping the needle on a simple instrument, called the PDI, centered. Unlike the visual bombing system, the SHORAN computer was not interfaced with the aircraft's autopilot. Nevertheless, the operator's manual cautioned that the PDI should only be used as an aid because of the inherent lag in the comparator (a device that compares two items of data). Coordinated smooth turns were essential because skidding and slipping varied airspeed, in turn affecting when the bombs would be released and where they would impact. Before the autopilot was engaged, the aircraft commander (A/C) would trim the airplane to fly hands-off to cut down on altitude deviations. On the bomb run the A/C would rotate the autopilot turn control to keep the PDI needle centered, while throttle control to maintain airspeed usually fell on the right seat pilot's shoulders. Maintaining precise control was further complicated if AAA or searchlight evasive action became necessary for survival.

Evading flak and staying out of the spotlight was more like juggling than flying an airplane. Altitude and heading had to be veered away from the threat, all the while maintaining a position near enough to the SHORAN arc so the aircraft could be returned to the arc with the proper heading and airspeed at bombs away. The largest bombing errors occurred when bombs were released while the aircraft was still in a banking turn. A split second before bombs away the airplane had to be straight and level. A good pilot could anticipate the needle deflection and roll out with the needle slightly deflected so that it was centered at the precise moment of release. One mission we really goofed and tossed our bombs into the next county--with spectacular results. Unintentionally, we hit an ammunition dump that lit up a small portion of North Korea for many minutes afterward.

When more than one B-29 attacked a particular SHORAN target, the bombers usually flew in trail three minutes apart.

Like all bombing methods, SHORAN produced mixed results. I can, however, vouch for the fact that on my 26th mission against the No Pong railroad bridge, the night photoflash pictures showed that we hit the 6' X 45' span.

Nonetheless, employing SHORAN under visual conditions against aggressive enemy defenses practically insured the kind of disastrous failure that befell the 307th on the mission to Namsi.

Antiaircraft Artillery (AAA)

A year before Black Tuesday, in October 1950 one additional air defense artillery regiment, ten independent antiaircraft artillery battalions, and two antiaircraft machine gun companies were formed to counter the rising tide of UN bombing missions deep into North Korea. Moreover, when Chinese entered the war they brought along their own antiaircraft artillery divisions as well as independent antiaircraft artillery regiments. On Black Tuesday, in addition to 297 35 MM AAA, 76 of the big 85MM guns were in place. By early 1952 the Communist forces had four antiaircraft artillery divisions, 18 independent antiaircraft artillery regiments, more than eighty AAA battalions, and around twenty independent antiaircraft machine gun companies.

Until the Soviets secretly entered the fray, there weren't enough ground radar stations to meet the needs of the Chinese and Korean antiaircraft artillery regiments. Only five Chinese units had weapons-aiming stations for all of their medium caliber antiaircraft weapons   The rest of the Chinese and Korean artillery units had, at most, only one aiming station per unit.

Until late spring, 1951, Korean and Chinese antiaircraft artillery provided cover for the Pyongyang area and lines of communications in the belt just behind the front. Beginning in June, additional air defense protection was organized to cover river crossings, railway stations, operational airfields, hydroelectric stations, storehouses and supply centers. AAA was grouped to ensure the highest density of fire along the best bomber routes to probable targets based on a bomber speed of 260 mph at 24,000 feet, not coincidentally, the B-29's airspeed and bombing altitude.

The grouping of AAA coverage was influenced to a large extent by the mountainous terrain. Wherever there was room, guns would be deployed on the peaks along the probable bomber routes. An exception to this sort of grouping was the railway bridge over the Yalu at Sinuiju. Based on the assumption that UN aircraft would not cross the border into China, the bulk of the medium and light AAA batteries were concentrated on Korean soil. Where the guns were radar-directed, the seeker antenna was located on the crest of a hill where it would have the greatest possible range throughout the most sectors.

On 12 April 1951, the deadly combination of fighters and antiaircraft artillery destroyed or damaged beyond repair six B-29s, a harbinger of what was to come on Black Tuesday six months later. A little over two months after the April B-29 raid, on 22 June 1951, sixteen F-80 and F-84 fighter-bombers twice attempted to destroy the Sinuiju railway bridge. According the Soviet records, antiaircraft fire claimed five aircraft shot down without any damage to the bridge.

At operational air bases, some of the light antiaircraft batteries were moved away from the airfield in the direction of landing or takeoff from the runways to cover against enemy fighters attacking during these vulnerable flight phases. Air defense command posts, which controlled the overall mission to repulse air raids, were placed on hills in view of both AAA and potential targets. Individual AAA control was permitted only when Communist fighters occupied in the same firing zone at the same time.

To ensure survivability, AAA units were moved frequently and always at night. Communications nodes were placed under cover, and telephone lines were buried in shallow trenches. In case the antennas were attacked, all posts had a spare that could be set up in a minute or less. To protect against surprise attack, fifty percent of the AAA assets were manned and ready at all times.

When repulsing large enemy bomber raids during daylight and cloud ceilings 18,000 feet or higher, fighter aircraft were used against UN bombers, ground based antiaircraft artillery held their fire until their fighters disengaged from combat. When ceilings were between 3,000 and 10,000 feet, fighters intercepted attackers above the clouds while AAA targeted those below. In isolated incidents, fighters were directed to attack incoming aircraft below the cloud deck. In these instances, light AAA was activated while medium antiaircraft guns went to standby readiness.

At night, fighters flew 3,000 feet above the estimated altitude of the target aircraft and held a parallel course until searchlights illuminated the target so they could see to attack. AAA had no limitations during night operations. Many training hours were devoted to acquainting pilots with the location of AAA batteries as well as making sure AAA personnel knew the differences in the radar signature between the MiG-15 and F-86. Specific entrance and exit points to the area of operations were also defined to help establish who was friendly and who was foe.

As the number of AAA units increased, UN bombers were forced to fly significantly higher altitudes and make more raids against the same targets. By late 1951, bombing targets within the boundaries of MiG Alley became chiefly a night operation. During the same period, the UN decided to concentrate on bombing railway river crossings in terrain where repair work would be more difficult. To cover these new targets, the Communist forces formed mobile AAA groups, including radar and searchlights, which could be trucked along roads, secretly under cover of darkness. At each predetermined target, the batteries would select multiple firing positions and move their equipment after one or two engagements.

Moving units sometimes proved costly in terms of men and equipment. At the start of the war, UN air power managed to inflict significant losses on antiaircraft artillery units when caught on the move. This led to the development of a march plan, which laid out instructions for the time, place and order of assembly of the convoy. These included the starting time, route, time to arrive at the last place listed on the plan; phase lines, locations for short halts, and measures for antiaircraft defenses; and controlling signals for the march. All light antiaircraft guns had to be prepared to fire either on the move or while on a short halt. They usually moved in eight convoys, four light antiaircraft battery convoys, two radar convoys, and two carrying ammunition and rear services goods. Four medium antiaircraft guns covered each light antiaircraft artillery battery convoy, while a six-gun medium antiaircraft gun battery protected the radar convoys. The medium antiaircraft guns followed the lead, center and trailing convoys. For covering the ammunition and goods convoys, a battery of medium antiaircraft guns was dispersed among their convoy. During the move, each convoy would deploy a radar station, from which the convoy leader would receive information on the air situation. Communications inside the convoys was organized to provide communications between the head and tail of the convoy to give the leader the ability to control movement, adjust the speed of movement, and provide assistance to halted vehicles.

On the morning of 8 October 1951 one of the mobile batteries was positioned to protect a railway tunnel and station at Koyu. Later that day, two waves of F-80 fighter-bombers raided the station. They were met by unexpected AAA fire that claimed six of the attacking aircraft.

By December 1951, daylight missions against railway bridges and crossings in the Anju and Sinuiju sectors had come to a halt. The mobile batteries carried on at night but were generally ineffective unless searchlights illuminated the attacking aircraft. During a two-month period in the fall of 1951 nine B-26 bombers were claimed to have been shot down at night after being illuminated by searchlights.

As UN bombing picked up, more mobile units were added, especially in the Anju-Sinuiju sector, primarily to provide additional fire power against B-26s operating at night as "free hunters."

Communist antiaircraft regiments were able to extend their area of coverage by setting up dummy AAA positions. Before dawn, soldiers would clear snow, create firing pads, and set up dummy guns. The real guns were well concealed. On one occasion, thirty F-84s attacked the dummy positions in the morning. After they departed, the firing positions were changed so that when they returned that afternoon, the UN bombers hit barren spots that had been occupied by the real AAA that morning.

All in all, the dummy positions and mobile units created the impression that the number of AAA batteries was much larger than thought. Deception and mobility proved decisive in the huge number losses of UN bombers during the course of the war. Afterward, Soviet calculations revealed that the average expenditure of ammunition for each aircraft shot down was as follows: 85mm – 560 rounds; 37mm – 630 rounds; and 12.7mm – 2,500-3,000 rounds. Heavy caliber machine guns were most effective when fired at low-level attackers with several firing simultaneously at the same.

It is not surprising that the Soviets drew from a vast reservoir of experience. When the B-29s, in particular, began to use SHORAN, the Soviets knew that they could mass antiaircraft batteries along the predetermined arcs that were flown from IP to target. This, and the fact that the number of guns necessary to create barrage fire against SHORAN directed missions was cut in half, contributed greatly to the disaster that befell the 307th Bombardment Wing on Black Tuesday.

The Boeing B-29 Superfortress

By delivering the only two nuclear devices detonated in actual warfare, the Boeing B-29 established itself a permanent place in world history. The bomber was largely responsible for ending the war with Japan, the first major conflict in history where an enemy was forced to surrender through the use of air power. Combined with the atomic bomb development, the B-29 also stands as the most expensive human undertaking in recorded history. Today, with the fifty-year old B-52 still one of our front line bombers, it seems inconceivable that the effective life span of what was, at the time, the world's most lethal offensive weapon, was so brief. Six years after B-29 raids reduced Japan to ashes, in the sky over Namsi, the B-29 fell victim to the jet age fighter, and was soon replaced by the jet bomber.

Development of the B-29 actually began in the late Depression, nearly two years before the United States entered World War II, when Boeing submitted plans to the Army for a prototype long-range heavy bomber, designated the Boeing 345.

Although it was referred to as the world's largest bomber at the time of its introduction, the B-29 didn't come close in sizing up to the Douglas XB-19. The XB-19, which flew in September 1942, fifteen months prior to the B-29's first flight, measured 212 feet wingtip to wingtip, compared to 141 feet three inches for the B-29. Unfortunately, the XB-19's speed topped out at a paltry 209 mph, whereas the Boeing bomber was capable of speeds up to 365 mph. In the early forties the high-speed bomber was as revolutionary as the jet fighter that was to become its nemesis a decade later.

Ninety-nine feet from nose to tail gun, the B-29 weighed 105,000 pounds and was powered by four 2,200 horsepower

Boeing B-29A Superfortress
Crew Positions

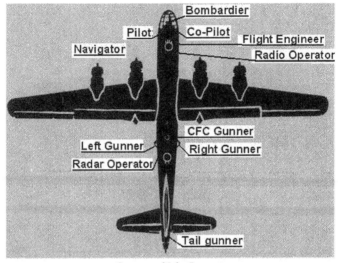

Bombardier
Pilot
Co-Pilot
Flight Engineer
Navigator
Radio Operator
CFC Gunner
Left Gunner
Right Gunner
Radar Operator
Tail gunner

Courtesy of John Duquette

Below: Interior of nose Section, forward-looking view

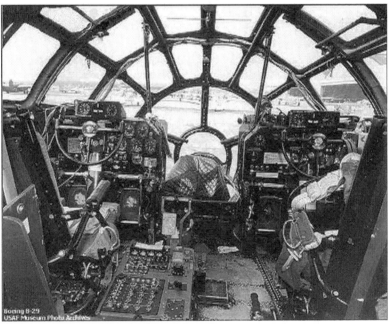

engines. Although the heaviest production bomber of WW II was capable of speeds up to 365 mph, in order to attain its maximum range with a full bomb load, its normal cruise speed had to be lowered to 220 mph. At optimum cruise, the pressurized aircraft could fly as high as 31,850 feet over a distance of 5,830 miles. In its day, no other bomber and few fighters could match those performance figures.

The B-29 was a study in streamlined innovation. The long, narrow, aerodynamically efficient wing mounted four engines, and was joined to a streamlined, tapered fuselage. Eleven crewmen manned stations in three pressurized compartments, the forward, aft, and tail gunner's sections. Built in the shape of a cigar, the aluminum tube with a glassed-in nose did not have a discernable cockpit. The two pilots and bombardier shared the greenhouse flight deck. The bombardier sat dead center in the foremost section of the greenhouse. Whenever clouds, smoke or haze did not obscure a ground target, he used the Norden bombsight to visually aim and drop the bombs. The Norden bombsight, a closely guarded secret during World War II, was a mechanical analog computer made up of gyros, motors, gears, mirrors, levers and a telescope. Once the target was acquired through the optics, the bombsight, coupled to the flight controls, automatically flew the airplane to the release point and dropped the bombs. When the target was obscured, the radar operator, located in the aft-pressurized compartment, took control of identifying the target aiming point. B-29 bombardiers also acted as nose gunners when the bomber was under attack.

Instead of looking out over the nose of the aircraft, as was the case in other Allied bombers before and since, the pilots sat toward the rear of the large greenhouse-like frame, much in the fashion of the German Heinkel He 111 bomber that devastated England during the Battle of Britain. Pilot seating was standard. The aircraft commander, the appellation used to designate the airline equivalent of "captain" in American military aircraft, sat in the left seat. The copilot on the right was called "pilot." Both looked out over either side of the bombardier's position. Their instrument panels, controls, and other paraphernalia were all contained within freestanding pedestals.

Because of this unusual configuration, most of the engine instruments and system controls were monitored and operated by the flight engineer who sat facing aft behind the bulkhead separating him from the pilot. Usually the ranking enlisted man on most crews, the flight engineer was the main man responsible for getting the most miles per gallon, maintaining the airplane's balance, and keeping an eye out for engine trouble.

A few feet further aft, to the left of the forward turrets, the navigator determined the aircraft's position using radar and various other tried-and-true methods, including celestial fixes. After determining the aircraft's position, the navigator would call out, over interphone, the headings necessary to stay on course.

Crammed up against the right fuselage wall behind the forward turrets, the radio operator also handled the electronics jamming equipment. When the aircraft was out of contact with line of sight radio stations, the radio operator would make position and post strike reports.

A 35-foot long, 28-inch diameter tunnel over the bomb bays connected the nose and rear compartments. At the forward end of the rear compartment, the right and left gunners, usually called "scanners," manned blisters on either side while the gunner who called the shots defensively, the CFC or central fire controller, occupied an elevated "barber's chair" between them.

Farther back, the radar operator monitored the aircraft's position on the radarscope, assisted in navigation and, if the weather precluded visual contact with the ground, acted as radar bombardier.

The unpressurized section between the aft and the tail gunner's compartment housed a gasoline-operated auxiliary generator called the "putt-putt." The unit provided the necessary power for starting the engines and served as an emergency electrical backup. It also made it possible for the B-29 to operate from any airfield with suitable runways where external power sources might not be available. Operation of the putt-putt was an additional responsibility of the tail gunner. Separated and alone in his own pressurized compartment, the tail gunner brought the total crew number to eleven.

The tunnel above the bomb bays that connected the forward and aft-pressurized crew compartments was large enough for a man to crawl through and allowed for opening the bomb bay doors without affecting cabin pressure. In the B-29, supercharged air was pumped into the pressurized areas to maintain the equivalent of 8,000 feet altitude when flying at 30,000 feet.

German and English air forces had experimented with pressurizing combat aircraft; however, the danger of explosive decompression seemed to rule out the possibility of pressurizing large crew compartments. Indeed, the B-29 experienced a few extreme cases where crew members were sucked from the airplane when a hatch or blister blew out. Not only was there the life-threatening possibility of being propelled from the airplane, explosive decompression had the unnerving effect of not only sounding like an explosion, but was also followed by a smoke-like fog as the air within the compartments condensed.

On a mission that should have been a milk run, our circular hatch to the forward bomb bay blew into the bay, striking and damaging several bomb nose fuses. The loud bang was followed by a whirlwind of maps, lunches, papers, dirt, and dust being sucked out through the opening and the sudden formation of an interior mist that looked like, but luckily did not smell like, smoke. More disconcerting was the unknown condition of the bombs themselves. You might say we "defused" the danger by dropping them on the nearest target of opportunity.

Although pressurized and better heated than its Boeing predecessor, the B-17, the Superfortress was still a typical military bomber, not designed in any way for crew comfort. It was pretty much bare bones construction, with additional padding and material to accommodate pressurization. At altitude it was not uncommon to have ice on the floor and other exposed metal parts that would inflict damage on exposed skin if touched. Warm gloves and boots were a necessity but not always available.

Most large bombers were designed around the bomb load and the B-29 was no exception. Its double bomb bays, arranged in tandem, could hold 20,000 pounds of bombs of various sizes. During the Korean War, the usual load was forty five hundred pound bombs. Individual bombs were attached to shackles by a trigger-like mechanism that was opened by electrical impulse. To keep the aircraft on an even keel, a device called an intervalometer released the bombs alternately from each bomb bay, fore and aft, either one at a time or salvoed all at once. When the B-29 dropped clusters in salvo or in bunches, the bombs would sometimes bang into each other, bend the fins, and send one or more wide of the intended target. Aerial photos of tight bomb patterns sometimes reveal bombs gone astray as individual impact puffs on either side of the aiming point. A more serious shortcoming was the tendency for bombs to hang up inside the bomb bay.

On a mission flown prior to Black Tuesday, Rolland Miller and Fred Spivey, gunners on Capt. Clarence Fogler's Able Lead crew, had used crash axes to chop away at a cable that had hung up a cluster of 100-pound bombs. The cable holding the cluster had snagged on a shackle in the rear bomb bay. The axes were not big or sharp enough to cut through the cable, so they had to take the bombs home. After landing and parking the airplane in their revetment on the Kadena ramp, Fogler, Capt. Joe Denson, and another officer from Wing that had flown with them checked the bombs. The bomb bay doors were opened, and they shook the cluster. One fell out on the hardstand almost landing on the Wing officer. Miller was under the tail of the aircraft and on his way to the edge of the hardstand to empty the aft relief can when he heard the "thump" of the bomb hitting the asphalt. Luckily for the crew it was a GP bomb and the fuse vane had not spun off, arming it so it could explode.

In late 1950 and early 1951, special radio-controlled weapons known as Razon bombs, were tried against the stubborn North Korean bridges. After release, the bombardier guided the bomb visually with a remote control that allowed him to alter range and azimuth as it fell. Razon bombs were mostly ineffective because they weighed only a thousand pounds. Their successors, Tarzon bombs, were packed with unstable RDX explosive left over from WW II and weighed 12,000 pounds. The bomb was so big and unwieldy that two-thirds of it protruded outside the bomb bay of the B-29. In all, thirty were dropped but only six bridges were destroyed. When results were tallied, the Tarzon proved to be as dangerous to the crew as it was to the enemy. At least two B-29s were destroyed trying to ditch their bombs into the sea, and Tarzons were withdrawn from service in late April 1951.

Like the XB-19, the B-29 was outfitted with tricycle landing gear. Instead of large single tires, its main landing gear wheels came in pairs that were called "trucks." Unlike the XB-19's massive high lift wings, the B-29's long thin wings looked incapable of sustaining the heavy bomber aloft. Designed from scratch by Boeing engineers, the wing, did, in fact, present a serious problem. With so little lift, approach and take-off speeds were predicted to be astronomically high. This was solved by the inclusion of another innovation, massive flaps that were approximately one-fifth the area of the wing itself. The huge flaps lowered the stall speed and made landing and take-offs more manageable.

Because of its more than one hundred electric motors, figuratively, the B-29 could have been called an "electric airplane"

Utilizing a primitive application of the computer, the B-29 came equipped with a General Electric remote control gunnery system, which corrected automatically for range, altitude, airspeed, and temperature. There were five gun positions, the forward and aft upper and lower turrets and the tail guns. All turrets (inaccessible in-flight) were electrically powered, remotely sighted and controlled. Throughout the Korean War, all except the upper forward turret were armed with two .50 caliber machine guns. The upper forward had been equipped with an extra pair of .50s to cope with Japanese fighter attacks, which were mostly head-on. Except for the tail gunner, but including the bombardier, any gunner on the aircraft could take control of two of the four B-29s turrets and verbally pass control on to another gunner who might have a better shot at an attacker. A further advantage was that remote control positioned the gunners within the pressurized hull, away from gun noise and vibration.

The bombardier/nose gunner was assigned primary control of the upper forward and secondary control of the lower forward turrets. In the secondary position he could fire both turrets in his line of sight from 270 degrees to 90 degrees—nine o'clock high or low around to three o'clock high or low. Aft of the bomb bay, the central fire controller (ring or upper gunner) had primary control of the upper aft turret, secondary control of the upper forward and tertiary control on the tail guns. The right gunner had primary control of the lower aft turret, secondary control of the lower forward and tertiary control of the tail guns. The left gunner had primary control of the lower forward, secondary of the lower aft turret and tertiary control of the tail guns. The tail gunner had only primary control of the tail guns and no other controls.

So they could see directly aft, the right and left blister gunners remote control sights were mounted slightly out in the blister. The gunner could put his head into the blister, set the sights at the 180-degree mark and fire directly aft under any of their three control conditions. If the attack came in high from the rear, the tail gunner and CFC would take control. If the fighter continued down, control would be passed to the left or right gunners. Gunners could track their gun sights without the turret following until they closed the "action switch" on the "cookie handle" on the sight.

Although B-29 turrets were equipped with mechanical interrupters to prevent gunners from firing into their own wings or tail surfaces, there was no provision to interrupt shooting into another B-29 flying in close formation. On more than one occasion, B-29s returned from a mission with more damage inflicted by gunners on other B-29s, who didn't let up on the trigger quite fast enough, than by the enemy cannon fire.

The original WW II tail gun configuration included a 20mm. When it became evident that the Japanese did not have anything fast enough to catch up to a B-29, the cannon was removed. Almost all Japanese fighter attacks against B-29s formations were frontal. The few rear attacks that did occur were accomplished by the fighter placing itself higher and in front of the formations so they could begin their dive while ahead of the formation and time it to come in on the bomber's tail as they pulled out of the dive at the same altitude.

This tactic had been developed and practiced with deadly precision since the beginning of WW II when Mitsubishi Zero pilots first tried to intercept the speedy Martin B-26 Marauder. In one early engagement, the great WW II Japanese Zero ace, Saburo Sakai, came close to changing the history of the late twentieth century when he miscalculated and pulled out of his dive behind, and shot down the second Marauder in the formation instead of the first. According to Sakai, the lead bomber had a special observer along for the ride, Lyndon B, Johnson, who succeeded to the presidency following President John F. Kennedy's assassination to become the 36th President of the United States.

When B-29s bombed from high altitude, the Japanese fighters could not climb high enough to get above the formations and were thus forced to make frontal attacks. Removing the 20mm cannons benefited the bombers by allowing them to carry more weight elsewhere, either fuel or munitions. With the advent of the jet fighter, the B-29s speed and altitude advantage vanished. Its fifty caliber tail guns were effective up to about six hundred yards; whereas the MiG's more powerful cannons could inflict devastating damage at eight hundred yards. MiG pilots were briefed to attack from the rear and fire their cannons beyond the range of the B-29's 50 caliber tail guns--a tactic that would prove lethal in the Korean War, and prompt the Chief of Staff of the United States Air Force to visit FEAF B-29 units and personally ask tail gunners if they wanted the 20mm cannon reinstalled.

MiG pilots never underestimated the danger presented by the B-29 gunners, but were far more concerned that Sabres might arrive and shoot them down over the sea or UN controlled territory.

Although B-29 gunners claimed a number of MiGs shot down during the Korean War, Soviet literature references only two confirmed kills due to return fire from a B-29 during the entire war. The first occurred on 6 December 1950, when Nikolay Serikov, 29th GIAP, 50th IAD, was shot down and killed by a B-29 tail gunner. Ironically the gunner did not claim this kill, so his name is unknown. The only other acknowledged casualty, V. M. Khurtin, survived to fly another day but was razzed mercilessly by his unit when he returned from pickup. The second shootdown occurred on October 23, 1951, Black Tuesday.

Many reasons have been given for the ineffectiveness of the B-29's twelve guns. The most common claim was that the primitive gunnery computer, designed to fire at slower prop-driven Japanese planes, could not keep up with the high-speed MiG-15. Soviet commanders, however, thought enough of the B-29s firepower that they instructed their pilots to open fire beyond the range of the fifty caliber machine guns. Moreover, records show that when the MiGs came within range, B-29 gunners could and did inflict serious damage. On 14 November 1950, Richard W. Fisher, of the 307th Bomb Wing, shot up the MiG-15 piloted by Nikolay I. Podgorniy (28th IAD), just after the Russian pilot damaged Fisher's B-29. On 24 October 1951, Harold M. Setters (98th BW) fired at a MiG-15 and wounded Aleksandr P. Smorchkov, a veteran who shot down three Superfortresses, including Setters' B-29. The actual reasons appear more complex and more often than not boil down to a question of meaning of the words "shot down."

Boeing built a total of 2,766 B-29s at plants in Wichita, Kansas and in Renton, Washington. The Bell Aircraft Co. built 668 in Georgia, and the Glenn L. Martin Co. built 536 in Nebraska. Production ended in 1946. Modifications of the original B-29A, used in both WW II and Korea, led to the RB-29 photo reconnaissance aircraft and B-29D, which was later developed into the B-50. The Soviet-built copy of the B-29 was called the Tupolev Tu-4.

Because of the demands of war, early B-29s were built before the testing phase had been completed. Although the plan placed the bombers in combat months before they might otherwise have flown, the decision to produce before testing would prove fatal to many.

Problems that had plagued the big Boeing bomber since February 1943, when the prototype crashed and killed test pilot Eddie Allen, the crew, and 19 on the ground, continued into and well past the Korean War.

Charles Stone, after training to become an aircraft commander at Randolph AFB, Texas, described the B-29's propensity for coming unglued in his *Recollections of an RB-29 crew in Japan*. While shooting touch-and-go landings, his B-29 developed a fuel leak in one of the engines, which filled the aircraft with gas fumes. Threatened with "a full scale explosion," Chuck wrote, "Quick ventilation action by the Instructor Pilot (and) complete electrical shutdown permitted a safe landing." On another night training mission two engines progressively failed. Old crew members often joke that the B-29 was the best three-engine bomber Boeing ever built. In Chuck's case we could add "two-engine" to the list.

The B-29 was powered by four Wright R-3350 Duplex Cyclone, 2,200 hp radial engines, each equipped with twin General Electric turbo-superchargers that enabled the R-3350 to maintain maximum power up to 30,000 feet altitude. The configuration also made the engine highly susceptible to fire. Magnesium used in engine and airframe components exacerbated the problem.

Another cause of the B-29's problems stemmed from the fact that in the five years since the end of WW II many of them had been parked at a storage site in open desert adjacent to Davis-Monthan AFB just outside of Tucson, Arizona. Although D-M was selected because of its dry, non-corrosive climate, six years in the Sonora Desert nevertheless took its toll. One unconventional glitch the airplane developed was an invasion of desert rats--not fictional gremlins, but factual, furry rats of the "pack" variety. During preflight they could be heard scurrying about, tiny rat feet against aluminum. Because of engine noise, we could not hear them in flight. However, on more than one occasion someone reached for a sandwich only to find a bite had already been taken. Pack rats became such a problem in our airplane that on the way home from one mission we climbed as high as the airplane would go, donned our oxygen masks, and flew depressurized. After landing and engine shutdown, the scraping of little feet continued. Although flying unpressurized had drained the crew, the rats continued their charmed existence. Later, after we'd returned to the states we learned that our plane had been shot down on a night mission over the Yalu, which caused us to wonder if our Sonora Desert pack rats might live on in North. Korea.

Rats notwithstanding, age-related deteriorations, like fuel and oil seal failures that could fill an aircraft with fumes or cause a prop to run away, were a constant source of concern for crews already faced with the possibility of flak and fighters.

B-29s were primarily used in the Pacific theater during World War II, where as many as 1,000 Superfortresses at a time bombed

Tokyo, destroying large parts of the city. On August 6, 1945, the *Enola Gay* dropped the world's first atomic bomb on Hiroshima. Three days later a second B-29 named *Bockscar* dropped a second atomic bomb on Nagasaki. Shortly thereafter, Japan surrendered.

Cognizant of the massive destruction rent to Japan's war-making capability, and lacking an equivalent aircraft, the U.S.S.R. set out to reproduce the B-29. Fortunately for the Russians, they were able to impound three B-29s that had made emergency landings on their airfields during WW II. From these, the Tupolev Design Bureau, headed by the renowned Soviet aerospace engineer A.N. Tupolev, reverse-engineered a near replica. Designated the Tu-4, the first Soviet intercontinental strategic bomber, first flew in 1947. An entire aircraft industry segment was created to produce the Tu-4, and more than 800 were built.

Between wars, B-29s were modified to perform several functions, including in-flight refueling, anti-submarine patrol, weather reconnaissance, and rescue duty. One particular B-29 played a vital role in breaking the sound barrier. On October 14, 1947, a modified mother ship carried Captain Chuck Yeager and the Bell XS-1 rocket powered aircraft to launch altitude. After release from the B-29, the XS-1 reached Mach 1.06, the first to officially exceed the speed of sound.

With the advent of the B-36 into the USAF inventory, what had been the heaviest operational bomber in the world had its designation reduced to "medium" bomber. As a medium, the B-29 saw military service again in Korea between 1950 and 1953, battling new adversaries: jet fighters and electronic weapons.

It can be argued that an even more potent adversary was the airplane itself. Besides the myriad of problems that plagued the rushed-to-service bomber in WW II, the resurrected B-29 presented a host of new and often baffling annoyances. One such was an individual airplane's erratic flight characteristic. Whether caused by sitting in the desert heat year after year or someone's unreported hard landing was impossible to determine. Some B-29s used more fuel than others, to the point where those operating out of Okinawa were restricted from flying the longer missions. First Lt. Jim Foster, a copilot in the 28th BS, 19 BG, recalled one B-29 that, while in flight, had an unmistakable sideways drift that could not be trimmed out. To correct the problem, a replacement

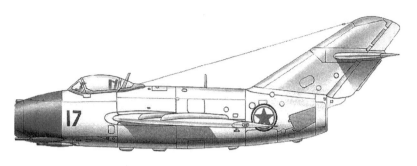

MiG-15 with N. Korean AF markings. *Yefim Gordon: MiG-15*

Today, MiG-15s (above) and B-29s (below) can be found on display throughout the world, such this pair at the Pima Air Museum, Tucson, Arizona. *Photos by author*

center wing section was shipped from California to Okinawa by barge--a fix that apparently wasn't entirely successful.

There were, however, a greater number of reliable B-29s such as Foster's "Lemon Drop Kid." The "Kid" did not miss many flights, most likely because Gene Gray, the flight engineer, lived with the airplane on all of its down days. Foster attributed a lot of their flying success "to Gene and the scanners for keeping it in good shape." Jim also worked part time in Maintenance at his own request. On one occasion, when a 307th B-29 crashed off the north runway and caught fire, he and the unit Maintenance Officer got in a Jeep and were within a quarter mile from the crash when the photo bombs exploded.

Jim and his crewmates spent most of their free time maintaining their bird ship-shape. It took that kind of dedication to keep the aging craft in the air and reliable.

The last B-29 in squadron use retired from service in September 1960.

Mikoyan-Gurevich MiG-15

Faced with a potential enemy that possessed atomic bombs, the Soviet Union scrambled to build an aircraft that could knock down attacking bombers before they reached their targets. The Mikoyan-Gurevich Bureau had been planning an advanced swept wing fighter with an ejection seat for just this purpose, but lacked a suitable jet engine to power the craft. As luck would have it, the British decided to license the Soviets their best engine--a move that prompted the Soviet dictator, Joseph Stalin, to ask, "What fool will sell us his secrets?"

Eight months after its first flight, MiG-15s powered by copies of the Rolls Royce Nene engines were rolling off the assembly line. The engine was a slightly modified version, designated the RD-45. Because inferior materials were used in manufacturing, the Soviet version had an extremely short service life of one hundred hours. Ironically, at the same time the Soviet MiG was in full production, the British had not yet installed the Nene in any of their service aircraft. MiG-15s were eventually equipped with better engines that also allowed more efficient fuel management, plus the larger 200-liter tanks.

The MiG-15 prototype, first flown in December 1947, was a study in simplicity and innovation. When viewed in cutaway we see little more than a stovepipe with a jet engine, cannon, cockpit, wings and tail. Yet the MiG-15 had been constructed using advanced welding techniques to enhance survivability, and carried its three cannons in a quick-detach package housed under the nose. It also had a pressurized cockpit, an ejection seat for the pilot, speed brakes to slow it down, wing fences to direct air flow, and drop tanks for extended range.

When the MiG-15 first entered service with the Soviet Air Force, veteran prop pilots were wary of a flying machine that had no visible means to keep it airborne. Nonetheless, the MiG-15 became fully operational in a remarkably short time and some units were deemed combat ready by mid-1950. Due in a large part to its rugged simplicity, the aircraft proved reliable, easily maintained, and more than capable of besting the best the West put up against it. Crews nicknamed the MiG-15 "soldier aircraft," in their jargon, the ultimate accolade.

Although the MiG-15 and America's best, the North American F-86 Sabre, were developed separately and independently, they were remarkably similar. In addition to the commonalities shared by most single engine fighter-type aircraft, both featured swept wings and stabilizers. Each had wings that were swept back at exactly 35 degrees. The two aircraft resembled each other so closely that later, in Korean air-to-air combat, each side resorted to elaborate paint schemes.

When it came to rate of climb, maximum ceiling, and simplicity of design, the MiG-15 was superior to the F-86. Although the Sabre could outmaneuver the MiG, especially combat turns, maximum horizontal flight speed was roughly identical for both aircraft. If a situation became disadvantageous, the MiG could usually climb away from the Sabre to an altitude that was often above the UN fighter's maximum ceiling. Contrary to many reports, the MiG-15 could not go supersonic no matter what the pilot did. Unlike its American counterpart, its built-in mach limiter automatically popped speed brakes as it approached Mach 0.97.

Within five years over 8,000 MiG-15s were built--more than any other aircraft in production at the time. Eventually, over 13,000 were built in the USSR alone. Its large production numbers led to another nickname, "The Aluminum Rabbit." In no way was it meant to be a character description--something the West would learn the hard way in December 1950, only three years after its first flight, when it was deployed against the United Nations air forces in Korea.

First used in combat against the Chinese Nationalists, the MiG-15s were painted with Communist Chinese marking and flown by Soviet pilots wearing Chinese uniforms. The fighting was limited and definitely one-sided. No MiGs were lost.

Looking back, it seems remarkable that apparently no one in the West took the MiG-15 seriously. The Soviet Union, always anxious to win bragging rights, traditionally flaunted its new weaponry in gaudy parades and air shows. The MiG-15 was no exception. Although it made its world debut at the Tushino Air Show, the initial response was to largely dismiss the airplane as sub-standard. Even its NATO designation, Fagot (a worthless bundle of sticks), reflected the West's initial attitude toward the jet fighter. However, when the MiG-15 appeared in the skies over Korea, disinterest turned to shock and awe. Its performance had been a well-kept secret outside of the USSR until UN fighter pilots suddenly found themselves up against silver swept wing fighter that could fly faster and higher and outmaneuver all but one American-built fighter.

On the first of November 1950, MiG-15s intercepted a flight of prop-driven F-51s near the Yalu River in what is generally recognized as the first encounter between USAF and Soviet jet fighters. Later that same day, Lt. Khominich, a Soviet MiG-15 pilot from the 72nd GIAP, attacked ten F-80 Shooting Stars out of the sun and reported that he shot down one with a three-second burst. Like many of the Korean War's reported "kills," this one could not be confirmed. A week later, on 8 November, the first jet versus jet battle officially acknowledged by the USAF took place between six MiG-15s and two flights of F-80 Shooting Stars in the same general location. Although the USAF recorded a MiG kill, like Lt. Khominich's claim, it is just as likely the aircraft made it back to his base without crashing.

The first confirmed jet-versus-jet kill took place on 9 November during an air battle between Soviet and US Navy pilots. Eighteen MiG-15s of the 1329th GIAP attacked twenty piston-driven F4U-4 Corsairs and AD-1 Skyraiders, again in the same Yalu River area. The MiGs were pounced by escorting Navy F9F-2 jet Panthers. Although the MiGs decimated the prop-driven attackers, Capt. Mikhail Grachov, Commander of the 1st Squadron, was shot down by a Panther piloted by Lt. Commander William Amen. This was the first jet-versus-jet kill acknowledged by both sides.

November 9 also marked the first loss of a B-29 to MiG fire. Because of heavy casualties B-29s inflicted on Communist troops, the bomber was considered a priority target. N. I. Podgomyy and Maj. A. Z. Bordoon were credited with shooting down one B-29 each. The MiG-15s cannons were capable of blowing off the bomber's wing, while the B-29's range-limited fifty caliber machine guns in combination with a WW II computer tracking system designed to combat Japanese propeller driven fighters, proved ineffective against the swift jets.

The improved MiG-15bis, dubbed in the West as the Fagot B, entered combat at almost the same time as the basic model. It was flown on its first combat mission on November 30 and became the Soviet mainstay. The older A models were transferred to Chinese and Korean units. Both models were superior to all of the USAF's straight-wing F-80 and F-84 fighters.

The MiG-15, as well as most American single engine jets, carried external wing tanks for additional range. At near maximum throttle, a MiG that took off, climbed to altitude, engaged a target for fifteen minutes and returned to home base could count on about 45 minutes fuel with a small reserve. The two additional wing tanks, which contained a paltry 53 gallons each, did not give them much more, but was sometimes the difference between being able to fight and not.

To counter the MiG threat, the United States rushed more of their new swept-wing North American F-86 Sabres into the fray. In the first aerial engagement between F-86s and MiG-15s, that took place on 17 December 1950, the F-86s scored first. Lt. Colonel Bruce Hinton, flying an F-86 named (*Squanee*,) poured

The Machinery of War ♠ 89

1,500 fifty caliber rounds into a 29th GIAP MiG, killing the pilot, Major Yakov Yefromeyenko. In the battles that ensued, both sides claimed more kills than the other side would admit to. Interpreting the records seems to indicate that during the first two weeks of air-to-air combat between the titans resulted in the loss of one F-86 and three MiGs.

January 1951 saw a drastic decline in MiG activity, due in large part to the inexperience of the first group of Soviet pilots, particularly in combat situations pitted against the formidable F-86. Their primary mission was to stop the bombers so they avoided dog fighting with F-86s, at times turning for home rather than tangling with the Sabres.

The omission of a G-Suit control mechanism is further evidence that the MiG-15 had not been intended for air-to-air-combat against fighters of equal stature. G-suits were not particularly avant-garde technology, having been introduced to the general public in the pre-war 1941 Hollywood film, *Dive Bomber*. The pressurized "suit" worn by U.N. pilots was a sort of half-pants that covered the legs and stomach section and inflated when subjected to higher gravity forces. The inflated bladders squeezed the pilot in critical body areas to prevent blood from rushing away from the brain. This action kept the pilot from blacking out, usually a momentary condition but one that could prove fatal with an F-86 in hot pursuit or during low level maneuvering. The strain of repeated high-g combat produced major debilitating effects that grounded more than a few Soviet flyers. Many were sent back to the USSR with serious internal problems from combat stress, and were humiliated for it even though it was not their fault--all because the designers failed to include the g-suit in the MiG-15's hardware.

The second group of MiG pilots to arrive in the Korean theater had more experience flying jet aircraft and a great deal more total flying time than the first. Many of the pilots in the 324th IAD were combat veterans of World War II. However, in spite of their experience, three aircraft were lost on their first sortie.

To cut down on losses due to friendly fire, the second group immediately painted the noses and fin tips of their MiG-15s red.

In the heat of battle, particularly in aerial melees fighter pilots nicknamed "furballs," it was often difficult to distinguish a friendly swept wing aircraft from an enemy aircraft sporting the same configuration. Sabre units marked their aircraft with diagonal body and wingtip stripes. The early black and white paint scheme was soon replaced by bright yellow. Other Sabres also had stripes or a checkerboard pattern painted on the vertical fin.

In April 1951 the new group of seasoned Soviet pilots was relocated to Antung on the Yalu, a few jet minutes from MiG Alley. For UN bomber crews the move would prove to be one of utmost tactical importance. Suddenly, American air power ceased to dominate the skies. From then on, American bombers venturing into MiG Alley would be in constant danger.

The April 12 1951 maximum effort daylight mission against the bridges at Sinanju included B-29s from the 19th, 98th, and 307th--all three of FEAF's Superfortress units. The bombers were escorted by 39 F-84E Thunderjets, with additional F-86s providing top cover. Fifty MiGs struck the lead formation of 19th Bombardment Group aircraft while they were still several minutes from the target. One B-29 went down in flames and five other bombers were damaged. A second wave of twenty MiGs scattered the outclassed Thunderjets and hit the 307th formation. One crippled bomber spun out of control and exploded on impact with the ground. A second 307th B-29 crash-landed at Suwon.

The April 12 mission was, by all accounts, a wake-up call that was, for a short while, heeded. However, by late summer and early autumn, someone had fallen asleep at the switch and the big bombers were once again venturing into MiG Alley in broad daylight. Black Tuesday would be the second wake-up call, one that would not be forgotten.

The Black Tuesday 307th mission was spotted by ground pickets, and forty-four 303rd Fighter Aviation Division MiG-15s from the 17th, 18th and 523rd Fighter Aviation Regiments were scrambled to intercept the bombers. The pilots were ordered to destroy the bombers and not tangle with the fighters. As on April 12, the MiG-15s dove through the bomber escort fighters and went straight for the B-29s. According to Maj. General G. A. Lobov, the Soviet pilots destroyed twelve B-29s and four Thunderjets. Factual records, however, indicate that some of the claims were duplicated. In other words, more than one Soviet pilot claimed the same B-29 shot down. Actual USAF losses were bad enough to bring daylight B-29 bombing to an abrupt halt.

Night operations resulted in fewer B-29 losses but they were still being shot down. Because the MiG-15 was not equipped with airborne radar, ground controlled intercept (GCI) radar stations would direct the pilot to the target, hoping the radar-directed AAA searchlights would light up the bomber. There were occasions when the GCI vectoring was so accurate that MiGs accidentally rammed their prey. If the searchlights didn't illuminate the bombers, the MiG pilots looked for exhaust flames. On moonlight nights they often were able to spot the bombers visually. Maj. Anatolly M. Karelin of the 351st IAP became the first to shoot down a B-29 after it got caught in the searchlights. According to Soviet records, Maj. Karelin became a night ace, with a total of six B-29s to his credit. In January 1953 Capt. Yurly was credited with two B-29s destroyed in a single night.

The ultimate success of the MiG-15 in the Korean War depends largely on whose records are considered most accurate. Loss figures are further obscured because of the nature of the combatants. Although many of the actual combatants, especially bomber crew members, suspected the MiG pilots were Russian, it was not until after the fall of the Iron Curtain that these suspicions were confirmed. Some Soviet pilots were even paid for shooting down UN aircraft to the tune of 1,500 rubles for each confirmed kill. It has also long been assumed that the high kill ratio (usually attributed to F-86 pilots) of ten to one over the MiG-15 was largely against the less experienced Chinese and Korean pilots. Subsequent Soviet records prove otherwise. The Chinese did not actively enter the combat arena until after the Namsi mission and it can be argued that North Koreans never actively engaged in air-to-air combat against F-86s while flying MiG-15s. Inexperience among Chinese and Korean pilots led to multiple take-off and landing accidents. To make matters worse, the Chinese pilot suffered from chronic malnutrition, which resulted in loss of consciousness in high-G combat maneuvers.

Although the MiG-15 was, in many ways, a superior machine, the aircraft was also extremely limited in both range and firepower. Listed as a fighter aircraft in virtually every publication where it has been written about (like nearly all MiGs up to the MiG-23), the fifteen was developed as a point defense interceptor, deployed to operate effectively against bombers within a radius of 75 miles of the MiG's home airfield. Range, or radius of action, was severely limited to a maximum of 370 miles. Some publications optimistically list the aircraft's range, with two 200-liter (53 gallon) drop tanks, at up to 2000 kilometers (1,243 miles)--a figure based on ideal peacetime cruise conditions. Wartime MiG-15s had ranges of around 1,200 km (746 miles), but not when operating at combat speeds up to 1,000 km/h (621 mph). In the combat mode, a MiG-15 ran at maximum or near maximum throttle, which translated to about 45 minutes with a small reserve. Fuel allocations in the Korean conflict allowed for 15-20 minutes to intercept the bombers, 5-10 minutes of combat, and 15-20 minutes for returning to the home airfield. The average planned combat mission lasted 45 minutes, and was seldom more than 57, the point where the fighter was likely to run out of fuel.

MiG-15 armament consisted of a 37mm (1.45 caliber) Nudelman N-37 cannon attached to the right underneath side of the nose, with a basic load of 40 rounds. The short-recoil gun, with an adjustable hydraulic recoil buffer, fired from an open bolt. An additional pair of staggered 23mm (.90 caliber) Nudelman/Rikhter NR-23 cannons on the left carried 80 rounds per gun. The rate of fire of 400 and 800 rounds per minute, respectively, translated to a six second continuous burst before running out of ammunition. The N-37 was developed in 1947 for use against US strategic bombers. Tests conducted against a Tu-4 bomber, a B-29 copy, proved that just one hit with a 37mm projectile was enough to bring down the bomber. On the UN side, the F-86 had six .50 caliber machine guns with a 6,600 rounds per minute rate of fire. Although both aircraft could use up their ammunition in fifteen seconds, the MiG's slower rate and fewer rounds made it clear that the intent behind the design was, from the beginning, to hit and run. Marginally suited for dog fighting, the MiG-15 was nevertheless deadly against B-29s.

As lethal as the MiG was against the slower, much larger target, it could have been much more so if their ammunition had performed more efficiently. On Black Tuesday, two of the three B-29s that crash landed at Kimpo Air Base near Seoul South Korea had unexploded cannon projectiles inside wing fuel tanks. There are numerous examples of cannon duds that would have certainly downed the aircraft they ripped into had they exploded. Many B-29 crew members credit their survival to faulty fuses or whatever it was that caused the failure to explode.

Designed specifically to shoot down B-29s armed with atom bombs and flown against targets within the Soviet Union, meant the MiG-15 basically had to take-off, make one firing pass at the B-29 and glide back down for a landing. Three cannons maximized the likelihood that one attack would do the job. The larger caliber ammunition also limited the MiG-15 to one six-second burst from all three cannons before running out of ammo--not exactly the best situation for dog fighting. In actual engagements with F-86s, the better Soviet pilots would select either the 37mm or the two 23mm guns and fire them separately, giving them a bit over eleven seconds of ammo. By contrast, the F-86 could fire a fifteen second burst, gaining a one to four seconds added opportunity of firing on the MiG after it ran out of ammunition.

Limited ammunition was just one reason that Soviet pilots were often under orders to avoid combat with F-86s. Indeed, MiG groups would usually climb to altitude before crossing the Yalu, fly over the fighter screen above the F-86's maximum ceiling, and swoop down on the B-29s from behind.

The dogfights depicted in most dramatizations of MiGs vs. Sabres were more often engagements between MiGs designated to protect their comrades' recovery to home base with F-86s hot on their tail. Hollywood and fighter pilots notwithstanding, a fair number of F-86 aces scored victories in pursuit of MiGs that had already exhausted their ammo and fuel.

Bad weather was also a major factor that severely limited MiG operations. The airplane was pretty much a VFR airplane. One account tells of a unit's fighters being grounded for over a month during the monsoon season. This probably accounted for the fact that B-29s conducted so many daylight-bombing missions into

MiG Alley between April 12 and late September 1951 without being intercepted.

As already noted, the MiG's most limiting factor was its short combat range. Almost without exception, all of the early clashes between MiGs and F-86s took place within the boundaries of MiG Alley. Although it is generally concluded that the Soviets limited their combat arena so their presence would not be exposed, a more cogent explanation would be that their combat radius did not much exceed these boundaries. In a significant way, this limitation also saved many pilots and airplanes that might have otherwise been lost. As long as the pilot was alive, even severely shot-up MiGs were within gliding distance of their bases on the other side of the Yalu. Dead-stick landings were not uncommon. One lucky soul landed with 154 bullet holes in his airplane, including 39 in the engine compartment.

Concerning actual losses, the truth probably depends as much on interpretation of the records as what the records report. For example, if the pilot wasn't careful, the MiG-15 had the nasty habit of becoming uncontrollable at high Mach numbers. This problem, called *valezhka* by Soviet pilots, caused the airplane to fall off into a spin that sent the aircraft plummeting earthward as though it had been shot down. An experienced pilot almost always recovered from this unusual maneuver, although usually forced to return home due to low fuel or ammunition. It was also during this recovery phase that the MiG was most vulnerable. To engage an enemy or even to take evasive action under these conditions meant running out of fuel and crashing.

It is well documented that the MiG could take what often appeared to be an enormous number of direct hits from the F-86's fifty caliber machine guns and keep on flying. Although there is considerable debate as to whether the MiG-15 suffered losses as high as those reported by their counterparts in the F-86, there is none on the issue of its effectiveness against slower straight wing fighters and the B-29.

Early encounters in the Korean War led designers to upgrade the MiG-15 with hydraulic aileron boosters and an engine that developed 900 additional pounds of thrust. The later aircraft, designated the MiG-15bis, could climb faster and higher than the F-86, but was limited by poor turning performance and high mach instability. The MiG-15bis manufactured in September 1950 carried 375 US gallons of fuel weighing roughly 2,259 pounds. Its top speed of 657 mph and 10, 000 feet per minute rate of climb at sea level dropped off to 616 mph and 4,000 fpm at 32,000 feet. Its turning time of 65 seconds and the 4,265 feet it was capable of gaining in a yo-yo maneuver gave it an edge over its competitor, the F-86 Sabre.

Like all new combat aircraft, the MiG-15 underwent extensive modifications throughout the Korean War. To improve performance, its airbrakes were enlarged, and new cannons and gun sights were installed. To increase pilot survivability, the ejection seat was replaced and additional armor was added. Early on, stabilizer tips and elevator hinges were reinforced after two aircraft crashed when the original elevators buckled during high-G maneuvers.

Early jet engines were notorious fuel hogs. The range listed on performance charts (best described as "combat radius") meant that the aircraft, at max cruise settings and best cruise altitude, was capable of flying a certain distance before having to turn back. In practice, the MiG-15 often came into direct combat shortly after climbing to altitude. Combat maneuvers cut into this range figure severely, reducing the aircraft's ability to stay aloft from hours to minutes. Fortunately, the protected Manchurian bases were within gliding distance, which allowed pilots to make highly vulnerable dead-stick landings if necessary.

For MiG-15s operating in daylight out of Manchurian bases, Pyongyang (the capital of North Korea) was too far south for a MiG-15 to take off, fly to Pyongyang, engage in combat, and return home. On occasions they landed, refueled, and then flew combat, but those occasions were relatively rare because of the continued bombing of North Korean airfields.

When intercepting daylight bombing attacks, MiG pilots usually climbed to an altitude above the ceiling of the F-86 escorts. This burned excessive amounts of fuel but also allowed them to fly uncontested above the fighter escort and swoop down on the B-29s. Night bombing, intended to protect the bombers from visual air-to-air cannon fire, fell victim to the Law of Unintended Consequence. Night MiG interceptors did not have to climb above the fighter escort because there was none, so they were able to intercept B-29s farther south than during daylight.

The MiG-15's legendary survivability grew out of its resistance to standard American fifty caliber machine gun bullets. MiGs were reported to have returned to their bases with as many as 204 holes in their fuselages and wings. One, flown by a wounded Soviet pilot, Lt. Veshkin, made an engine-out, gear-up belly landing three miles short of his intended runway. When the aircraft was examined, the ground crew counted 154 bullet holes. The engine had been hit 39 times and all of the compressor and turbine blades were bent. It is also reported that this MiG was returned to flight status eight days later. Accounts abound of the MiG's incredible durability. During a dogfight in September 1952, a MiG flown by Maj. Karatayev, took 24 hits in the engine that punctured two combustion chambers and bent 16 turbine blades. The aft tank exploded and the forward fuel cell and hydraulic tank were punctured. The left airbrake was also burned away, yet the pilot was able to land.

A partial reason for the MiG's amazing survivability was due to the use of armor-piercing slugs by F-86 units. A Sabre would get on the tail of a MiG and pour a load into it without apparent effect because the slugs were going all the way through.

Unlike the Sabre, which had excellent cockpit visibility, MiG pilots complained of bothersome reflections from the canopy and misting caused by water seeping between the glass layers and freezing at altitude.

*　　　　　*　　　　　*

Soviet MiG squadrons were divided into three groups: attack, cover, and reserve. As the names imply, the attack group would go after the UN bombers while the cover group provided protection, and the reserves served as backup. In order to intercept UN bombers in the least amount of warning time, the MiGs were placed on quick-reaction alert (QRA). The three squadrons in each regiment would alternate two-hour shifts. When the duty shift received the signal from the control tower the pilots would climb into their fighters and scramble to get to altitude ahead of the incoming enemy force. Typically, the Soviet pilots would climb to altitude and loiter above the objective they were assigned to defend in order to have an altitude and speed advantage over the fighters escorting the UN bombers.

When forced to engage the F-86, Soviet pilots usually employed a head-on, hit and run tactic directed by ground controlled radar control. Having secured an altitude advantage and using the sun whenever possible, MiG pairs would execute high-speed diving attacks and climb away, avoiding sustained combat. Fuel permitting, they would repeat the tactic.

MiG combat activity declined whenever a new outfit entered the theater of operations. Unlike the American practice of replacing individual crews, the Soviets rotated entire units. This basically deprived them of the hard-earned combat experience that had been gained by the departing unit.

Less than two months after the ceasefire, in September 1953, a North Korean pilot defected by flying his MiG-15bis south to Kimpo AFB. The aircraft was then shipped to Kadena AFB, Okinawa where it underwent flight tests, including evaluation by America's most famous living pilot, Chuck Yeager, the man who broke the sound barrier. With an F-86 escort tagging along to observe, Yeager climbed the MiG to 55,600 feet, which was 4,600 feet higher than the F-86 could climb. Although the tests proved that the Sabre was a better aircraft insofar as equipment and armament was the measure, the MiG's quickness and ability to climb higher than the Sabre made possible the debacle that occurred on Black Tuesday.

5: **Prelude to Disaster**

Except for an occasional maximum effort that involved all three B-29 groups, during most of 1951 the 19th, 98th and 307th shared the burden and risk of bombing targets in heavily defended MiG Alley. After months of relative calm, the week leading up to Black Tuesday suddenly became deadly. On Sunday, October 21, the 98th Bombardment Group came under MiG attack and lost one B-29 over the target. The following day, the 19th had one go down over the Yellow Sea.

On missions he flew prior to October 22nd, Jim Foster recalled that the MiGs had stayed well away from the B-29s, clearly visible but not attacking. The author also remembers seeing a MiG at a distance, probably on our September mission against the Sunchon RR Bridge. Although I was never certain that the swept wing silhouette wasn't an F-86, the fighter appeared to enter a pursuit curve-type attack but broke off in what is best described as a stall that literally dropped it out of the sky. In recent years I've learned that the MiG-15 had a nasty high speed stall characteristic that made it appear as though it had been "shot down." Most of the Russian pilots recovered from the stall but a few did not. This disagreeable characteristic also made the MiG highly vulnerable when pursued by an American F-86.

Even though the presumed MiG was definitely out of range, several B-29 gunners in our formation fired at the fleeting target, and a couple tried to take credit for a "kill." We found out later that they'd scored a number of hits--on unintended targets. More than one B-29 in the formation that day came home with .50 cal holes in a wing tip as a result of gunners on other B-29s not releasing the trigger soon enough.

MiG pilots who stalked our formations leading up to the week of October 21 were apparently taking the measure of the B-29s and were, in retrospect, harbingers of what was to come. Unfortunately for the B-29 crews, in the days leading up to Black Tuesday, FEAF showed signs that it was suffering from amnesia, apparently having forgotten the lessons learned on the bloody B-29s vs. MiGs air battle on April 12.

Six months before Black Tuesday, on April 12, 1951, a daylight mission came under attack by a large number of MiG-15s. The Soviet jets inflicted crippling damage on the B-29 force that was sent to bomb the Sinuiju rail crossing, a multi level bridge over the Yalu River between Uiju, North Korea, and Antung, Manchuria. FEAF put forth a maximum effort by launching forty-six B-29s, with eighty fighter escorts. Bombing was carried out by three bombardment groups, the 19th, 307th, and 98th, each representing one of the B-29 units assigned to fighting the Korean War. Each group bombed in a column of flights formed into diamonds, a combat formation that provided the maximum in defensive firepower. The first group, the 19th, had one aircraft armed with the radio-guided, 12,000 pound Tarzon bomb. The Tarzon aircraft made its bomb run parallel to the bridge, while the second and third groups came in from angles of 30-35 degrees to the bridge's longitudinal axis. Unlike other missions, the four B-29s in Charlie Flight split away from Able and Baker Flights to attack the same target from a different direction. MiGs intercepted the first two bomber groups while they were 18 to 27 miles from the target.

On that day, Cpl. Rolland Miller, left gunner on the 307th's lead aircraft that would also become Able Flight's lead aircraft on Black Tuesday, remembers the heavy black exhaust smoke from the Soviet jets as they climbed out from an airstrip in Antung. Miller's radioman was also monitoring transmissions from a spotter plane that called out, "A train is leaving from the station" each time a flight of MiGs took off. As they listened to the count rise, their hearts sank. They knew they were in for a rough day and they were right.

Miller's navigator, Lt. Fred Meier, remembers the 125-150 knot winds that caused such excessive right drift that their bomber had to fly into protected Manchurian airspace due to an effect called "cross trail." Because of the strong wind effect on the falling bombs, aircraft were forced to release north of the target in order to hit it. They were so far north of the aiming point that Meier's bombardier had to be shown on the map that they'd not chosen the wrong initial point. "The Airborne Commander, Col. Curnutt was

April 12, 1951 Mission. Target: railroad bridge over the Yalu between Sinuiju, N. Korea and Dandong, China. The pair of blobs in the upper left of this photo are reported to be attacking MiGs. The B-29 tail belongs to Miss. N. C., Able 3 on this ill-fated mission.
Courtesy of Lyle Patterson

Dramatic photo of Dragon Lady just after taking a cannon hit in the cockpit under the Aircraft Commander's window. The bombardier and Aircraft Commander were both killed. The Copilot landed the B-29 in Korea. Note: both bomb bays are open and the turrets are tracking the MiG attackers. *Courtesy of Lyle Patterson*

having a fit," Meier recalled, "(and) the Air Force never admitted that they actually flew over a MiG base."

The maximum effort mission was also plagued by other unanticipated glitches. In addition to hundred-plus knot crosswinds that resulted in twenty-one degrees of drift and put them seven miles into Manchuria, the twelve 2000 pound bombs dropped by each aircraft went through the bridge to the ground before exploding. To destroy the bridge, the fuses should have been set to detonate several feet above ground impact. They were not.

As he would repeat six months later, Meier's aircraft commander, Capt Clarence Fogler decided to land in Korea before returning to Okinawa. In Meier's words, "We landed at Kimpo to count the holes ... General Kelly met the crew after debriefing and recommended the entire crew for the DFC. It (the mission) was a good idea," Meier granted, "but badly planned."

No one who flew on or against the April 12th mission would forget it, or that it was a preview of what was to come, six months later, on Black Tuesday.

Russian ace, Sergey Kramarenko remembers that he and his fellow MiG pilots arrived at the airfield just as the morning light began to unfold the shapes of the swept wing fighters parked on the ramp. After checking over their airplanes, the duty flight went to readiness condition one. Four pilots manned their aircraft, cocked for immediate takeoff, while the others either rested in their aircraft or went to the hut where they waited for orders from Command. Shortly after breakfast, they received word for all regimental pilots to go to their aircraft. Minutes later they were ordered to scramble.

After the 196th Regiment, led by Lieutenant Colonel Pepelyayev, took to the air, three squadrons of the 176th Regiment followed. Only a duty pair of aircraft remained behind on the ground. This was the first time all of the 324th Fighter Aviation Division's combat ready aircraft were sent to intercept an Allied bomber force. Kramarenko's group of six MiGs was to provide cover for the two forward squadrons that formed the strike group and whose mission was to attack the bombers.

Later, Kramarenko would learn that the Soviet radar stations had acquired a large group of enemy aircraft heading towards their airfield. In order to repulse this mass raid they decided to send up every single fighter in the division.

For Ralph Livengood, a B-29 navigator in the 19th BG, the April 12 mission began with wake-up shortly after midnight. Briefing was at 0200. In his book, *B-29 Navigator*, Livengood recalls that the usually noisy briefing room became deadly quiet when the target, Sinuiju, was announced. They saw that the rail crossing over the Yalu River between Sinuiju, North Korea and Dandong, China was as deep into MiG Alley as they were allowed to fly. Many of them had been there before and knew what was in store. Just across the river, protected by political decree, the Manchurian airfields were packed with MiGs anxious to shoot them down. Livengood wrote, "As the briefing came to an end the usual buzz of conversation was absent. Each person was contemplating the day ahead and what it might bring." This would be the 202nd mission for the 19th and number sixteen for Livengood and his crew. They would be flying *Miss N. C,* serial number 44-86376.

Four days earlier, Livengood had been happy to see that they would be flying their 15th mission in *Miss N.C.* again. In his words, "The B-29 was . . . almost another home as we spent so much time in it." Their mission was scheduled to be at night in support of frontline troops. Two hours and twenty-four minutes after takeoff their airspeed and altitude began dropping as an engine began losing power. Six minutes later, the engine developed a severe vibration and had to be shut down. Within the hour a second engine did the same thing and also had to be shut down. With their airspeed hovering just above stall and losing altitude the A/C gave the "prepare to bail out" signal, but was in a quandary because they were flying over heavily populated Taegu, South Korea in an airplane with a full bomb load. In a last ditch attempt, they restarted the engines and babied them through the rest of the successful mission.

Early on the morning of the 12th, Livengood was not enthusiastic about flying *Miss N.C.* Although the previous mission had somewhat renewed his faith in the airplane, in addition to a pair of engines they now had flak and fighters to worry about.

At 0439 *Miss N. C.* lifted off of the Kadena runway. The 30th Bombardment Squadron led the pack as Able Flight, followed by

Although nose art was absent from 307BW B-29s, other units, such as the 19BG shown here, encouraged the practice.

(Above) Miss N. C., participant in the notorious
April 12 mission to the Yalu (p. 102).

(Below) Command Decision, "ace" B-29 flown on the
October 22 mission (p. 112). *Photos by Author*

the 93rd in Baker and the 28th comprising Charlie Flight. After crossing the coast-in point, the three flights proceeded to the assembly point where they formed-up at 17,000 feet into three flights of four each and were joined by fourteen F-84s. Charlie, however, left the main formation at the fighter rendezvous point and proceeded toward a different initial point for the bomb run. Livengood's aircraft flew in the number three position off of the left wing of Baker Leader. When the main force reached the IP, they turned on course for the bombing run. Able one carried a 12,000 lb. remote radio-guided Tarzon bomb. Each of the remaining aircraft in all three flights were loaded with eight 2,000 bombs each. The targets were precise points on the bridge span. For the Tarzon, the aiming point was the 8th span from the south abutment while the others aimed at the 3rd pier from the south abutment.

Thirteen minutes into the bombing run, the dreaded word "MiG" broke the intercom silence. They were coming in level on the left side. Livengood could see a wave of them flying toward Baker Flight, gun muzzles "blinking like fireflies" along with the bright flashes from their 37 mm cannon. Tracer trails poured into the formation as gunners turned all of their turrets toward the fighters and opened fire. Someone reported a B-29 on fire, then Baker two damaged and leaving formation, "Baker one hit in the cockpit and going down nose first." "Watch for chutes, Able Two hit and leaving formation." The first pass lasted only a few seconds. The second attack was even more determined.

Leading seven F-86s from the 334th Fighter-Interceptor Squadron that had joined the fighter escort, Captain James Jabara latched onto a MiG-15 that was lining up to attack the bomber formation. Jabara closed from behind and fired several bursts. Pieces flew from the Communist jet as it fell into a smoking dive and crashed. It was Jabara's third victory and he would go on to become the first American jet ace in history.

For the bombers, the nightmare continued. Baker one crashed without a single parachute spotted. Hit hard, Baker Three dropped out of the formation. Able one took a pounding. Able Two turned for Taegu with wounded aboard. Livengood's CFC, Lyle Patterson, reported hitting a MiG that was "on fire and going down." Then came the third pass. Baker Four had two engines shot out. As the MiGs pulled away from their third pass, the bombardier called "bombs away." It was 1020 as they broke away from the target. Only two of the original eight aircraft remained in the formation and would make it home. *Miss N. C.* was one of the two.

Records show that the 19th BG lost five B-29s on 4/12/51 and the 307th one. A small number of MiGs made passes at the 98th bringing up the rear, but failed to shoot any down. The radio-guided Tarzon bomb landed 500 feet from the bridge and did no damage. Only the third group succeeded dropping several bombs in the vicinity of the bridge.

Although April 12 turned out to be a very black day for FEAF and UN air superiority in general, during the next four months B-29 daylight bombing formations were seldom attacked--except for sporadic encounters, usually with individual MiGs. One such attack took place on the first of June 1951. First Lieutenant Yevgeny Mikhailovich Stelmah (18th GIAP/303rd IAD), the element wingman of a MiG-15 quartet, spotted B-29s attacking the Kwaksan railroad bridge. In spite of the bad weather, Stelmah (described by his comrades as young and impetuous) called for the others to cover him as he dived towards the bombers. Unfortunately Stelmah's radio was not functioning properly and the others didn't hear his call. He jumped the 98th Bomb Group B-29s and after several passes, brought down B-29 # 44-86327 by setting its number three engine on fire. Four aircrew members were seen parachuting from the burning bomber but sea and air rescue efforts were unsuccessful. Stelmah was already over the sea near Pyongyang, but erroneously thought he was being covered and pressed the attack against the remaining three B-29s. He shot up another B-29 that was so heavily damaged that it was written off after an emergency landing at Taegu, South Korea. By then Stelmah had allowed himself and his aircraft to venture too far into Allied-dominated airspace where he was shot down by an F-86 piloted by Capt. Richard Ransbottom. Stelmah ejected and landed in UN controlled territory. After evading capture for several hours, to avoid revealing Soviet involvement in the war, he committed suicide by putting a bullet through his heart. Ironically, his body was recovered by Chinese troops and sent back to Antung. Stelmah was posthumously awarded the highest Soviet military decoration, the Golden Star.

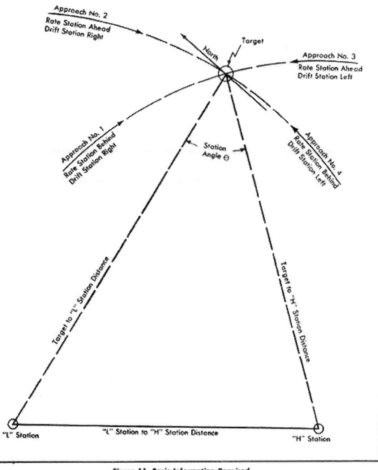

Approach No. 2
Rate Station Ahead
Drift Station Right

Approach No. 3
Rate Station Ahead
Drift Station Left

North

Target

Approach No. 1
Rate Station Behind
Drift Station Right

Approach No. 4
Rate Station Behind
Drift Station Left

Station
Angle Θ

Target to "L" Station Distance

Target to "H" Station Distance

"L" Station

"L" Station to "H" Station Distance

"H" Station

Figure 11—Basic Information Required

The four possible SHORAN arcs for bombing a specific target.

To read some of the Russian accounts of this period, a student of the Korean air war might come to the conclusion that the MiG pilots in general were waging a relentless war against the B-29 raiders. In spite of all that has been written about the "brave volunteers" attacks on the "fortresses," there was very little organized MiG resistance between April 12, 1951 and the final weeks of October 1951. One Russian manuscript takes note of the low morale among B-29 crews because of their high loss rates. It would be closer to the truth to say the opposite was true. Because there had been so little organized resistance for six months, the crews had, if anything, become complacent. In retrospect it appears foolhardy or at least arrogant that on Black Tuesday the 307th would launch a formation of B-29s on a daylight mission in the clear between cloud layers, in loose trail, maintaining a SHORAN arc at the expense of massed firepower and without immediate fighter cover against a target less than fifty miles from the Soviet MiG-15 bases. This slap in the face, "come and get us if you dare" attitude was indicative of thinking among the majority of bomber crews that the MiG was less of a threat than the B-29's often unreliable cyclone engines.

Especially in light of what was still to come, reasons for the relatively few hot encounters during the summer of 1951 are not entirely clear. On the Korean Peninsula, the monsoon season, which traditionally begins in late June and ends a month or so later, apparently kept the MiGs grounded. In the area around Antung, the steady downpours, along with occasional typhoons, made flying nearly impossible for long periods during the summer months.

To further complicate the Russian operation, the radar network in China was so primitive that it wasn't until 1952 that Soviet technical personnel got an efficient operational network up and running. While the Russian early warning radar network was still under construction, it is probable that UN electronic intelligence (ELINT) gathering aircraft located gaps in the coverage. It appears that the flight paths of several B-29 missions, especially those on 23-25 August were planned to enter North Korea through corridors not adequately covered by Russian radar.

The Russians also contend that FEAF escaped serious losses because Soviet fighters were either launched too late to intercept the B-29s or the forward barriers of F-86, F-84 and Meteor F. Mk 8 fighters engaged and prohibited them from reaching the bombers before they were out of range.

On 22, 23, 24 and 26 June, 1951 pilots of the 303rd IAD scrambled several times to intercept B-29s but were unsuccessful on all except the 26th when pilots of 17th IAP intercepted four B-29s and First Lt. Georgiy T. Fokin damaged one. In the entire month of July there was one encounter on the 29th against four B-29s escorted by forty F-86s. FEAF B-29s continued without opposition until 23 August when sixteen were intercepted. Carrier-based F2H Banshees thwarted another group of MiGs from attacking a formation of eight bombers. On the 25th while homing in on a large formation of B-29s (my first combat mission), MiG-15s of the 17th IAP encountered a group of Meteors from the No.77th Sqdn, RAAF. Nikolay Sutyagin and Grigoriy Pulov were each credited with shooting down a Meteor. Although the RAAF did not officially admit a combat loss, their reports show that two of their pilots, Reginald Lamb and Ronald Mitchell were "killed in action" because of a mid-air collision on a training flight. Igor' Seidov, co-author of *Red Devils on the 38th Parallel*, reminded this author that he should "say 'thank you very much" to the F-86, F-84 and Meteor F. Mk 8 pilots who did not allow the MiGs "to catch" our B-29s on 25 August, "in which he and his fellow crew members flew and escaped that day." I should be especially grateful to the RAAF Meteor pilots who perished while foiling the 17th IAP aimed at attacking our formation. I could well owe my life to those brave Aussies.

I hope it's not too late: *Thank you very much.*

During the summer of 1951, records indicate that Fokin was the only MiG pilot who damaged a B-29.

Two weeks before Black Tuesday, the Pacific Ocean coughed up the strongest typhoon of the season. Like a large number of Western Pacific typhoons, this one named "Ruth" was spawned in the tropical waters south of Guam. Ruth took off on a northwesterly direction, aimed directly at Taiwan, eighteen hundred miles distant. After maintaining an unwavering course for nearly fifteen hundred miles, she suddenly veered sharply right, setting her sights on Okinawa, less than a day away. A mad scramble followed. Kadena had to evacuate its aircraft or risk losing them on the ground.

While aircrews evacuated the B-29s to Japan, Dewell Turner, whose tour as a spare gunner with the 307th had begun a month earlier, was a part of the group that remained on Okinawa. When told a typhoon was bearing down on the island, ground personnel and spare gunners were formed into work groups to stow the tents and equipment in an attempt to minimize the expected damage. Among the seven men in Turner's work group was his friend Paul Stainbrook. Their assignment was to strike the squadron's tents and store them in one of the few permanent buildings in the area. Although most work crews sought shelter in the 19th Bomb Group's more permanent shelters, Turner's took refuge in the 307th's new Quonset that housed the latrine, lavatory, and shower room. The metal structure's low, streamlined silhouette, anchored cables, and dearth of glass made it the ideal place to ride out a typhoon. As Ruth moved closer, the work group made sure they had plenty of flashlights, rations, and water, and set up cots in the shower room. For the first few hours, their choice of shelter seemed perfect. The sound of rain was amplified by the tin roof, and in the wind's howling they could hear things being tossed about, but they heard nothing that seemed imminently threatening.

Eight hours into the storm, their sense of security was dramatically ended by a loud crash of something thrown into the side of their Quonset. The force of the impact shook the building and was followed by an indescribable screech, which seemed to the occupants would never end. Turner and his fellow riders of the storm rolled out of their cots onto the floor, fully expecting to find themselves blown into the bay. After the screeching subsided, Turner and his buddies-- thankful for having been spared some horrible fate--speculated about what could possibly have caused such a racket. As they talked, they realized that the relative quiet meant the eye of the storm was directly over them, and dashed outside to see what had happened.

Turner recalled, "It wasn't funny at the moment, but later we had a good laugh about our 'narrow escape' from the storm. Our new Quonset hut was built right next to the old latrine and shower house. That structure was also tin, but it was built tall and square. There was no way it could withstand the force of hurricane winds. The old shower room and latrine had blown over onto our Quonset hut and then the wind slowly forced it up and over the roof until it was completely on the other side. The only other damage was to our psyche. And that was because the sound was like a thousand fingernails scratching on a blackboard."

The 19th Bomb Group managed to launch all but one B-29 (ours), which was missing an engine. The rest of the crew evacuated another B-29 to Tachikawa, an air base in Japan, leaving me behind to take turns with other spare copilots and ground crew flying the aircraft into the wind as the typhoon surged through. This meant starting engines and changing directions as the powerful winds shifted. It also meant flying out gusts that sometimes exceeded take-off speed.

Unknown to me at the time, Fred Meier, the lead navigator on the Black Tuesday mission was riding out Ruth in another B-29. Twenty-nine of the 307th's assigned thirty B-29s evacuated ahead of the typhoon, leaving behind Fred and his crew sitting in the airplane on a 307th hardstand for 76 hours. Like us, they ran the engines to keep the nose pointed into the wind. His pilots, he recalled, said it was like flying the plane on the ground.

When the winds finally subsided, we were rewarded for riding out the storm by a rare sight. Mongooses, brought to the island to destroy the deadly habu (snake), suddenly emerged from hiding in broad daylight and swarmed around our airplane, apparently searching for something set loose by the storm. We weren't able to determine what they were looking for, and after that one instance never saw another mongoose on Okinawa.

The NCO club was severely damaged and the 30'/th mess hall took a serious hit. Some of the 307th's tent floors had missing planks. One had sailed through the side of the NCO Club. There was roof damage where Turner's work group had stored their tents and all of the tents and clothing that had been inside were soaked. They were able to erect the tents before the flight crews got back, but forced to rough it for several days until local civilians repaired the damaged structures. Turner and his fellow Americans marveled at how well the village structures weathered the storm. "Many of them did not look strong enough to withstand a good Oklahoma breeze," Turner observed, "much less a typhoon."

Ruth continued northeast, striking Japan once, then again after changing direction over the Sea of Japan. Sasebo, a Japanese port used extensively by UN naval forces, was devastated by 100 mph winds and 45-foot waves. Warships and transport vessels, including HMAS *Sydney*, an Australian aircraft carrier that would lead rescue operations on Black Tuesday, put out to sea to escape the dangerous harbor. Even so, wave damage was substantial and four of *Sydney's* aircraft were tossed overboard.

Typhoon Ruth left 943 dead, 2,644 injured and 359,391 homes destroyed or inundated. Although devastating, she caused barely a ripple in bomber operations.

Without fully appraising the possible consequences, the sudden proliferation of airfields under construction south of the Yalu inside North Korea spurred FEAF planners to act hastily. Their special concern focused on Namsi, Taechon, and Saamchan. All three airfields would be able to handle MiGs when completed. From these more southern bases, the jet fighters could then provide air cover for ground attack aircraft targeting UN ground forces. This, FEAF planners reasoned, would upset the balance provided by Allied airpower, and drastically affect the outcome of the war. They apparently overlooked the facts that the location of these airfields added less than ten minutes to the combat radius of the attack aircraft or that MiG survivability depended to a large degree on its being able to climb, unfettered, to an altitude above the F-86's maximum ceiling.

Bomber Command's campaign against the airfields began on the night of October 14, with B-29s using SHORAN, an electronic system that had been designed and tested for night bombing. The first two missions, flown by the 307th on 14 and 15 October, were unsuccessful, which prompted planners to switch their thoughts to daylight raids. By providing massive fighter screens, they hoped to ward off the MiG attackers so the B-29s could obliterate the airfields. On October 18, five days before Black Tuesday, FEAF sent nine B-29's from the 19th to bomb Saamchan, the southernmost of the three airfields, and nine B-29's from the 98th Wing to attack Taechon. After missing their fighter escort rendezvous, the 98th diverted to a safer secondary target. The 19th's Superforts forged ahead to Saamchan without encountering MiGs and cratered the airfield with 306 one hundred-pound bombs. On 21 October the 98th was again diverted from its scheduled target when the bombers failed to meet up with friendly fighters, except this time the MiGs caught up with the bombers and shot down one. After the 98th failed twice to bomb Taechon, the 19th was given a shot. On 22 October, the day before Black Tuesday, nine 19th Bomb Group B-29s picked up 24 escorting Thunderjets, as scheduled, and pressed on toward the airfield.

One of the nine targeting Taechon was a 30th Bomb Squadron B-29, SN 44-61656, best known for its nose art, *Cream of the Crop*. The name was splashed in red-bordered yellow letters across the entire right side of the nose section. Above the lettering, the well-endowed blonde who soared Superman-style had recently been censored with a black patch painted across her bare breasts. Censoring, some thought, was bad luck, and for *Cream of the Crop* it proved to be. This was her last mission.

To spread MiG defenses and prevent them from concentrating on the main bomber force, FEAF had scheduled F-80 and F-84 ground attack aircraft to strike railway stations and other targets in the Sukchong-Anju-Sunchong area at the same time as the B-29s zeroed in on Taechon with Australian Meteor and American F-84 and F-86 fighters flying protective cover.

Less than five minutes after the bomber force was picked up on Soviet radar, twenty MiG-15s from the 17th IAP, fourteen from the 18th GIAP, and another twenty from the 523rd IAP launched out of their Manchurian base to turn back the bomber and ground attack forces. As they headed out for the attack, the 17th and 523rd broke off to cut off the F-80s and F-84s.

After leveling off 4,000 feet above the F-86 bomber escort patrolling the Taechong-Pakchong-Anju corridor, the fourteen 18th GIAP MiGs followed directions from Soviet ground radar to place them in contact with the B-29s nearing Teysyu. Lt. Col. Aleksander P. Smorchkov, group leader, recalled the intercept: "We took off in heavy weather conditions, and we were not 'rated' pilots for that. As there was a break in the clouds, we headed right for it, but when we climbed out at ten thousand (meters), everything was completely covered. Then they gave us the command to take up such-and-such a course to where the 'big ones' were. We dove down--the entire regiment following me, but we maintained a good formation. 'We will dive,' I told them, 'everybody stay alert and don't smack into each other in the clouds!' I dove down, fighting the desire to fidget, looking for my wingman--there he was, right beside me, but other than him I could see no one else in the dark. I only had one thought in mind--please let nobody collide! I led, as commander, and was responsible for providing the morale of all of my pilots. For that I would be judged later. Only one pair had to collide--and I would be the guilty party!"

After penetrating the cloud layer, the fourteen-MiG formation emerged intact less than two miles from the twelve bombers and their immediate escort of twelve F-84s and eight Gloster Meteors. Elated, Smorchkov told his pilots to "Take on the big ones and don't worry about the small fry!" The fourteen broke into pairs and fours in a spread formation and, at full throttle, closed on their prey with a 373 mph speed advantage. Focusing his attack on the four B-29s bringing up the rear of the formation, Smorchkov opened fire at 900 meters. His initial burst missed low, his second to the right. Pressing his attack to 300 meters, the next few cannon shells split the right-side engines and wing fuel tanks. The B-29 burst into flames and started falling. As the stricken bomber entered the lower cloud layer, Smorchkov counted six parachutes. The second pair in his flight, Senior Lieutenants Stepanov and Shebanov, attacked the other two B-29s in the four-ship formation and damaged, but did not shoot down another B-29. Smorchkov told his wingman, Lieutenant Voistinnykh to move over and he would cover him. Voistinnykh fired but was out of range. At the same time, ground control gave the order for everyone to land due to low fuel.

Most of the badly outclassed F-84 escorts had been drawn off by the forty MiG-15s from the 17th and 523rd shortly before Smorchkov's group dropped down out of a cloudbank and attacked so suddenly that the B-29 gunners were unable to return the fire. Already crippled by flak hits, *Cream of the Crop* was a virtual sitting duck. After slipping under the lower cloud cover, the heavily damaged bomber managed to limp to the Korean coast, where the crew parachuted into the sea. Miraculously, Allied ships rescued all twelve crew members.

To Jim Foster, flying copilot on the 22 October mission, the B-29s were easy targets for the MiGs to pick off at will. In his words, "One came in on us...did not hit us with cannon fire but I swear that he went between the antennae and airframe on my side--he was that close!" Foster's airplane was not hit by cannon fire.

C. J. Christ, the pilot on crew S-26, remembered the mission: "The attack came from three o'clock and four o'clock high. CFC put six guns on him (four upper forwards, two upper aft), and began firing when he was in range. The front of the attacking MiG-15's was aglow. My navigator Louis Schilinger was squatted next to me watching the show. My first remark to Louie was, 'Hey, I think we got him!' Louie's remark as he ducked behind the improvised flak shield was, 'Got him, hell. We're looking into his gun barrels!'"

C. J's airplane was flying in the fourth or slot position, below and behind a B-29 that would eventually claim ace status, *Command Decision*, whose aircraft commander was Captain Donald Covic. As the gunners on Covic's B-29 opened fire, spent cartridges and casings spewed from their turrets, shattering the slot aircraft's nose windows, navigator's bubble, and CFC dome. The impact peeled rubber boots off of leading edge between engines on both sides of the airplane and the vertical stabilizer. The spent ammo also broke the HF antenna, which then trailed behind the airplane still attached to its tailfin point. The CFC was so nervous he vomited on gunners Paul Schaeffer and Hacker, on both sides-- but never stopped firing at the incoming MIG whose tracers were going between the HF antenna and his dome. As the MiG peeled away at 8-9 o'clock, the CFC put the lower two guns on him.

Just ahead of them, Covic took a hit in the port inboard engine section that caused the left main gear to drop and the engine to start smoking. Covic feathered the prop.

"One strange thing we noticed about the MIG," C.J. recalls, "he was bobbing up and down in a Dutch roll. I don't know if we hit him or not. Since the four upper forward guns were firing right behind me, I know that at the time, the tail gunner in Covic's airplane was also firing. I think Covic peeled off and landed in South Korea."

With his leftover ammo, Smorchkov shot down one of the five F-84s claimed by the Russians. Stepanov and Shebanov claimed they shot down another B-29, but subsequent records indicate that this claim was likely based on separate sightings of #44-61656 crashing into the sea. I was assigned to the 19th at that time and know for a fact that only one B-29 failed to eventually return to Kadena.

Recent Russian reports concede that the intercept of the B-29 formation was, in their words, "a bit of an accident," and that two 18th GIAP MiGs received several bullet holes they presumed came from the F-84 escorts.

Actual Namsi target photo (taken on 14 October 1951) used by Able Lead bombardier, Nick Kourafas, to plan the visual aiming points for Able ("A"), Baker ("B"), and ("C") Charlie Flights on the Black Tuesday mission. *Courtesy of Nick Kourafas & Fred Meier*

6: Target: Namsi Airfield

Of all of the claims made by Russian historians who have written of the Soviet involvement in the air war in Korea, the repeated reference to B-29 "carpet-bombing" is the most annoying. I cannot recall a single mission that was ever targeted against non-strategic targets or where the bombs were "spaced," as in carpet-bombing. While it was normal for the B-29 to carry a total of forty 500-pound bombs, the hope was that a few of them would hit what was aimed at. The Russian view often appears to be that we were indiscriminately targeting whomever and whatever happened to be in the way. Our orders were always the same. If we could not acquire the primary target we went to the secondary. Our third course of action was to dump the entire load in a designated salvo area. Had we been given the option to carpet bomb, it would have been no great task to muster an armada of B-29s to lay waste a swath across the Korean peninsula that would have isolated the Communist troops and essentially put an end to the debacle.

An even more important factor, largely ignored by Russian writers, is the fact that the American Medium bombers were prohibited from conducting true strategic bombardment. This farce was most evident in the bombing of Yalu River bridges separating North Korea from Manchuria only on the Korean side. The policy that prohibited strikes outside Korean borders required B-29 units to fly their bomb runs down the river to avoid violating Manchurian airspace. For MiG pilots, B-29s were sitting ducks. On one bridge mission (not on the Yalu--I never had that pleasure--probably Sonchon) a particularly clear day allowed us to see the Antung area. Someone on the crew said, "Let's go get them." Of course, we never did. Had we done so, the Russian pilots would not have had airfields to fly out of.

Not only were UN aircraft restricted from attacking MiG bases across the Yalu in Manchuria, MiG-15 pilots were also prohibited from attacking UN positions from their Manchurian bases. To make matters even more peculiar, documents indicate that there was no such restriction if the MiG pilots took off from airfields in North Korea. Because of this and other factors, the Communists decided to repair damaged airstrips in North Korea in addition to building new ones, apparently to take advantage of this twisted sort of logic.

The lack of airfields in North Korea frustrated the Sino-Korean Unified Air Army command. If they had them, they reasoned, the UAA could protect their lines of communication and attack UN forces in their rear areas. Ground attack aircraft, however, required cover that could only be provided by MiGs flying out of Manchurian airbases that would be unable to reach the front lines. Realizing this, apparently without understanding the reasons for doing so, the Koreans attempted to build an airfield at Uiju, just across the Yalu River from the Soviet MiG base in Antung, Manchuria.

James Johnson wrote, "Bringing them (MiG-15s) to Uiju was a stupid idea from the moment of its creation, as the Americans, who were constantly using offensive tactics and were the first to have the chance to attack an enemy 'jet' base, hit the airfield day and night. ... Just after six weeks of combat the North Korean aviation moved to Manchuria, from where they only returned (to S. Korea) after the ceasefire."

At the beginning of the war, the North Koreans decided to build eleven airfields on its own soil. Construction was carried out in river valleys that were at least 1.5-2 kilometers wide and had bordering peaks no more than a hundred feet above field level. Several antiaircraft artillery regiments were positioned on the peaks around the airfield at the corners of a quadrilateral or triangle at intervals of two to three kilometers, and one to one and half kilometers from the runway. Light antiaircraft artillery (AAA) was scattered around the airfield at intervals of 50-1500 meters and at ranges of 300-400 meters from the runway. Six-gun batteries were established at intervals of 200-700 meters between emplacements.

As the MiG airfields neared completion in April and May 1951, B-29s carried out an intensive bombing campaign and systematically destroyed them, usually when the work was 80-90% completed.

As the numbers of MiGs pouring into the airfields across the Yalu increased, it became evident that there were not enough operational F-86s on hand to effectively counter the MiG threat. To make matters worse, the see-saw movement of Communist and Allied ground forces had moved the newly arrived American F-86 fighters from S. Korea to Japan and back again, which placed them out of range of MiG Alley, thus unable to protect bombers penetrating that far north. The situation changed in March 1951 when the 4th FIW moved to Suwon, South Korea, where it would remain until the ceasefire, over two years later. Conditions on the ground were poor at best. Inadequate facilities and a shortage of spare parts made it difficult to repair malfunctioning or damaged aircraft. When maintenance problems became even worse, F-86 and ground attack aircraft missions into MiG Alley were temporarily halted and the North Koreans promptly returned to constructing airfields.

In early October, allied photoreconnaissance aircraft revealed eighteen nearly completed airfields. Three of them, Namsi, Taechon, and Saamchan, were capable of handling jet aircraft and would provide bases for Ilyushin Il-10 two-seat ground attack aircraft. Although the prop-driven Il-10 had proven obsolete against jet interceptors, it was believed that with MiG cover it could attack supplies and troops beyond the front lines, in the UN's rear area. Driven by this thinking, the three-airfield complex became an immediate FEAF priority and the B-29 units were assigned the task of destroying them.

Plan A recognized that the least dangerous method to accomplish this would be to bomb the airfields at night using SHORAN. The first two night raids, however, produced no results. When it was determined that all of the SHORAN aimed bombs had missed the target, FEAF elected to go with the less desirable alternative but one proven highly effective against strategic targets such as airfields: daylight precision bombing. To protect bombers flying in daylight and using the Norden bombsight to acquire targets visually, FEAF ordered up a potpourri of fighter and fighter-bomber cover to ward off the MiG threat.

The mix did not go as planned. Two of the first three bomber forces failed to rendezvous with their cover and bombed the secondary targets instead. On Monday, 22 October 1951, after failing twice in the three previous days, the 19th BG attacked Taechon and ran head-on into some of the most intense MiG defenses of the war. This, the day before Black Tuesday, marked the beginning of the end of daylight precision bombing.

Shortly after Black Tuesday, FEAF's B-29 attacks on airfields were restricted to night SHORAN bombing missions, either single ship or pairs flying at altitudes ranging from 24,000 to 27,000 feet. AAA defenses against these attacks usually consisted of four batteries of medium antiaircraft guns. Two batteries would fire using radar data and two would lay down a screen of barrage fire along or just downstream from the probable bomb release line. Because of the constrictions imposed on the bombers, both by terrain and political decree, the release line could be predetermined. Out of 3,470 bombs dropped on the Taechon airfield, only 167 fell within the limits of the airfield and the rest landed as far as two miles away. While claiming credit for such inaccuracies is often attributed to effective ground defenses, it is more likely the result of a combination of factors, such as the inherent inaccuracy of electronic bomb aiming systems, jet streams incongruities, and incorrect target selection and/or identification. Those who manned the batteries like to think of their defenses as "repulsing" attacks whereas there is no evidence that any B-29 ever turned back because of flak.

Light antiaircraft batteries were also deployed along the final approach flight paths, 4.5 to 5 kilometers from the airfield, to ward off UN fighters that attacked North Korean based aircraft that were taking off or landing. Eventually, however, experience showed that four medium antiaircraft batteries and four light antiaircraft batteries were not enough to protect an airfield.

On the Namsi mission, the three visual aiming points were evenly spaced on the centerline of the runway.

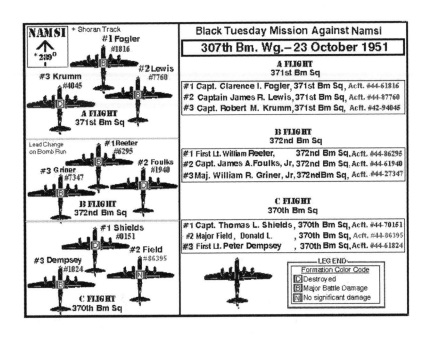

NAMSI

↑ *Shoran Track
* 219°

Black Tuesday Mission Against Namsi

307th Bm. Wg. – 23 October 1951

A FLIGHT
371st Bm Sq

#1 Fogler
#1816

#3 Krumm
#4045

#2 Lewis
#7760

A FLIGHT
371st Bm Sq

#1 Capt. Clarence I. Fogler, 371st Bm Sq, Acft. #44-61816
#2 Captain James R. Lewis, 371st Bm Sq, Acft. #44-87760
#3 Capt. Robert M. Krumm, 371st Bm Sq, Acft. #42-94045

B FLIGHT
372nd Bm Sq

Lead Change
on Bomb Run

#1 Reeter
#6295

#3 Griner
#7347

#2 Foulks
#1940

B FLIGHT
372nd Bm Sq

#1 First Lt. William Reeter, 372nd Bm Sq, Acft. #44-86295
#2 Capt. James A. Foulks, Jr, 372nd Bm Sq, Acft. #44-61940
#3 Maj. William R. Griner, Jr, 372nd Bm Sq, Acft. #44-27347

C FLIGHT
370th Bm Sq

#1 Shields
#0151

#3 Dempsey
#1824

#2 Field
#86395

C FLIGHT
370th Bm Sq

#1 Capt. Thomas L. Shields, 370th Bm Sq, Acft. #44-70151
#2 Major Field, Donald L., 370th Bm Sq, Acft. #44-86395
#3 First Lt. Peter Dempsey, 370th Bm Sq, Acft. #44-61824

LEGEND

Formation Color Code
D Destroyed
B Major Battle Damage
N No significant damage

7: Black Tuesday, October 23, 1951

It was still early morning when their F-84 escorts joined the nine B-29s at the fighter rendezvous point. Ahead and far above, 34 F-86 Sabres of the 4th FIW were providing a fighter screen south of the Yalu to intercept MiGs attacking the 307th from above while the 55 F-84 Thunderjets of the 49th and 126th FBGs were assigned to fight off any that broke though the Sabres. Able Lead navigator Fred Meier remembers seventeen F-84s joined on time, at 0935, and stayed with them until 0958, but he never saw a single F-86.

So far the bomber formation had remained intact. Captain Clarence Fogler led Able Flight, with Capt. James Lewis on his right wing and Capt. Robert Krumm on the left. Behind them, Lt. William Reeter, headed up Baker Flight with Capt. James Foulks on the right and Major William Griner, flying left wing. Capt. Thomas Shields led Charlie Flight with Major Donald Fields and Lt. Peter Dempsey on his right and left wings. Colonel Henry Ledbetter, Group Director of Operations flew in Fogler's lead aircraft as Airborne Commander. As they neared the target, Colonel Ledbetter and Fogler's copilot, 1st Lt. Stan Pyfrom exchanged positions. Ledbetter took the right pilot's seat while Pyfrom was relegated to the aisle stand.

Overhead, the much faster F-86s and F-84s were forced to slow down and fly extended figure eight and racetrack patterns in order not to get too far ahead of the bomber force.

As the bombers and fighters groomed for the assault, Soviet radio interception personnel who were monitoring enemy radio communications noticed unusually high traffic, suggestive that a significant attack was in the making. This was confirmed a short time later when Soviet radar screens picked up echoes of the approaching fighters and bombers, reported to be "along the Kaysyu-Kinsen-Isen-Iotoku line at altitudes of 6500 to 8000 meters (21,000 to 26,000 feet), each consisting of eight to thirty-two aircraft, and with an overall number of around two hundred aircraft of the F-86, F-84, F-80 and Gloster Meteor Mk. 4 types and two groups of ten to twelve B-29 bombers." The sighting, which considerably overestimated the size of the attacking force, was reported to 64th IAK Headquarters.

Throughout the war, rumors persisted that someone was tipping off the Russians that B-29 strikes were on the way long before they got there. In fact, the bomber force was seldom off of the Soviet radar screen--not because of someone slipping them notes under the table but because their radar tracked the bombers far enough out for the MiGs to scramble and intercept them before bombs away. MiG pilots were on constant, hot alert, in their cockpits, ready to launch at a moment's notice. On Black Tuesday, roughly half the interceptor force was either in the cockpit or by their MiGs. According to one Russian source, the presence of increased F-80 reconnaissance flights over the Namsi area the previous day had tipped them off that something big was in store.

After assessing the situation, the commander of the 64th IAK decided to launch two divisions sequentially, the first wave of 58 MiGs from the 17th, 18th, and 523rd. Their mission was to strike the main group of enemy bombers and ground attack aircraft. A second wave of 26 MiGs, from the 176th Guards and 196th IAP, would cover the withdrawal of the first wave, joining the battle where necessary.

As Soviet radar followed the progress of the B-29 force up the Korean Peninsula, the Soviets became concerned that such a large force might have been sent to attack their airfields north of the Yalu. Based on this possibility, the entire available combat MiG force was ordered to launch.

First Lieutenant Aleksey Nikolayev recalled the morning: "Since dawn there was a thick overcast over the airbase, but despite that we were ready to scramble at the first warning. Suddenly, in our headphones, sounded the command, 'air.'" The alarm sent the pilots of the three squadrons of the 303rd IAD scrambling for their MiGs. Fifty-eight MiGs launched, 44 to engage the enemy bombers, with fourteen kept over Antung and Myaogou to protect the take offs and landings of the intercept force.

In *Red Devils over the 38th Parallel,* Senior Lieutenant Dmitriy Aleksandrovich Samoylov describes his role as Dmitriy Os'kin's wingman: "I saw the commander (Os'kin) taxi out, but the wingman just sat there. Others had already begun to taxi, but he still sat there. I then signaled to Zykov, that he had stopped, and I moved up to take over."

Major Maslennikov led the first twenty MiG-15s that took off. Another twenty under the command of Lieutenant Colonel Smorchkov followed, plus an additional eighteen led by Major Os'kin. The second wave, launched 24 minutes after the first, consisted of two flights totaling 26 MiGs commanded by Colonel Vishnyakov and Major Mitusov. Keeping to the north bank of the Yalu, the regiments assembled by executing 90 and 180 degree climbing turns that allowed the fighter groups to close on one another. Approaching 20,000 feet the interceptors set course for the Anju-Taysen area, guided toward the enemy fighter and bomber groups by their ground command post radars.

Weather conditions turned out pretty much as predicted. The bomber force was between clouds decks, the deck beneath topping out around thirteen thousand feet. From their bombing altitude of 22,550 ft, the forecast lower cloud deck obscured visual reference to the ground. This forced the 307th to go electronic, which meant they would have to intercept the pre-selected SHORAN arc at the initial point (IP) for the bomb run. Although the geographical location of the IP has not been pinpointed, it was usually about fifty-five miles short of the target and as close to the SHORAN arc as possible. From crew member reports it appears as though Able and Baker Flights intercepted the arc at a point that was thought by Charlie Flight to be in error. Francis Kroboth, Flight Engineer on Charlie Two, heard someone say over interphone, "They went to the wrong IP." Other reports by MiG pilots and B-29 aircrew support the proposition that the three B-29 flights split into two groups, the six ship Able and Baker group and the three ship Charlie Flight. The apparent disagreement as to where the bomb run was to begin further fractionalized the defensive firepower by splitting the force into two groups that were roughly three miles apart.

To prevent explosive decompression in case the aircraft's pressurized hull was punctured by flak or cannon fire, each bomber depressurized for the run from the IP to the target. All crew members attached their oxygen masks to their faces. Gunners also switched from the normal "demand" setting on their regulators to "one hundred percent" to sharpen their vision.

On their run to the Namsi airfield, the SHORAN arc took them through the flak field near Taechon. Able Flight encountered several minutes of the most accurate and intense AAA they'd experienced on any mission in either the Korean War or WW II. The 1777th and 151st AAA Regiments had put in place fifty-nine 85mm and fifty-six 37mm guns to protect the airfield at Taechon. The 85's were the advanced radar-directed designs developed by the Germans and captured by Soviet forces at the end of WW II. The bursts were the deadly big stuff, similar to the flak Fogler had encountered when he flew B-24s over Europe in WW2. Both of Fogler's blister gunners had a chilling view of the puffs of smoke-cloaked shrapnel as the black mushrooms walked up on the formation as though being attracted by a magnet. Several ships, Fogler's included, were damaged by the flying steel. Miller still has a piece about the size of a walnut that penetrated the fuselage, ruptured one of the yellow oxygen tanks, and lodged three feet under his seat. Except for a few odd pieces, Fogler's crew had no flak protection gear. Baker Leader's B-29, commanded by Lieutenant Bill Reeter, received two direct hits, one on the right wing a foot from the fuselage and one directly under the Central Fire Controller in the aft pressurized compartment. Pieces of shrapnel pierced the thin aluminum skin, tore through the pressurized interior and lodged deep in the CFC's right thigh. Another piece apparently hit a vital component of the SHORAN equipment at the radar operator's station, a few feet back, knocking it out.

Having honed their skills on Able and Baker Flights, the AAA gunners on the ground zeroed in on the third flight. As Charlie Flight passed over the big guns they were pummeled. Shields' aircraft, Charlie flight leader, took several hits and appeared to be in serious trouble.

To view what was going on outside, Sgt. Edward Moore, radio operator on Charlie Two, squeezed out of his cramped, windowless crew station behind the forward turrets, hoisted himself into the tunnel over the bomb bay, and slid in under the astrodome. He recalled, "Scanning right, all I could see was flak. Shields was to our left. I remember during the run in I watched his gunners 'cutting up' . . . with ours." Moore watched the flak tail off before dropping back down by the window to the forward bomb bay to report its condition after bombs-away.

Timeline of Events – "Black Tuesday" 23 October 1951

Real Time (CKT)	Event
0415	Mission takes off from Kadena AFB
0645	Over Cheju-do Island
0845	Mission enters North Korea
0910	Soviet radar picks up attack group
0912	64th IAK goes to Readiness No. 1
0924-0933	20 MiGs from the 17th IAP, 20 MiGs from the 18th GIAP, and 18 MiGs from the 523rd IAP take off.
0935	B-29s began bomb runs
0940-0945	14 MiGs from the 176th GIAP and 12 MiGs from the 196th IAP take off
0940	18th GIAP spots B-29 bombers and launches attack
0943	523rd IAP spots B-29 bombers and launches attack
0945	17th IAP spots B-29 bombers and launches attack.

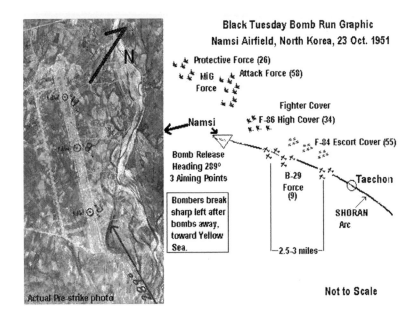

Black Tuesday Bomb Run Graphic
Namsi Airfield, North Korea, 23 Oct. 1951

Protective Force (26)

MiG Force   Attack Force (58)

Fighter Cover

Namsi   F-86 High Cover (34)

F-84 Escort Cover (55)

Bomb Release
Heading 289°
3 Aiming Points

B-29 Force (9)   Taechon

Bombers break
sharp left after
bombs away,
toward Yellow
Sea.

SHORAN Arc

—2.5-3 miles—

Actual Pre-strike photo

Not to Scale

Once the bombers were clear of the initial flak field an uneasy calm set in. The Taechon area was only 15 miles or about four minutes flight time from the target. The crews knew that the MiG pilots would not have flown into their own flak barrage, but now they were clear of it.

Baker Flight Leader scrambled to recover their SHORAN bombing system. Unable to get it working, Reeter called for Griner to take over the flight lead position. Foulks' aircraft in the number two position was handling the electronic countermeasures chores and was not SHORAN capable. They were rapidly approaching the target and in the process of changing leads when their fighter escort CAP radioed that MiGs were inbound. Caught in the act of playing "musical chairs," one of the MiG pilots mistakenly assumed Baker flight had panicked and later took credit for breaking up the "bombing attack."

Lt. Col. Aleksandr Pavlovich Smorchkov led twenty MiGs of the 18th GIAP and Major Dmitriy Pavlovich Os'kin of 523rd IAP led an additional group. They knew that the American fighters would be flying slow to stay with the bombers and concluded that the best chance to beat the Americans was to jump the Sabre screen at the MiG's best airspeed and keep them engaged, leaving the B-29 force open to attack by the squadron assigned to hit the B-29s.

At 0940, five minutes before bombs-away, Smorchkov's strike group, flying at 26,000 feet, spotted a fighter screen of "up to forty" F-86s on an intersecting course. The Sabres were flying a snake pattern of eight groups in arrowhead formation and Smorchkov dispatched 14 MiGs of the 1st and 3rd AE to go after them. The F-86 Sabres, the 307th's main line of defense, was about to be isolated from the action that was about to erupt. Moments later, he saw the B-29s ahead and to the left. From his northern approach the bombers in loose formation flying a SHORAN arc curving toward a WNW bombs-away heading created the impression that they were flying "abreast" on a southerly heading. The "eight bombers," Smorchkov reported, had "an immediate cover provided by up to thirty F-84s, which were located to the left, right, and above them at distances of six to eight hundred meters ... flying in groups of six to eight aircraft."

Baker Flight's "musical chairs" apparently blocked Smorchkov's view of one of the nine B-29s.

Trailing 3,000 feet above Smorchkov's element, Os'kin's group turned ninety degrees to the right to avoid eight F-86s intersecting their course from above. While entering the turn, he spotted the nine B-29s escorted by an estimated "forty F-84s, F-86s, and eight Gloster Meteor 4s" ahead and to their left. Two groups of F-86s in arrowhead formations patrolled to the right, six to nine miles behind the B-29s.

Os'kin's angle provided a better view of the bomber force and he reported that the "B-29 combat order consisted of a left hand flight of three aircraft in a level wedge formation." Following Able and Baker Flights, Charlie was two to three miles behind and to the right, the three aircraft more or less abreast. Os'kin was given the order to attack Charlie Flight. As they maneuvered to intercept the bombers, their regiment was, in turn, attacked by two groups of Allied fighters.

Os'kin's wingman, Samolylov, recalled, "My commander, making a vertical maneuver, got out from under their attacks and then he himself went over to the attack. (He) got on the tail of an F-86 and closed (within) decisive firing range, less than 800 meters. At that moment, when I thought he was firing at long range, I saw the nine B-29 bombers below us and called over the radio to my leader that we had 'big ones' to the right (as we called B-29s)." Os'kin broke off his attack on the F-86, flipped his aircraft over in a half roll to drop down on the B-29s, and gave the command, 'To all – attack the big ones.'"

Meanwhile, Major Maslennikov's cover group of twenty MiG-15s engaged twenty of the bombers' F-86 fighter screen.

Up front in Able Lead, Fred Meier made a note of the bomb run true heading, 289 degrees and predicted target time, 0945. He vacated his navigator's table, and moved to the front of the flight deck to sit on a piece of folding plywood erected behind the bombardier's flimsy back-rest. This was Meier's normal position on all bomb runs and afforded him perhaps the best view of any crew member. Two sets of eyes, reasoning went, were better than one. Standard operating procedure called for the navigator to be that extra set of eyes. If the target should suddenly appear under the 5000 ft cloud deck, he could help the bombardier locate and synchronize on it. Then, on a normal mission, after bombs-away

Moments after Rolland Miller snapped this picture, the B-29 in the photo (#045, commanded by Captain Robert Krumm) was shot down by MiGs.

he would return to his seat to the left of the forward turret, fill out the strike report, and hand it to the Radio operator for immediate transmission.

Meier scanned the cloud deck underneath for a break and a glimpse of the target. Instead, he saw tracer bullets crossing in a tight acute angle about 100 feet in front of their aircraft.

As the countdown for the bomb drop began, Rolland Miller, left gunner on Fogler's lead B-29 reached for his camera. He'd not received any radio warnings about MiG's so he thought they were in the clear. He wanted to get a picture of the bombs actually being dropped. At the "bombs-away" signal he snapped a picture of the number three aircraft, 42-94045, piloted by Capt. Robert Krumm, just as the bombs began leaving the bomb bay.

Farther back, Capt. John Wagenhalls, Dempsey's bombardier aboard Charlie Three, was busy scanning for breaks in the lower cloud deck in hopes of spotting the target so he would pick up the specific aiming point. "At some distance from the target but surely within sight of it," he remembered, "we were attacked by what seemed like a large number of MiGs."

A moment later, all hell broke loose.

Miller's first warning came from Fogler's radio operator, T/Sgt. Marvin Hoke. Over intercom, Hoke announced that MiG's were in the vicinity. When Miller looked up they were everywhere. One MiG made a pass on Krumm's aircraft and hit him. Smoke and flames erupted from the #2 engine and wing and the aircraft started an immediate descent. Miller began shooting at an incoming MiG and had to look away from 045. Just before the stricken bomber went into the clouds he caught a glimpse of it and two chutes a distance behind the aircraft.

Smorchkov emerged from the clouds and saw a B-29, surrounded by fighters, directly in front of him. He came in high from the right side of the formation, lined up behind the bomber, closed to within cannon range, and fired his 37 and 23mm cannons. His target was Charlie lead, commanded by Capt. Thomas L. Shields. As Shields' tail gunner returned fire, Smorchkov recalls the bomber going to full throttle and turning away (possibly to maintain position on the SHORAN arc). Smorchkov's first burst missed low, so he raised the nose and fired again. This time the projectiles hit their target. The B-29's engines burst into flames that spread into the wing. Smith, Gross, and Stainbrook bailed out. Goldbeck was the last to go. Moments after he cleared the airplane it exploded in mid-air. The four landed in the Yellow Sea and were later picked up by Search and Rescue. They were the only ones who survived.

The sudden import of combat sharpened Edward Moore's vision and sense of awareness. He remembers the moments that followed as vividly as if they'd happened today: "Suddenly the bomb bay doors snapped shut with the bombs still in place. The engines surged and I stood up and said to no one (no one was within hearing,) 'what the hell is going on?' I was standing next to the B-29's upper forward, quad-fifty turret when they fired and I said, 'Oh shit!'" Moore had been listening to the HF radio and missed out on the warning. He remembers waiting for "cannon from the MiGs to start taking us apart." He could hear the engines of the MiGs and their cannon fire as they repeatedly pressed home their attacks. Although Moore was wearing a harness for a chest parachute, he'd left the pack off to avoid accidentally catching the ripcord and spilling the chute while moving around in the tight quarters. He'd missed the interphone call on the fighters coming in and did not want to miss the bail out signal. When he saw that the navigator had moved out of his seat and gone forward to aid in target identification, he went to his position so he could see the flight deck. Instead of all of the crew being in their assigned positions, someone was on the deck between him and Arch Cummings, the flight engineer. "Who in hell is flying the ship?" he wondered. Then he heard Major Field on interphone speaking in a normal tone of voice. He trusted his aircraft commander and started to return to his crew position behind the turret. As he passed the navigator's window, he saw a MiG or an F-84 flash by off the left wing. As he took his seat he detected a popping noise coming from his headset on the radio table. He turned down the RF gain on his receiver and heard an SOS, loud and clear, coming from Sgt. Daugherty, Shield's radio operator. "Dougherty," Moore remembered, "was very cool under what had to be a bizarre situation. His message was 'on fire going down track 270,' then the key closed." Moore immediately repeated the message with an emergency Y precedence to the 307th special communications detachment at 20th Air Force Headquarters on Okinawa.

He remembers the attack as the most hectic and raucous period of his life. "I thought there was no way I could stay alive, but eventually it became quiet and all I could hear were those 3350s."

The first Soviet kill occurred at 9:43. A few minutes later one of Smorchkov's wingmen, Nikolay L. Korniyenkom, hit Dempsey's B-29, Charlie Three. At the same time, fourteen of his regiment MiGs lunged head-on into the fray with the F-84s. Lt. Lev Kirilovich Shchukin fired at 150 meters and the F-84 flown by Capt. John Shewmaker of the 111th FBS exploded in an orange fireball. A second F-84 was reported to have crashed fifteen miles northeast of Sensen. F-84 pilots of the 154th FBS would claim four MiGs destroyed. Major Richard Creighton recorded his fourth kill, while Capt Ralph Banks and Lt. Fame D. Fortner each claimed their first. The famous future astronaut, Lt Walter Schirra, a US Navy pilot on exchange duty with the Air Force, was credited with the fourth MiG. Schirra would fly twenty missions with the 154th.

Edward F. Unser, veteran of 100 combat missions with the 154th FBS, had this to say about his airplane: "What bothered us the most was anti-aircraft fire which caused most of our losses.... the MiGs were after the B29s, not the F84s, (which were) not very good at escorting B29s because the MiGs were slightly faster and, with swept-back wings, could dive & climb faster. The F84 escort pilots felt bad because we couldn't keep the MiGs away from the B-29s."

On his first attack, Os'kin met them on a converging course and with a salvo from all three of his cannon flamed one B-29. When he made a maneuver to repeat his attack, a pair of F-84s from the immediate cover tried to stop him. Samoylov, his wingman, fired a burst as a barrier to break off the attack of the Thunderjets. Barrier bursts, Samoylov acknowledged, were not aimed. "You could never aim those, just blaze away..." Os'kin made a second attack on another B-29 from behind and set it on fire as well. With their fuel nearly exhausted, he ordered the regiment to break off combat. "We were down to less than five minutes of fuel remaining for combat," Samoylov recalled, "and had to head for home. Our regiment shot down several enemy fighters and bombers in this battle, but we ourselves suffered no losses; only one pilot had a bullet hole which he received from a B-29 gunner."

At the same time that twelve MiGs of the 523rd IAP were engaging the F-86 fighter escort, Os'kin and his five wingmen attacked Able and Baker Flights. On his first pass, Os'kin's cannon fire struck both Krumm in Able and Foulks in Baker. In a matter of minutes, two more B-29s, commanded by Griner and Reeter, were shot-up by Captain Stepan Antonovich Bahayev, Lieutenant Georgiy D'yachenko, and Captain Sergey Bychkov. Cannon fire from Bahayev's 37mm took out Griner's number three engine and one of his 23mm shells pierced a fuel tank in the right wing.

D'yachenko wrote: "We hit our terminal limits in the dive, and the aircraft popped their air brakes to ensure we did not exceed them. In order to avoid accurate fire from the B-29s, I flipped the nose of my aircraft to the left and right. I opened up on the third B-29 [Griner] with all three guns, saw shell strikes on the aircraft, but my leader went after the center B-29. [Reeter] . . . after the attack we slipped into the upper cloud layer. We turned around and once again moved to the attack, which we made when we dropped out of the clouds and spotted three B-29s below us. Lead shot one down [Foulks], but I was beaten off by attacking enemy fighters."

The first MiG to attack Able Leader came in low, at an extremely high rate of closure, from the eight o'clock position. Rolland Miller picked him up and got off four bursts as the MiG rolled towards the front of the B-29. Miller yelled over interphone to the bombardier, Nick Kourafas, that one was coming his way at 10 o'clock. Nick picked him up and fired. Nick wasn't able to see what happened next because almost immediately he got busy firing at another MiG coming in from the nose. Fogler said, "You got him, Greek." Nick smiled and replied, "No kidding," and started shooting at the next one. Totaled, Kourafas fired about a thousand rounds.

"How lucky we were," Fred Meier recalls, "the MIG started firing too late--what dumb luck. I wanted to grab Nick's gun sight but he was hot on it. The six forward 50 cal. guns were either in Nick's hands or the CFC's. It was so exciting I couldn't hear the 50's." Meier would later write in his diary, "At 0944, just before bombs away, the MiGs came in and on first pass (at bombs away) they knocked out #2 & 3 men."

By this time, the F-84s that had been flying escort were no longer in sight, probably forced to turn back because of low fuel.

Another MiG, that Miller was later credited with shooting down, came in at about eight o'clock low in what appeared to be a pursuit curve. Miller spotted him about a half mile out and had him framed in the orange dotted reticle ring of his gun sight. Whitish-gray puffs of smoke were coming from the MiG's three nose cannons and trailing out behind him. Rolland fired several short bursts and saw pieces of sheet metal come off the MiG's left wing and Fogler heard a loud "bang." Miller assumed that the MiG would turn towards the front of their aircraft. Instead, it rolled to his right and passed under the tail. Although this was originally listed as a probable, Miller's aircraft commander, Captain Fogler, said later that it had been confirmed as a kill from the gun camera film.

Fogler's plane had the radio antenna shot off at one connection, a hole in the #3 inboard gas tank, thirty holes in one bomb bay door, and a couple in the tail section. A piece that went into the gas tank was believed to have been a section of the main wing spar.

On the second pass, from head-on, the MiGs got Krumm. The burning B-29 peeled off to the left, headed for the ground, and impacted on a mud flat near the coast. Six days later, South Korean guerrillas found three crewmen dead inside the wreckage and three more under the tail of the crashed aircraft. One crew member had apparently been executed. Two others were unaccounted for, although it was reported that the pilot, Lt. John Horner bailed out, landed in water, got tangled in his parachute, and drowned.

Able Flight leader counted a total of 25 MiG passes. SSgt. Fred Spivey was credited with downing one and Miller hit another coming in low on the left side. When the MiG got in front of the lead bomber, he pulled up and to the left and Nick let him have about a hundred rounds. Kourafas recalls, "Fog said he could see the tail of the MiG shudder back and forth. He just seemed to be hanging in the air, not more than a hundred yards off and evidently the shuddering he saw was my bullets hitting him." Rolland

Miller and Sgt. Fred Spivey were each credited with destroying a MiG-15. A fighter pilot confirmed Nick's hits, so Miller and Nick each received credit, along with SSgt. Jerry M. Webb, Lewis's tail gunner.

Griner had taken over Baker Flight Lead as they neared the target in tight formation at 22,000 feet. As soon as the bombs dropped clear, they rolled into a left turn toward the Yellow Sea. They knew (but did not know the reason) that the MiGs would not chase them out over a sea controlled by Allied ships.

Dewell Turner, Griner's substitute left gunner, was responsible for the lower forward gun turret. Because the attacks were coming from the rear, it was not possible for him to pick up a MiG in his sights and fire while the enemy aircraft was within range. Griner's right gunner, Paul Dickerson, had the same problem because he controlled the lower aft turret. Both gunners were, in effect, reduced to the role of observers. By leaning out into his blister, Turner could see a MiG approach, tail high with flaps and gear down like it was preparing to land--a tactic employed to reduce speed so the pilot could improve his aim. As the attacks continued, a MiG dove by, trailing smoke and Turner saw it go down. The CFC, Clyde Slagowski, would be credited with the kill. One of the MiG's 37mm shells had ripped into their right wing and punctured the number three main tank. Fuel spewed out of the tank, poured over the wing, down the right side, and over Paul Dickerson's right side blister, making it milky opaque. Another 37mm exploded in the rear of the airplane, peppering the compartment with shrapnel. Pieces hit the radar operator, Glen Thornton, in the arm. The rest shattered the equipment around him, including the SHORAN set. Dickerson couldn't see to aim, so he turned to help Thornton. Their aircraft was so badly damaged that Griner gave the crew the option to bail out rather than ride out a risky crash landing at Kimpo. They all elected to stay with the plane.

Later, Griner's crew would count over 200 holes in their airplane.

As Baker Flight rolled out of the turn, Foulks' plane was hit from the rear on the first pass. The MiG cannon shot slammed into the left wing around the #2 inboard engine, passing through fuel lines, controls, 85-gallon oil tank, firewall, fire extinguisher, and magnesium accessory section. The entire section burst into flames. Unable to control the wing fire, Foulks dropped out of formation and, rapidly losing altitude, headed southwest toward the relative safety of the Yellow Sea. The MiGs broke off their attack as the crew initiated their mayday calls and the bail out signal was sounded. For those in the forward compartment this meant lifting the entrance hatch, and lowering the nose gear with an electrical switch in the wheel well. If the gear failed to extend, their alternate escape route was to squeeze around the forward turrets and use the forward bomb bay. Crew members in the rear pressurized compartment bailed out through either the aft bomb bay or rear entrance door. The tail gunner exited through the escape window on his right, another reason most tail gunners were slight in stature. Non-essential personnel went first. The last to leave the rear compartment was SSgt. Kenneth Kiser, the CFC. Up front Capt. Ara Mooradian, the bombardier, was followed by TSgt. William Botter, the flight engineer, Lt. Fred Beissner, pilot, and Foulks, the aircraft commander.

Reeter, delegated to the number three position because of inoperative SHORAN, was too busy maintaining formation to look around. He saw only two MiGs. One was making a head-on pass and he could see clearly the tiny puffs of smoke from the nose cannons. His wounded CFC called out that one was coming in from behind. There was an immediate explosion. The MiG passed in front and turned away. In the back of the airplane, a 23mm projectile hit the tail compartment. A large piece embedded in the heel of the tail gunner's left foot, and flying fragments from the projectile grazed the left gunner's forehead. Up front, a 37mm had creased the fuselage, lodged above the navigator's window, and exploded. The radio operator was badly injured and pieces of plastic from the window were embedded in Colonel Carroll's right calf. When the MiGs hit, he was riding on the aisle stand, slightly ahead of SSgt. Edmond Wilson, the flight engineer. Wilson was wearing a steel flak helmet, but still ended up with a sore face and internal hemorrhaging of the right ear. He reported that the navigator, Captain Morton Edwards, was slumped forward, face down on the navigation table. Edwards would never regain consciousness. Reeter felt wetness on the back of his neck. He also felt something sticking out of his jaw and pulled it out. It was a blue piece of tubing, probably part of the oxygen system. The airplane had numerous holes in it and was leaking gas out of the number three fuel tank. They had little or no aileron control, and., without pressurization or oxygen, had to descend immediately.

Reeter sent his copilot, Jim McQuade, back to check on the navigator. McQuade reported that Edwards was alive but his left eye was lying on his cheek and a piece of his skull was flipped back. He could see the navigator's brain.

Because of hypoxia, Reeter was having trouble staying focused and remembering what he should do. Realizing that their lack of oxygen was beginning to take its toll, he called over formation frequency that they needed to descend. Unaware of Reeter's loss of pressurization as well as oxygen, Griner requested they stay in formation to maximize firepower.

While still under attack, Dewell Turner watched Reeter's aircraft go into a steep descent. From that point on he would not see another B-29 until they landed at Kimpo.

Charlie Flight Leader's B-29, commanded by Capt. Thomas Shields, had been mortally wounded by Taechon's intense AAA. Shields broke from the formation to bail out his crew. As the aircraft spiraled away it came under MiG attack. Enemy cannon fire ignited a fire in the left wing near number two engine. Still descending, still burning, Charlie Leader headed southwest toward the Yellow Sea. Gunners in other aircraft saw several parachutes, but most of the crew was still inside when the plane exploded. Paul Stainbrook was one of four crew members that bailed out over the Yellow Sea and was rescued. Shortly after he got out of the hospital he was reassigned to fly as tail gunner with Major Field, who flew Charlie Three on the Black Tuesday mission.

Dempsey's right side bomb doors were shattered from cannon fire. His bombardier, John Wagenhalls, watched the B-29s scatter. Wagenhalls recalls, "It was almost as if each airplane was on its own since at least one aircraft from each flight was destroyed almost immediately in the first attack. Not one of the three flights remained intact. Firepower effectiveness was severely reduced as, basically, no formation still existed. It seemed almost like "panic" in the air. I don't know if any B-29s in the formation reached the target; we didn't. Still some distance from the target and having sustained unknown damage, which really didn't seem to affect the airworthiness of the aircraft, the pilot ordered the immediate and complete release of the entire bomb load. I salvoed forty 500-

pound bombs. We then made a descending left turn. I believe the pilot was trying to connect with other airplanes for protection from enemy fighter aircraft and escape . . . cannon fire from the MiGs. The gunners of our crew fired at several attacking fighters but none indicated that they had inflicted any damage. The enemy aircraft that I saw were all out of range by the time I spotted them." Wagenhalls believes that had the MiGs continued their attack they could have shot down the entire formation. Instead, fortune smiled on Dempsey's crew. No one on board was injured in the melee.

At "Bombs Away" and still under fighter attack, Able Lead broke to the left. The lower aft turret that Miller had control of during the previous attacks stopped firing when the turret cam switch interrupted the firing circuit. The mechanism had been designed to prevent bullets from the B-29s own guns striking parts of the bomber. But this time, with the fighter framed within the orange dots of the gun sight reticle ring and the firing button depressed, the mechanism prevented Miller from firing at the MiG.

The actual battle lasted fifteen minutes.

Three of the nine B-29s had gone down in flames, most probably from air-to-air cannon fire; however, a Russian Archival Record, TFR 138-86 claims that the gunners of the Soviet 1777th Antiaircraft Artillery Regiment shot down two B-29s on that date, that both aircraft crashed and the crew of one perished. A battery commanded by Lieutenant Colonel Medyantsev claimed one of the two.

Almost out of fuel, Os'kin's regiment reached the Yalu where the "duty six" (MiGs) waited to protect their recovery into their Antung airfield. The Americans were also waiting, and a MiG-15 piloted by Senior Lieutenant Khurtin was shot down by four F-86s over Chinese territory after crossing the Yalu.

Because of the fighter attacks, several minutes elapsed before Miller could look through the aft bulkhead door and report to the bombardier that the bombs had indeed released. What he saw did not give him a good feeling. Clusters of bombs still hung from racks in both bomb bays. Fogler began descending to 4,000 feet so Kourafas, Miller and Loren Richards could enter the aft bomb bay to manually release the 19 one hundred pound bombs that

were hung up. While the aircraft was descending, Richards and
Fred Spivy, the central fire controller, worked their way aft to
check on Sgt. DePratter, the tail gunner. They'd lost
communications and, although they feared he might be injured, he
was OK and brought forward. Concerned that a parachute might
catch on something, accidentally pop and drag them out, Miller
and Richards left theirs in the rear compartment before entering
the bomb bay. By manipulating the retaining shackles by hand,
they were able to dump the bombs into the China Sea. After the
bombs dropped, they flew on by themselves. Fred Meier
remembers they had "a hell of a tailwind on our way to Kimpo."

Probably due to combat damage, a bomb had hung up in
Griner's airplane as well and had to be manually jettisoned by the
bombardier and CFC.

When they were safely out of harm's way, Dempsey's crew
assessed the damage to determine where they should land. It was
decided that if Wagenhalls could secure the damaged bomb bay
door in the closed position they could continue to Kadena. While
still in flight, he was able to get hold of the bottom of the bomb
bay door, connect the bomb safety wires taken from the bomb
shackles to the bottom of the door and connect the other end to the
catwalk and other structural members within the bomb bay
enclosure. He repeated this process until all of the loose pieces of
the bomb bay door were closed and secured.

Dempsey's crew continued to Kadena where they landed after
nine hours and 35 minutes of continuous flight time from take-off
until landing. Fifty-two years later, Wagenhalls would remember
it as, "all in a days work!"

Field's crew diverted to the secondary target and dropped their
bomb load on Chinnampo, the supply port for the North Korean
capital of Pyongyang.

After bailing out, Fred Beissner fell free until he was out of the
overcast. Orienting himself over water, but in sight of the coast,
he pulled the ripcord. After his parachute blossomed he looked
around and saw three other chutes in front and above him. A
moment later he saw the plane hit the water with the left wing
following.

The Australian frigate, *HMAS Murchison*, had been assigned to
the rescue effort, assisted by two Sea Furys from Australia's first
aircraft carrier, the *HMAS Sydney*. While searching for mines

ahead of the *Murchison*, A Sea Fury spotted something that looked like a mine and strafed it. Four other Furies escorted a Fairy Firefly equipped with a 'G' dropper, which was dropped to a downed B-29 airman who was later picked up by an allied warship.

Four more Meteors were scrambled to provide CAP for the airmen downed in the sea, but Flt Lt Cannon and his flight were unable to spot any survivors. USAF SA-16 amphibian rescue aircraft picked up most of the downed airmen. Aboard one of the rescue amphibians, Squadron Leader Kater, 77RAAF's Senior Medical Officer, helped rescue four of the airmen while Cpl D.H. Sinclair, a Medical Orderly on board a second SA-16, assisted in the rescue of another survivor. Kater dived into the sea in an attempt to recover the body of another (probably Horner) who had apparently drowned. Hampered by rough seas and the constant movement of the amphibian, Kater himself was almost lost.

After splash down, Beissner inflated his tiny one-man dinghy, scrambled aboard, and floated for eight hours in dangerous, mine-infested waters. Just before dusk, a Sea Fury pilot spotted his flashing signal mirror and relayed his position to the *Murchison*. A Fairey Firefly, dispatched from the *Sydney*, dropped a larger dinghy and supplies that landed within ninety feet of Beissner. Braving shallow water which, at times, was less than a fathom deep, the *Murchison*   closed in for the rescue.   Once she momentarily grounded.. A sea-boat was directed to the position and rescued Beissner.   Of the thirteen on board Baker Two, Beissner was the only one who survived the day. Corporal Arthur Coffey's remains were recovered from the Korean Bay. Wentworth, Jones, Kiser, MacClean and Strine were taken prisoner and later repatriated. It was reported that Botter was captured but, like Foulks, Cogswell, Mooradian, Fueher, and Black, his body was never recovered and he was officially listed as missing in action.

As the battle boiled in the skies above Namsi, twelve Meteors swept the Anju area without seeing any other aircraft. Suddenly, B-29s returning from the mission were spotted just south of P'yongyang. The Meteors caught up with the B-29s and escorted them to the mouth of the Han River. Two more Meteors, flown by W/O Bill Michelson and Sgt. Frank Blackwell, were scrambled out of Kimpo to intercept unidentified incoming aircraft. Ground radar controllers initially vectored them to four B-29s and a single F-84.

Reeter's crew began calling in their damage assessment. Large pieces of the rudder, flaps, and ailerons were missing. The gunners reported that fuel was leaking. The original flap motor, located in the bomb bay, Reeter remembered, wasn't explosion proof. He asked someone to check the bomb bay for fumes. When the hatch that connected the forward compartment to the bomb bay was opened, the high-octane fumes were so strong that it had to be closed immediately.

They had no choice. It would be a no flap landing.

As they slowed for their approach to Kimpo, the airplane became harder to control. A cable to the left aileron had been severed. Reeter gave the crew a choice. If they wanted to bail out, they could. In Reeter's mind he had no choice. He had two wounded crewmen who couldn't bail out if they wanted to, so he had to land the airplane. The rest of his crew stuck with him. Although he used full aileron, as the aircraft slowed on final approach it was almost impossible to control. Then, just as it was about to get away from him, the airplane touched down. He was able to stop and taxi off the runway.

When they evacuated the airplane, fuel was running all over the place. Even so, people began gathering around the airplane and marveled that it had been brought down safely. They couldn't believe Reeter had landed it.

Pieces of the shell hit Reeter on the left side of his face, but he said he was okay and "up and around." Another piece hit Col. Carroll in the right calf and looked like a buckshot wound. Reeter's tail gunner took a 23mm in the foot. It entered at his toes and the point of it was sticking out slightly at the heel. When Reeter got outside the airplane, he asked where Edwards was. No one knew, so he went back inside and pulled him out. Ignoring his own wounds, Reeter helped remove his mortally wounded navigator from the airplane.

Nick Kourafas remembers that Edwards was still alive but was evacuated before Nick landed. Although half of Edwards' face was shot away, he lived another three days.

Reeter knew he had a facial wound but didn't know the piece of flak was still in his cheek until he went to the dispensary. The

Above: Battle damage to left landing gear truck on Baker
Three, 44-27347, commanded by Maj. William Griner.
(USAF photos taken after landing at Kimpo)

Below: Battle damage to lower aft fuselage on Baker One,
44-86295, commanded by Lt. William Reeter.
Courtesy of Dewell Turner

**Battle damage to right flap (above) & navigator's window (below) on
Baker One, commanded by Lt. William Reeter. (USAF Photos)**
Courtesy of Dewell Turner & others

piece was about 3/8 of an inch long and 1/4 of an inch wide. It had made a cut about 3/4 of an inch long and about 1/4 of an inch deep in his left jaw that required stitches in the cheek about half way between the point of his jawbone and the point of the cheekbone. Bill Reeter kept the piece as a remembrance, and, as a final note, added, "They took us to the BOQ and to the officers club (and) treated us real well. We got steaks for free."

Without exception every crew member on Griner's crew also chose to ride out a crash landing over bailing out. Dewell Turner, who was along as a replacement gunner, remembers, "Major Griner gave us the option of bailing out, but all the regular crew wanted to stay with the plane, probably because the radar operator was wounded and could not jump and they did want to leave him. I wasn't about to jump alone. Everyone had great confidence in Major Griner and he did a fantastic job getting us down safely."

After the bomber touched down, Griner locked the brakes to stop the airplane, which caused the tires to blow out.

Fogler followed Griner and Reeter, and was the last B-29 to land at Kimpo that day. They had battle damage to the fuselage and right wing and number three-engine propeller.

On the ground at Kimpo, Douglas Evans watched as the three B-29s limped in, shot up with wounded aboard. In his words, "I joined Pat Green and some of our guys who had just returned from the mission and we gathered by the side of the runway to observe the first twenty-nine come in with an engine burning. As he touched down we noticed the tires on his left main gear were flat and evidently shot out. He bounced and another tire exploded as he swerved to the left and went into a sideways skid, going off the runway right toward our crowd. I don't know about the rest of them, but I scratched out on a new world's sprint record and the big bird skidded through our spot in a thunderous cloud of dust. As it came to rest our crash crew and medics were right there and helped those poor shaken-up guys out.

"The rest of the shot-up twenty-nines came in, though not quite in the same hair-raising fashion. The wounded were rushed off and we noticed some of the equipment they unloaded was splattered with blood. One of their pilots was really worked up and indignant over the contest: "Those SOBs, they came in so fast we could hardly shoot. What a lousy deal!" As he explained it, the CFC (central fire control system) could barely hack jet intercept speeds.

"When we looked over the MiG cannon shell holes in the B-29s we didn't envy them a bit. You could crawl through some of those holes--37mms, I guess. That's the kind of fireworks we dodge in our dogfights; if a MiG nails an eighty-six like that it won't be coming back, that's for sure. Three of the B-29s were knocked down up north by that stuff.

"A share of the returning mission excitement was furnished by the escort 84s coming in from the same mix-up in a big sweat--very low on fuel, landing hot and blowing tires in their hurry to get on the ground. A real able sugar mission."

Colonel Ruffin W. Gray, who'd flown RB-29s in SAC and was commander of the 15th TRS (photo-jet) at Kimpo during the Namsi raid, recalled, "I will never forget watching those poor SOBs in the badly shot up B-29s struggling not to spin, crash and burn. I was out at the Mobile jeep when one came in either with gear retracted or it collapsed on landing and the B-29 skidded down the airfield out of control and damn near wiped out the GCA trailer. One '29 was so shot up with cannon holes that you could stand on one side and look through the fuselage. Watching the medics haul out the dead and wounded wasn't one of the better days at Kimpo. During the mission, the F-86's had the call sign of John Able. One of the tragic radio transmissions was, 'John Able Black, catch that flight of MiGs as they come off the bombers.' This was followed by a wavering, earnest plea of 'Catch them before they get to the bombers'. Again followed by, 'Sorry guys, we can't do it.'

"LeMay (SAC commander) was convinced that the B-29, the first tri-motor since the Ford--normal landing, three turning and one burning--was invincible. After this tragedy, he came to Kimpo to interrogate the F-86 guys about what happened. He ended up chewing them out and alleging that they were cowards, inept, etc."

Gray thanks God for small favors that he was not part of that B-29 debacle. He'd reported to Camp Stoneman, the embarkation port for the Korean War, a few days after the war broke out and surmises that had they'd found out about his B-29 experience his orders would have been changed--and he may well have been one of the crew members on Black Tuesday.

Captain John Masterson, Flight Surgeon of the 15th TRS remembered, "The thing that bugged all of us was that the nose gunner was nowhere to be found and was presumed to have fallen out. However, when we all got back to the hospital he was sitting on a bench, shaking like a leaf, but was able to get out, 'Can I get a double shot, Doc?' Hell, we gave him the bottle. He could not remember how he even got there through that tiny space between the pilots. The pilot (or co-pilot, I don't recall) told me that they were so busy they never saw the gunner get out even though he must have brushed against them." (The bombardier was most likely the "nose gunner" mentioned--author)

Although not wholly accurate, the Russians claimed that Os'kin had shot down two B-29s, plus one each for Shevarev and D'yachenko, while incurring only minor damage to the MiGs that amounted to a few bullet holes in their tails.

The full Russian report, released half a century after the battle, confirms that most of the MiGs had attacked the B-29 formation in flights and pairs from the rear. The report also states (in fighter pilot lingo) that the attack was carried out "on deflection courses of 0/4 to 3/4, firing from 1000 meters down to 400 meters range using two to three medium length bursts while making use of the deflector gun sights with moving reticles." Eighty-four MiG-15s were committed to the battle. Seventy-two pilots engaged in aerial combat and 36 fired their guns, expending 865 rounds of N-37 and 2,619 rounds of NS-23 cannon ammunition. This same report claims ten B-29s were shot down and one damaged--two more than actually flew the mission.

Eventually, four of the nine B-29s that took off on the mission made it back to Okinawa. Lewis, who had been flying in the Able Two slot, had a cannon hole just below the vertical stabilizer, a few feet ahead of the tail gunner, S/Sgt. Jerry Webb, that a man could squeeze through.

Fogler's crew was the last to return to Kadena. In addition to their own crew, they brought back Col. Carroll from Baker One and Majors Griner and Markel from Baker Three. Nick Kourafas wrote in his log, "Ledbetter was flying with us today. Five boys reported picked up at sea. They (the crew) didn't think they hit the target but the fighter boys said they did. It was a SHORAN run. They got back about 9:00 last night and got to bed about 1 am.

Bomb load was 144, 100 lb. GTs....Target was 40 miles from Sinuiju."

8: Aftermath

The first thing Griner's gunners did after landing was to clear the guns. Dewell Turner put it this way, "You recollect such strange things from an event like this. When we looked for the lower forward turret cover to remount it after clearing the guns, we could never find it. No telling what happened to it. Someone probably thought it would never be needed again. They were right." The crew was debriefed at Kimpo. During debriefing, a 4th FIW pilot confirmed CFC Slagowski's MiG kill and the intelligence officer said the MiG pilots were Russian. The crew was fed in the Officer's Mess, and waited several hours for a DC-3 to transport them to Itazuke Air Base in Japan where they spent the night housed in the transit barracks. The following day they were flown to Okinawa in a C-54.

After bombing Chinnampo, Field returned directly to Kadena. Edward Moore recollected, "When we landed at Kadena we were met by a reception party. I asked one of them 'where is everybody?' and he said that we were first back . . . we could see a ship flying around with major damage to the empennage. That could have been Lewis."

Fogler's crew had flown over eight hours on the mission, five of it in daylight. On the ground at Kimpo they counted over 500 holes in the airplane and had lunch at the fighter base mess hall. Miller remembers the steak and eggs as the best meal of his life, in his words, "simply because we were having another meal." After cutting the broken antenna loose, they assessed the damage. There were dollar-size chips out of the back of the number three prop blades and a hole in the wing, but the self-sealing fuel tanks had done their job and there were no leaks. After talking it over, they decided their airplane was safe enough to continue to Okinawa. They refueled and took off with Colonel Carroll and Majors Griner and Markel joining them for the trip to their home base.

While Fogler's crew was returning to Kadena, First Lt. Ernest R. Harden, III flew an RF-80 Shooting Star over Namsi Airfield to take photos of the bomb damage. Harden was provided an F-86 escort led by legendary ace, Colonel Francis S. Gabreski. When he met with Gabreski on the ground prior to takeoff to coordinate the mission, he recalled seeing a B-29 crew member still wearing a bloody flight suit.

To make the Chinnampo rendezvous point on time, Harden had to take off minutes ahead of the Gabreski's F-86s. While taxiing from his parking ramp, Harden's right tip tank was punctured and he had to switch planes. Nevertheless, he arrived at the rendezvous on time. Northeast of Sinanju the flight was met by a line abreast of MiGs coming at them head-on. As the MiGs closed to within shooting range, the F-86 escorts released their drop tanks. They tumbled by so close, Harden thought he might hit one. The engagement that followed did not involve him. It was the last Harden saw of either MiGs or F-86s that day. He recalled, "They had their own ball and apparently I was not invited." Except for a few bursts of 85mm anti-aircraft artillery fire, Harden got his photos of Namsi Airfield, did a split-S to a lower altitude and made it home without encountering further enemy fire.

That night he visited his unit's Photo Interpretation section to see his pictures. The photos had turned out well, but his heart sank when he saw there wasn't a single bomb crater on the airfield. "The B-29s," Harden later noted, "eventually did get to Namsi and were able to do their job at night."

Fogler's flight from Kimpo to Kadena added another 3:40 of flight time, and they didn't get back to Kadena until 2130 hours. Even at that late hour they were put through an extensive debriefing. It was customary to furnish battle weary crew members with a shot of something that was euphemistically called "combat" whiskey. Normally the limit was one shot of a brand that was basically rotgut. This time they were allowed as much Canadian Club or Seagram's VO (premium whiskey in those days) as they wanted. Finally, nearly twenty-four hours after their wake-up call for the Black Tuesday mission, at one in the morning, they were able to go to bed.

The following morning, Wednesday, 24 October 1951, Fred Meier learned that other B-29 crew members had been plucked from the sea, but his old cadet classmate, Lloyd Wentworth, was not one of them. He was also told by their crew chief that they found an unexploded 37mm cannon shell in the number three wing fuel tank. Fogler's crew had led and survived the April 12 mission

(Above) Able Lead crew after the mission:
"Fog" on far left, next to Fred Meier.

(Below) Enlisted members on Able Lead crew
waiting outside their "tent city" quarters.

to Antung and now, the Black Tuesday mission. They went on to fly a total of "68 exciting missions," Fred Meier recalls, "some more memorable than others--for obvious reasons," but these two missions that he'd flown as lead navigator, were melded in his memory. "Fortunately I have my diary," Fred confessed, "to separate the two." Namsi was Meier's 45th and final daylight mission. He would fly his 68th and last mission exactly ten years after the Japanese bombed Pearl Harbor, on December 7, 1951. It was at night, using SHORAN, but again they were shot up and forced to make an emergency landing at Itazuke. While waiting for their plane to be patched up, Meier got together with his brother Tex, a C-119 aircraft commander. It was the last time they would spend a day together. Tex was later killed in a helicopter crash.

On the 27th of October, three days after the Namsi mission, Fogler's crew met with Gen. Ridgeway to discuss what had happened. They'd been sweating out another daylight mission before their scheduled R & R, which fortunately came through on the 29th. After their meeting they left Okinawa, scheduled to spend time at the Fuji View hotel in Fujiyoshida, Yamanashi Prefecture on the Japanese main island of Honshu. Located at the base of Mount Fuji between two of the Fuji Lakes, Fujiyoshida was one of the most beautiful and unspoiled cities in war-ravaged Japan, in large part due to its specialization in high quality textiles rather than war materials.

Meier and his bombardier, Nick Kourafas, stayed in Tokyo for some shopping on the 30th and 31st before taking the train to join Fogler and Pyfrom at the Fuji View hotel bar. They visited the silk mills on the first and later met Colonel Ledbetter at Yokota Air Base. Meier remembers staying at the BOQ in Yokota with "my comrades, Nick and Gill. The cost was $.50 per night (no Geisha), $1.50 total for the three of us ...separate rooms too." On 5 November they returned to Tachikawa Air Base where they were supposed to pick up their Black Tuesday B-29, 44-61816, but the airplane was still being repaired.

On their first night mission after returning to Okinawa (Meier's 46th), Fogler's crew encountered flak and fighters over the target. On 10 November they flew to Namsi again, but this was a night SHORAN mission. On the 13th the crew were summoned to appear before General Vandenberg, Air Force Chief of Staff, who presented the crew with DFC's and, more importantly, told them their replacements were on the way. Meier would fly eleven more missions before they were given the green light to go home. When it was learned that all the spaces on MAC and Commercial Air had been taken, Fogler's crew was fortunate to have a friend, General Kelly, who made sure they had a B-29 to take back to states They picked up the aircraft at Yokota AFB, Japan, and flew it across the Pacific to Travis AFB, located midway between Sacramento and San Francisco in northern California. Meier arrived home in New York City on December 23rd. The one-way trip on a Constellation cost him $600.

In 1966, Able Lead aircraft commander, Clarence Fogler, and navigator, Fred Meier, would crew up again, this time flying B-52s in the 306th Bomb Wing stationed at McCoy AFB, Florida.

Edward Moore would fly a total of 26 missions with the 370th BS, but never again on Major Field's crew. He completed his tour, first with Captain Robinson's crew until they rotated home, and finished with Captain Heims' crew. After returning to the United States, Moore volunteered to go back to Okinawa where he flew another 14 with the 19th Bomb Wing, for a total of forty combat missions. Fifty-five years later, his email address contains these four letters: n-a-m-s-i.

A few days after the Namsi mission, Reeter wrote to his wife: "We got back to the airfield at Seoul and landed a little less than an hour after it all happened where we got the best of medical attention. The airplane was a wreck and I don't think they've decided yet whether to fix or junk it. That evening they loaded us on a C-54 and took us (except the three injured personnel) to Tachikawa Air Base in Japan where we went to bed about 1:00 o'clock at night . . .

"The two injured gunners kept right on shooting at the MiGs even though wounded. I guess there will be about seven Purple Hearts passed out to the personnel on the airplane . . . Everybody had their nerves shattered up a little on that mission and it wasn't any fun that's for certain. Was a little surprised that Edwards didn't make it. They were giving him a 50/50 chance when they first saw him and that evening they were giving him a little better than that. For about three days after the 23rd, whiskey tasted like plain ordinary drinking water. I have got additions to the crew, making it complete, and have flown one mission since . . . "

While it is generally accepted that October 23, 1951 marked the end of daylight precision bombing of targets located within the borders of MiG Alley, records indicate there were at least three more such missions after Black Tuesday. The following day, on 24 October, the 98BG flew against Sunchon and, although Sunchon is roughly twice the distance from the Antung MiG base, received essentially the same greeting that had been given the 307th. Again, on the 27th the 19BG was met with deadly resistance from a determined MiG force that resulted in the loss of one B-29. Eleven months later, On September 19, 1952, thirty-two B-29s with F-86 escorts attacked an enemy barracks and supply areas southwest of Hamhung.

The late October missions are indicative of either a fundamental gap in communication between units or total lack of appreciation for the potential danger on the part of the other two bomber groups. More likely it was one of those military bureaucratic mishaps that seem unable to stop the machine once it is in motion. Simply put, once the missions were planned, they went--regardless of whatever catastrophe loomed in the interim. Examined more closely, one might consider the entire concept of "units" as a bad idea. Instead of concentrating the bomber force on one base under a single command, one B-29 unit was stationed in Japan, the other two on Okinawa. Although the 19th and 307th could not escape sharing some mutually beneficial experiences, there seemed to be a reluctance to do so. In many ways the competition between units harkened back to school rivalries, sometimes with disastrous results. One can only wonder why the 307th ignored what had happened to the 19th just one day before, when they proceeded to fly the mission under such dangerous conditions. It is even more difficult to comprehend why the 98th was apparently unaware what had happened the day before over Namsi. None of the crew members I talked with recalled being told of the Namsi calamity before they took off for a daylight mission on October 24, 1951.

Max Nelson, who flew on the 24th as a Radar Operator, has documented the mission with photos on his web page, *98th Bomb Wing Korea 1951*. Their target that day was a railroad by-pass bridge at Sunchon, roughly ninety miles south of the MiG bases on the Yalu. Max and his crew, commanded by Captain Dave Holder, flew in the Baker Two position in a formation of eight B-29s. They were on board # 44-27341, a.k.a. *Dreamer*, accompanied by # 44-61932, *SAD SAC (T.D.Y.)* on their left wing, *Our Gal*, # 44-61676, in the slot, and *Miss Behavin'* leading the pack. The four Able Flight B-29s were *To Each His Own* in lead, *Miss Minooky*, right wing, *Chotto Matte* on the left, and *M.P.I.* in the slot.

At 1458 hours the Soviet radar picked up the 98th crossing an imaginary line drawn between Pyongyang-Nampo. Three minutes later, 303rd IAD fighters were brought to "readiness condition one" and three minutes after that began to take off. The total force involved sixteen MiGs from the 523rd IAP, twenty from the 18th GIAP, and 18 MiGs from the 17th IAP, all under the overall command of the same Lieutenant Colonel Smorchkov who'd led the kill on Black Tuesday. Following a procedure similar to their successful intercept the day before, one regiment acted as the combat screen while the other two went after the bombers.

After assembling between Hamhung and Wonsan on the Korean coast, the formation proceeded toward the target, Stan Kavrik, copilot on *SAD SAC*, recalls the first sign of trouble--radio transmissions telling them, "Trains are leaving the station." The message was being sent by radar monitoring sites, and each train was a flight of MiG-15s coming at them from the protected bases north of the Yalu. The American 4th Fighter Wing had put up a screen along the Yalu. Sixteen Aussie Meteors from No. 77 Squadron flew cover with an immediate escort of ten Thunderjets. The best the fighter escorts could hope for was to engage the MiGs until they were so short of fuel they wouldn't be able to intercept the B-29s. Closer to the ground, F-84s strafed and bombed AAA emplacements.

While the 523rd IAP clashed with the Meteor and Sabre screen, the twenty MiGs from the 18th IAP attempted to catch the Superfortresses that were headed for the sea. Because Sunchon was roughly fifty miles farther from their Antung airfield than Namsi, by the time they got there the B-29s had already dropped their bombs. Running short on fuel, the MiGs stayed at 31,000 feet until they were close enough to initiate the attack. At 1535 hours, Smorchkov directed the 1st Squadron take on the fighters while the 2nd and 3rd Squadrons assailed the bombers. The MiGs hit Baker Flight coming in four and five abreast, using what is known as the Abbeville technique. It was the only time during their combat tour that Max's gunners ever fired a shot in anger, but by the time the MiGs were in range, *Dreamer* was already on fire. It received several direct hits, the most serious a 37mm that entered the right wing and became embedded in the main spar. Fortunately, it did not explode, nor did the 21mm that punctured one of the main gear tires. The A/C rang the warning bell to prepare for bail out. Max recalls, "I grabbed my camera and forgot my chest-pack chute. Luckily the flames from #4 blew out and we made it to Taegu." *Dreamer* never flew again.

Because the encounter took place just north of the Pyongyang-Wonsan line that Soviet pilots were prohibited from crossing, each MiG was limited to a single firing pass. Most fired at one to two kilometers, well out of effective cannon range. Smorchkov, however, closed to 700 meters before opening fire and broke off his attack at 300 meters. The B-29 caught fire, but this time Smorchkov did not come away unscathed. In his words, "I was bracketed by a burst of fire as soon as I shot down the B-29 … There was a 'Fortress' off to my right and below, and all of its gunners were firing. I made a chandelle to the left and saw their tracers undershooting me. The cabin depressurized and I took a bullet in the leg, in the thigh, but it (his Mig-15) remained intact (and) somehow I managed to get back."

Smorchkov's lethal burst had found its mark in *Our Gal*. The aircraft staggered and fell out of formation, but that didn't deter Harold M. Setters, a gunner on the stricken B-29, from returning fire that may have wounded Smorchkov. He made it home. *Our Gal* was not as lucky. With fuel gushing out of a hole in its wing, the crew began bailing out.

A few days before the mission, Luke Fyfe, copilot of the stricken B-29, had gotten lucky by winning the thousand-dollar BINGO jackpot at the Officer's Club. This time he was not so lucky. Kavrik recalls one of the gunners calling over interphone, "He's going down," and another, "Guy's chute's not going to open."

A cannon shell shattered the tail gunner window on Kavrik's *SAD SAC*, but didn't explode. Another embedded itself directly underneath the radar operator. Luckily, no shrapnel penetrated the flak suit he'd placed on the floor under his feet. Ahead, and slightly to the right, *Miss Behavin* was getting hammered. A cannon round took out a prop, and the number one engine had to be shut down. With *Our Gal* out of the way, one of the MiG pilots, apparently out of ammo and emboldened by the successes of the past days, pulled into the slot position to the right, slightly behind and below *SAD SAC*, extended his air brakes, and parked. Stan Kavrik could see the MiG pilot plainly at a distance of about 25 yards. Moments later the MiG pilot must have decided he'd stretched his luck. He retracted his air brakes and banked away, exposing his entire underbelly of his machine to the six fifty caliber machine guns in the top turrets of the B-29. The CFC took aim and opened up, but the slugs appeared to bounce off or pass through the MiG without significant damage. Whether or not the MiG pilot was Aleksandr Smorchkov has not been determined.

The next turn in the bombing rotation belonged to the 19th. Mission briefing confirmed the worst. The wing navigator (mortician before he was recalled) we'd nicknamed "Digger O'Dell," showed up wearing his black top hat, the one he donned for funerals in civilian life and for briefing tough missions in the military. We were going back to MiG Alley. I vividly recall attending the briefing, going through our preflight, engine start, and moving out to the taxiway without a spare word spoken. There was none of the kidding around or usual jokes. Each man was stuck in his private reflections of a life that in all probability would, within a few hours, come to a violent conclusion in the skies over North Korea. In a letter to my mother the night before I'd willed my new fly rod to my old trout fishing buddy, Johnny Jose. Others on the crew had made similar arrangements. The line of bombers stopped short of the runway, each one canting so, during engine run-up, the blast from its propellers would not blow debris into following aircraft. As we waited for the take off order, that had never before been issued more than a few minutes after run-up, it began to rain. Sitting there, the only sounds were the idling engines burning fuel that, if we were lucky, we would need to get home. To make us wait seemed, at first, callous, and finally cruel--as though those in charge had decided to give us time to

General Hoyt S. Vandenberg, Chief of Staff USAF, listens to B-29 crew members shortly after Black Tuesday. The first thing the general said was, "I want to talk to a tail gunner."

Photo by Author

"Yea, though I walk through the valley of death, I know you are with me." Late evening, during the walk-around lull before take-off.

Courtesy of Fred Meier

dwell on our past indiscretions and inevitable demise. Unexpectedly, the tower told us to shut down our engines to await further instructions. With the silencing of the engines came the sound of rain pelting the aluminum fuselage. Even today, I think of those minutes, listening to the raindrops while awaiting the order to proceed on the mission, as interminable. Sitting in a B-29 copilot's seat on a rainy day on a Kadena taxiway I felt the cold clutch of real fear--and never more alone. It became the epiphany of my existence, so much so that sometimes I feel as though I've been living a frozen moment in time all of these many years since that day more than half a century ago I was certain would be my last. Sometimes I wonder if everything since that moment has been a dream, that I might wake up and we'll be swinging out onto the runway, engine power coming up, taking off for Namsi.

The voice from the tower was our salvation: "Return to your parking spots, all daylight bombing has been canceled, by order of General Hoyt S. Vandenberg, Chief of Staff USAF."

Not long afterward the man himself visited B-29 units in search of better ways to deal with the MiG menace. I have a color slide of the four-star general surrounded by B-29 officers while listening to an enlisted tail gunner. We'd been lined up in parade formation on the ramp in front the operations shack when his motorcade rolled in. The youthful general jumped out of his vehicle, walked briskly past the group brass at the front of the ranks and motioned everyone to gather around. Haltingly, we closed in. One of the first things General Vandenberg said was, "I want to talk to a tail gunner." One gunner eased forward. Vandenberg asked him, point blank, "Would you guys like the 20mm reinstalled in the tail?" They all replied in the affirmative, but I don't think it was ever done--probably because the trajectory of the shells fired from the 20-mm cannon was completely different from that of the bullets from the 0.50-inch machine guns, which made aiming in combat even more difficult.

General Vandenberg proceeded to question gunners one-on-one about the effectiveness of the B-29's guns against the MiG, and it is more than possible that their answers had a lot to do with the permanent cessation of daylight bombing in MiG Alley.

One definite result the meeting accomplished was to raise morale. We were at an all-time low. Crew officers were talking among themselves about refusing to fly "suicide missions." Our new bombardier, who'd flown numerous sorties against Japan, said we were being used as MiG bait. He may not have been far wrong. The pattern of several daylight missions, including Black Tuesday, defies basic common sense. Many ran counter to existing tactical doctrine that set up formation patterns to provide maximum firepower protection.

Records show that another daylight mission was flown in which still another B-29 fell victim to Aleksandr Smorchkov's cannon fire. According to Russian records, and verified by a listed KORWALD loss, Saturday 27 October was "the last day of the Black Week" for Bomber Command when nine B-29s from the 19th BG were targeted against railway bridges in the Anju area. By planning most of the route over water, FEAF planners had hoped to exploit the protection provided by the Soviet edict that prohibited MiGs from flying over the sea. The B-29s crossed over the coastline in the immediate vicinity of the target, released their bombs, and headed back for the coast.

Senior Lieutenant Dmitriy Samoylov recalled attacking the bombers, " . . . there, right in front of me, were nine B-29s. They were leaving smoke behind them, as they were heading towards the Gulf at full power where they knew we could not fly after them ... I was doing just over a thousand (kilometers per hour) and they were only doing about seven hundred, so I was closing on them quickly. They were firing their machine guns, and while the tracers could not be seen on a converging course, from the flashes from all of their turrets it was clear that they were shooting. I made an attack and flamed one of them... (We) could break off, but instead turned around and made a head-on attack... But I could not hold a converging course as I had from behind them (because of high rate of closure) . . . and just as soon as I opened fire I had to immediately begin a chandelle . . . Zykov called out: 'I'm hit!' When we had gone under them he had been drilled. Well, he may have only been hit once, but we had to break off combat."

The Russian report concedes that Allied fighter cover had prevented most of the attacking MiGs from reaching the B-29s; however, serial number 44-62071, a 30BS B-29 commanded by Capt. Vito Fierro, was so severely shot up that it was forced to crash land at Kimpo. Seven of the eleven on board were wounded and the aircraft listed as a loss.

For B-29s, switching from day to night missions kicked in the *Law of Unexpected Consequence.* No longer faced with being forced to climb to altitude north of the Yalu to avoid interception by F-86s, at night MiG pilots were free to climb on course at optimum range throttle setting, thereby extending their effective range. This much lower fuel consumption meant that a MiG could be flown farther south, and even orbited while awaiting the bomber's arrival. As a result, the boundaries of MiG Alley were greatly expanded. Because of the added exposure to MiG attacks, it could be argued that missions against targets in North Korea actually became more dangerous as a result of switching to night operations.

Although night sorties may have proved statistically safer, for many aircrew members they seemed more dangerous and fearsome than daylight missions. Bomber crews in particular had been trained to attack targets in daylight. There was something reassuring about being able to see the ground and even the threat when you could see it. In daylight the distance to flak or attacking fighters could be approximated. At night each burst or muzzle flash seemed perilously close. Bailing out of a crippled airplane was never a pleasant possibility, and at night it took on terrifying proportions. Even the electronic method employed to bomb a target at night, SHORAN, came to be dreaded by many. Dewell Turner, for one, hated SHORAN. Turner wrote to me, "They knew where we would go when we flew our missions and that gave them an advantage in setting up their lights and flak placements. We would often get more flak along the approach than over the target . . . it was also frustrating to attack the same target time after time. It made us feel as if we couldn't hit a thing. In addition, on the ground no gains seemed to be made. The whole thing felt futile. MacArthur was an egotist, but I agree with him that if it was worth fighting for it was worth finishing."

During my tour of duty as a combat crew member or throughout my research for this book I cannot recall a single veteran of the air war over Korean who did not or does not share Turner's view.

9: Analysis, Conclusions & Reflections

While researching the Black Tuesday mission for an article that was to appear in the October, 2001 VFW Magazine, I kept running into inaccuracies and contradictions in both published records and eyewitness accounts. Obvious bloopers in official publications clouded the picture of that day--such as the report that no F-86 Sabres were lost on 23 Oct. '51, yet showed three F-86 pilots were missing in action on that date, causing one to wonder how the F-86s returned without their pilots. Another official source document contained repeated references to Kimpo, "Japan," an air base in South Korea. These and numerous other inaccuracies, large and small, deepened my mistrust of nearly everything I read.

Many of the errors contained in official documents were detected without really trying, yet it was easy to see how small, inadvertent mistakes and omissions had, over decades, created a snowball effect that turned casual inaccuracies into unassailable facts. Many of these errors, omissions and inaccuracies, I knew from experience, were the result of having been recorded by those whose lives were restricted to offices far removed from the sphere of aerial combat. In the process of chronicling these events from word of mouth debriefings and second hand notes, truth was often further denigrated by less-than-motivated orderly room clerks' poor typing skills and training deficiencies. When it came to unit histories, the low man on the totem pole was often the one assigned the task. This seems evident in all of the records I read, and especially in the 307th Bombardment Wing archives for the month of October 1951. Even so, and although much of the recorded information appears to have reflected the interests of the archive author, tangentially many archive entries helped clarify, support, and add to the information gathered from eyewitness accounts and other sources.

As the number of disparities mounted, both in published records and eyewitness accounts, I began to doubt that I could ever unscramble what really happened that day long ago in the skies above Namsi. Just about the time I was ready to chuck the entire project, I made contact with John Duquette, chief honcho of cottonpickers.org, the *Everyman a Tiger* web site. The site covers the history of the 8th and 15th Tactical Reconnaissance Squadrons that flew lone missions into North Korea, particularly in the late summer and early fall of 1951. The RF-80 pilots, known affectionately as "Photo Joes," operated out of Kimpo Air Base (K-14) near Seoul, South Korea. Their motto was "Alone, Unarmed, and Unafraid" and above the bar in the squadron's "Cottonpickers Club" tent was posted, in large, brazen letters, the words, "Every Man A Tiger." John's father, a Second Lieutenant at the time, was one of the RF-80 pilots who photographed Namsi the day before Black Tuesday. Coincidentally, when we first corresponded, John was in the Army, stationed in Korea. Probably because of this dual connection, John had become a Korean Air War historian in his own right. When I expressed my dismay regarding the incongruity between various reports and witnesses, he consoled me with these words:

My ... experience with historical research has left me with the general view that one can--at best--only capture the shadow of truth. The ability to collect and interpret the shadows is what makes one historian "better" than another-- because all that is left are the recordings of observers of things that were of varying levels of interest to them personally--few of which had a sense of the history they were making and/or recording--nor should it be expected of them. They were just trying to live their lives. Little did they know that many years later, folks interested in telling their story, would be perusing their each and every word trying to glean the nuances of every sentence--trying to reconstruct the truth.

Two men can observe the same event, and see different things--perhaps even contradict each other. Perhaps both are true; perhaps both are false. We then have to rely on corroborating evidence and sometimes the laws of physics to reconcile the differences. At the end of that process, our best guess on the shape and form of the shadow is what we are left with. Sometimes, it is left to the reader to judge from the options presented as to what really happened ...

Diary entries are as good as the proximity of the individual to the event and his level of knowledge about what he is observing; the closer he is to "eyes on" and the more he knows about what he is looking at, the more veracity one should give to his account. A private watching or participating in an attack may think everything is FUBAR; his General may think that everything is going according to plan except for that confusion down there in 1st Platoon, A Company. Ah...the shadows of truth ...

Amen, John.

When I researched and wrote the VFW article, that is all I wanted to do. As more information poured in from former crew members who'd read the article, and from others who'd been at Kimpo, flown fighter cover, or inherited photos and memorabilia from a parent crew member, I began to see that the story had not been told at all. Missing were the circumstances that led to the incredible miscalculation that a mission that departed so drastically from tactical doctrine could succeed. Three flights of three B-29s flying a SHORAN arc in broad daylight within forty miles of protected air base bristling with MiGs invited disaster. When Soviet radar picked up the incoming bombers it must have been, for them, like Santa Claus coming to town. I imagine they could scarcely believe what they were seeing.

As I struggled through my research notes, a far different impression of the Korean Air War that I had lived with since my involvement over a half-century ago slowly emerged. Hollywood's gung ho cinematic concoctions, hyperbolic "war stories" that inflated and distorted the reality of aerial combat, plus my own relatively narrow views and notions had transformed the Korean Air War into something it was not.

John Duquette not only drew up the route charts and maps used in this history, he also provided plenty of research--including the following report filed by the 4th FIW's intelligence officer to explain the ineffectiveness of the fighter escort:

"First . . .there was confusion on the part of the fighter escort and the B-29s in the rally point and route of return which greatly impaired the mission of the fighter escort aircraft. Secondly, the MiGs were aggressive and in numbers which made possible the temporary supremacy of the enemy in aerial warfare over North Korea. Their tactics seemed to be well planned, their formation appeared excellent, and their discipline appeared superior to that seen thus far in the Korean War. Thirdly, the enemy aircraft were in sufficient numbers to engage the F-86s in areas away from the bombers."

The report concluded, "These factors could well presage a new phase of aerial warfare over North Korea."

While most accounts of the air battle over Namsi tend to stress the disparities between the speedy state-of-the-art fighter jet and lumbering obsolete bomber, a closer examination of tactics--or lack thereof--employed by the B-29 force reveals deviations that are incongruous with tactical doctrine that had been adhered to from the very beginning of daylight mass bombardment.

Contrary to popular legend, the Soviets had designed and deployed their airplane with one purpose in mind--to shoot down bombers. In spite of several new features, such as an ejection seat and pressurized cockpit, the MiG-15 more closely resembled a stovepipe with cannons. Early models carried only forty 37mm and 160 23 mm cannon rounds. By comparison, the MiG-15's chief adversary, the F-86, carried nearly nine times as many rounds for six .5-inch Colt-Browning machine guns. Because two hundred rounds were insufficient to engage in an active dogfight, MiG pilots had standing orders never to initiate a combat engagement with the F-86. They were also instructed to open fire on B-29s while still outside the bomber's defensive range--made possible because their cannons had a significantly greater range and impact power.

Much of what we read about the MiG-15 also either ignores or does not take into full account what is perhaps a fighter aircraft's most important performance factor. Saburo Sakai, the famous Japanese Zero ace, with 64 confirmed kills, maintained that a fighter's worth is determined, above all, by its range. In a 1998

Interview with Scott Hards, the Japanese Zero ace said, "I can't tell you how much that affects you when you're in the cockpit. When you know you've got plenty of gas, it really lets you relax ... When you are worried about your gas, it really affects what you do with your plane, even how you fight." Sakai once flew a Zero for twelve continuous hours. He felt sorry for German ME-109 pilots because "they could barely get to altitude and fight for a couple of minutes before they had to start worrying about their fuel supply." He wondered how many were at the bottom of the English Channel because they hadn't enough fuel to get home. If the Nazi's had built a fighter with range, he speculated, they could have operated from airfields near Paris, hit targets anywhere in the British Isles and still had plenty of fuel in reserve--and England would no longer exist.

The severe limitation on how far from its home base the MiG-15 could intercept an enemy bomber force created the false impression that they were deliberately avoiding combat because the pilots were either unskilled or afraid. The prevailing mood among American airmen at the time I was over there was that we were fighting "a bunch of gooks--" a disparaging term that contained a great deal of contempt as well. This general attitude could well have been at the heart of the decision to proceed with the daylight mission using the largely untested electronic SHORAN bombing system. SHORAN had been designed to allow a bomber to strike a target with a high degree of accuracy in darkness or in weather. Key in both instances is the word in. On Black Tuesday, a decision was made to launch the strike even though the bomber force would be above a cloud layer, in the clear, fully exposed to attacking MiG-15s that were not radar-equipped and therefore could not accurately aim and fire on aircraft that were obscured by clouds or darkness. Later, when the B-29s switched to night operations, the word in would again come into play when MiG pilots would knock down aircraft illuminated by moonlight or searchlights.

The deeper I dug into the particulars of the Namsi mission, the more dismayed I became at the apparent apathy among Allied planners. The Black Tuesday mission clearly should have been aborted and rescheduled for night or instrument conditions with maximum electronic countermeasures. They had the capabilities but (apparently) not the patience.

Other missions leading up to Black Tuesday, notably those flown by the 98th BG, had been diverted to secondary targets because of failure to rendezvous with fighters. Even if the B-29s had linked up with their escort, it had been fairly well established that the straight-wing F-84 and Gloster Meteor were next to useless against the MiG-15. Regardless, FEAF kept sending them as fighter "protection" that the Russians pretty much picked off at will. Although F-86s scored well after the MiGs had already delivered their blows against the 29s and were out of ammo, F-86s weren't especially effective when it came to preventing MiG attacks on the bombers.

The situation was made worse by the practice of what amounted to inter-group competition between the three medium bomber units. Competition between the 19th, 307th, and 98th eventually reached the point where one unit presumably figured out how to cluster and carry up to 192 one hundred pound bombs (vs. the previous 144) and did not tell the other two units how they did it. In this instance, none of those I interviewed who flew the Namsi mission were aware of the intense MiG opposition the 19th encountered the day before--nor were the 98th crews advised of the 307th's devastating losses before flying their mission the day after Black Tuesday.

Throughout the conflict, the Soviets believed that B-29s would someday cross the Yalu and bomb their airfields. For that reason they kept large numbers of MiGs in reserve to protect their airfields and so few committed to intercepting our formations south of the Yalu. From what they saw on their radar screen on 23 October 1951, the Soviet commanders thought it was possible the day had arrived; yet a sizable MiG force was retained as backup in case the main bomber force was still over the radar horizon.

Almost all existing US records, published and otherwise, state unequivocally that 150 MiG-15s attacked the 307th's B-29s. We now know this number couldn't have been accurate because it exceeds the total of operational MiG fighters available on 23 October 1951. The "150" is apparently based on an interpretation of the number of radar echoes observed taking off from the Manchurian bases. The method used to determine how many MiGs were in the formations that appeared on the radar scopes as a single larger return is not known but has to have been an educated guess. The reports also do not differentiate between combat and training aircraft or whether a particular aircraft took off, landed and took off again--perhaps several times. The Soviet record, which this observer believes to be accurate, shows 84 MiGs were launched against the attacking force. Of these 84, approximately a third of the force committed to combat was assigned to physically attack the bombers. Another third engaged the F-86s to divert them from the attacking force, while the remaining third were on guard to protect the tails of the attackers returning to base, low on fuel and out of ammo. On Black Tuesday 84 MiG-15s were launched, with 44 assigned to intercept the bomber force.

One of the biggest differences in American and Soviet versions of the air war is the numbers of opposing aircraft shot down. Some Russian versions of the Black Tuesday battle allege more B-29s destroyed than flew the mission. Likewise, American gunners claimed more MiGs than the Russians admitted were shot down by B-29 gunners during the entire Korean War. Air Force records and subsequent chronicles, for example, categorically state that the 19BG B-29 named *Command Decision*, which flew into MiG Alley the day before Black Tuesday, became a B-29 bomber "ace" by having shot down a total of five MiGs. A representative nose section of the aircraft is, in fact, on display at the National Museum of the USAF near Dayton, Ohio. Accompanying text for the Museum website photo of Command Decision reads:

> This fuselage is painted in the markings of *Command Decision*, the famous B-29 Superfortress. During the Korean War, gunners on *Command Decision* shot down five Soviet-built MiG-15 jet fighters. This qualified the aircraft for unofficial recognition as a bomber "ace."

The purpose here is not to dispute *Command Decision's* qualification or other claims. It is, instead, an attempt to root out a hypothetical but reasonable explanation for these differing views.

Both sides were apparent victims of honest misinterpretation. In the tumbling confusion of aerial combat it is possible for a split second impression to become an indelible memory that may or may not be a complete picture of what really happened. Under these conditions, a snapshot of a smoking aircraft can easily become a "kill," where, in fact, the aircraft made it back to its home base. In another hypothetical scenario, a flight of MiGs swoops in, shoots, hits, and sets two B-29s on fire. A few seconds later a second flight fires at the same burning B-29s. Result? Four B-29s are reported destroyed with the end result that the tally taken after the battle has more B-29s shot down than flew the mission. This same hypothetical can be applied to the B-29 gunners. The tail gunner fires and hits a MiG attacking from the rear. As the MiG comes abeam, the CFC and LG also score hits; then, as the MiG passes the nose, the bombardier puts a few rounds into the fuselage, perhaps knocking off a panel. As the MiG passes out of range, it rolls over and dives as though shot down. In this case, when the tally was taken, two people received credit for a MiG kill, plus one probable. The MiG, however, made it back to Antung and landed--albeit perforated with .50 cal holes.

Although there are few outright concessions, records indicate that both sides were aware of the exaggerated nature of "kill" claims. The Russians, for example, concede, "... it is completely possible that at regimental level the number of B-29s was correctly counted, but then at division level their summaries combined the regimental assessments, as did the single corps description of the air battle." In other words, regimental unit figures were added to other regimental unit figures by higher headquarters to arrive at a total that included duplicate claims.

For fighter pilots, the number of kills appears to have had a great deal to do with pride and what would later come to be known as "machismo." As old fighter pilots put it, "There are only two types of aircraft, fighters and targets." For bomber crews, MiG claims probably had more to do with survival than pride--the sense that they could fight back and destroy a superior machine. Knowing there was an "ace" bomber provided the sort of lift aircrew members needed when faced with the grim prospect of being shot down by a MiG. For bomber crews it was more about their morale than about the grisly task of killing.

Throughout this book I've used the expression "shot down," but what does the term really imply? Do the words conjure up images of Spads and Fokkers on fire and spinning out of control, jet fighters exploding in mid-air? Parachutes? Does an aircraft that crash lands at a friendly base with dead and wounded aboard fall into the category of "shot down?" For reporting purposes it would at first appear that "destroyed" would be more precise in defining the final disposition of an opposing combatant, but even "destroyed" requires analysis and clarification. Two of the B-29s that landed at Kimpo Air Base on Black Tuesday never flew combat again. These two were not officially shot down, but how can it be denied that they were not essentially "destroyed?" In the same vein, the independent KORWALD aircraft loss report lists eight of the nine B-29s as losses, although three subsequently flew combat missions after undergoing extensive depot repairs.

According to an official Soviet record, only one MiG was "shot down" by a B-29 gunner during the entire Korean War. Again, semantics and interpretation seem to come into play. Numerous accounts tell how an F-86 on a MiG's tail blasted away, pouring fifty caliber slugs into the MiG that appeared to dive out of control while, in actuality, it was only damaged. It is likely that our F-86 pilot claimed a kill even though the MiG made it home. Still, this may not be an unreasonable claim. Had the encounter taken place outside of gliding distance to a friendly runway, it is probable that the MiG would've crashed and would, per se, have been "shot down."

In the heat of aerial combat it is never easy to judge closure rates or target movement. On Black Tuesday several MiGs flew through Able and Baker Flights and were hit several times. Although the attacking fighters were "shot up," there is no record that any were "shot down," as a few gunners claimed. Their retreat to their home sanctuary across the Yalu, perhaps coupled with an undesirable flight characteristic, may have led gunners to believe they'd shot down a MiG. The early MiG-15 fuel supply often limited it to a single intercept. With ammunition depleted and running on fumes, the pilot had to throttle back and dive toward home, sometimes creating the impression he has been shot down. Although their bases were just across the river from MiG Alley, there are numerous accounts of pilots making dead stick landings because they had run out of fuel. Adding to the illusion of a "kill," during combat maneuvers was the MiG's propensity to stall and literally tumble out of the sky. While his adversary would understandably assume the MiG had gone down, with training and experience, Soviet pilots were able to recover and make it home safely.

A factor that surely contributed to the debacle over Namsi might best be described as a poverty of expectations. Just as those in positions of authority never expected the Japanese would bomb Pearl Harbor or that our intelligence community never seriously considered that terrorists would hijack and crash airliners into The World Trade Center, it appears that FEAF did not believe that enemy fighters were capable of penetrating the considerable numbers of F-86s and F-84s screening the B-29s.

Exacerbating the potential risks engendered by the complacency of American commanders was their apparent lack of understanding the nuts and bolts of SHORAN bombing. Because of ground equipment limitations, to bomb Namsi, one of only four approach arcs could be used. Two of these approaches were reciprocals of two others. In other words, approach one attacked the target in the opposite direction from a continuation of the approach three arc. The same applied to numbers two and four. Because Namsi Airfield was so far north, approach number two could not be flown without crossing into Manchuria. Namsi's proximity to the border eliminated number three as well. Because approach number one required the bombers to fly inland from the Yellow Sea, the formation would have been subjected to intense post-release pressure from both MiGs and anti-aircraft artillery during an extended escape route that would have had them turning back to the sea. This left only approach number four as the arc of most probable choice. By a simple process of elimination, the Soviets were able to mass their large caliber radar-directed AAA defenses along this arc. Indeed, the formation encountered what has been described as the most concentrated and accurate flak that even WW II veterans of bombing missions over Europe and Japan had ever encountered. Following this line of thought, one cannot escape the conclusion that Namsi (which provided only a 40 mile additional range advantage for intercepting MiGs and would have subjected them to extensive and unacceptable launch and recovery risks) may have been an elaborate trap to lure B-29s into MiG range. The flip side is a school of conjecture that the B-29s were sent to lure the MiGs out of their sanctuary for the F-86s to feast on. If either or both of these were true, the Soviets clearly came out on top.

A question that puzzled me throughout my research was why so much brass flew on a daylight mission deep into MiG Alley. For all intents and purposes they had no function other than acting as observers (euphemism for "passengers"). Although it was not uncommon for 19th Bomb Group B-29s to carry passengers on combat missions, they seldom sandbagged aboard an aircraft that was certain to come under enemy fire--and never into MiG Alley. This was not just to protect the individual sandbagger from unnecessary risks; the policy also protected crew members by facilitating more rapid escape. Extra bodies further complicated what would, at best, have been a marginal survival situation. Nobody wanted someone in the way if they needed to bail out in a hurry. Few staff and ground personnel had been thoroughly trained in emergency egress procedures, as well as escape and evasion techniques while behind enemy lines. It's not inconceivable that the brass wanted to witness first-hand the MiG force being drawn into combat and destroyed by the "superior" F-86 air cover. Whether they had deluded themselves into believing Chinese and Korean peasant pilots (as some claimed) were flying the Russian jets will never be known. It is clear, however, that the American commanders who went along for the ride to Namsi demonstrated more arrogance than common sense.

Not only does the presence of ranking officers raise the question as to whether the raid itself was designed to decoy MiG-15s into the fray for F-86s to destroy, speculation that the mission had a darker purpose is further supported by the blatant disregard for many of the basic principles of tactical doctrine, such as massed formation firepower, or taking full advantage of cloud cover, darkness, evasive maneuvers, and electronic jamming to escape detection. Instead, the bombers were lined up like shooting gallery ducks, plowing straight ahead in broad daylight while using a bombing method (SHORAN) that had been fashioned primarily for night bombing. If there was another purpose, the experiment was a marvelous failure. The MiG's superior performance left the 86s far behind and the 307th decimated.

On the other hand, their expectations may have been reasonable. For all the hoopla, the MiG really wasn't the monster threat to the B-29 that Korean Air War historians have made it out to be. Although no one will admit it, combat experiences (including this observer's) indicate that MiG pilots were generally reluctant to attack B-29s and, with few exceptions, seldom entered a formation's cone of fire. At the time we assumed that the aggressiveness was a characteristic of Soviet piloted aircraft and reluctance indicative of less experienced Chinese or Korean pilots. Russians records indicate otherwise, that only Soviet pilots flew combat prior to November 1951 and when the Chinese and Koreans were finally permitted to handle the MiGs, they did so sparingly.

Like many of their American counterparts it must have been difficult for the Soviets to comprehend the rationale behind their involvement in the Korean conflict. This was further complicated by the unreasonable rules of engagement that (for both sides) favored the enemy. Morale problems became such a factor on at least one occasion that the Russians were trucked down south to hospitals in Pyongyang and elsewhere to personally view civilian casualties. The Soviet brass apparently thought the pilots could use this motivation because they weren't aggressive enough. A large number of ex-B-29 crew members agree. Personally, I always felt that the MiG pilots could've blasted our B-29 out of existence if they'd really put their minds to it.

Neither side's viewpoint is entirely correct. For all of its press, the MiG-15 was very limited in range and offensive firepower-- almost to the extent that it had to be where we were at precisely the same time or the intercept would fail. Hollywood has blurred the fact that aircraft are limited to what they <u>can</u> do based on fuel and rounds of ammunition--not unlike the old Westerns where horses ran forever and six-shooters fired a limitless number of bullets.

Most concepts about the Korean Air War are largely leftovers from Hollywood films and other unreliable sources. While researching this book, one crewman emailed, "Where were the F-86s?" He went on to suggest that the fighter squadron commander should have been court-martialed for dereliction of duty, reflecting the prevailing misconception that the F-86 was a vastly superior aircraft to the MiG-15, whereas the opposite would be a more accurate appraisal. For all of its limitations and quirks, the MiG-15 was a machine well ahead of its day. Whether it was a "better" aircraft than the F-86 depends to a large degree on which performance factors were compared. To hit closer to the truth, we should probably avoid overall abstractions, such as "best," "better," and "superior." Instead, each aircraft should be rated within the parameters of its designed role. The MiG-15 was designed to shoot down bombers (B-29s, B-50s & B-36s). In this role it was probably the finest aircraft of its type flying at the time. It could reach intercept altitude in less than five minutes and had a service ceiling of 51,000 feet. On the other hand, an F-86A with wing tanks and full ammo could barely make it to 40,000 feet. By most accounts, on Black Tuesday, the F-86s were significantly outnumbered--although it made no difference; the MiGs simply flew over the 86s and blew past the 84s.

Perhaps the greatest defeat the United States air forces suffered in World War II also happened in October. On 14 October 1943 German Fw.190s and Bf.109s shot down sixty B-17s out of about 300 unescorted bombers. These losses represented 20% of the total force, and the USAF considered these raids disasters. Over Namsi the Soviets shot down and inflicted major damage on all but one of the entire strike force of nine B-29s. For the Soviets, Namsi became an epic victory of Soviet MiG-15 pilots against a numerically superior force, so important that three of the pilots involved--Smorchkov, Os'kin and Shchukin--were awarded the Soviet Union's highest military honor, the *Zolotaya Svezda* or Golden Star, which also gave them the title of *Geroi Sovestkogo Soyuza* or Heroes of the Soviet Union.

It has been generally concluded that the Namsi raid marked the end of daylight bombing in Korea. It has also been claimed, mostly by Russian writers, that the MiG put an end to any notion of expanding the war through strategic airpower. Neither of these claims proved true.

In his autobiography, *In the Skies of Two Wars*, Korean War ace Sergey Kramarenko writes, "... the tremendous losses suffered by B-29 bombers forced the American command to cease sending them over on daylight raids to certain death, as one single five-second burst from the cannon of a MiG-15 would send a B-29 down in flames or cause it to blow up in midair."

While it is true that a single burst *could* down a B-29, throughout the Korean air campaign, B-29s absorbed countless hits without going "down in flames" or being "blown-up in midair." In several instances, cannon projectiles were found unexploded inside fuel tanks.

Far from ending daylight bombing, experiences in Korea solidified and accelerated plans that had been in the works for years. Namsi and other bombing missions verified what strategic warfare planners had suspected, that the slower propeller-driven bombers of the pre-jet age could no longer be relied on to deliver bombs on the target. The advanced version of the B-29, the B-50, and the high-flying, massive, ten-engine B-36 were no longer viewed as viable deterrents to nuclear warfare. Within months of the conclusion of armed hostilities in Korea, the six-engine B-47 jet bomber would begin making its way into the Strategic Air Command's inventory, and not long afterwards the B-52 jet bomber would replace the B-36 and the B-47 as SAC's primary global weapons system. Well over fifty years later, the B-52 is still in service with the USAF.

It could also be argued that Black Tuesday ended what was referred to as "visual precision Bombing;" but that would ignore the reality that the primary bombing method used on the Namsi mission was not visual, but electronic--or that electronic methods of bomb delivery would remain the priority for decades to come.

With the exception of missions flown during the "reaction" period, massed formation and visual (precision) daylight bombing ended with the October 23, 1951 Black Tuesday mission. Before the disaster, tacticians had advocated the use of massed firepower and fighter escorts to protect bombers from enemy interceptors. The air battle over Namsi proved that even a large force of fighters could not protect the B-29s. Nor could the bombers, in spite of their massive defensive firepower, defend themselves. Tactical doctrine was, in fact, turned on its head. Nothing about aerial bombardment was ever again the same. The Strategic Air Command (SAC) abandoned its fighter escort program and launched a crash campaign to replace the piston-powered bomber with aircraft that could operate independently. This meant jets: the B-47 and B-52 (I instructed in both). The jet bombers were no longer fortresses bristling with guns. Whereas the B-29 had five turrets, each jet successor had only one in the tail. Firepower was supplanted by electronic countermeasures. Radar operators, who could not even see outside the aircraft, replaced bombardiers. The new Tactical

Doctrine dictated bombing missions that were essentially single-ship sorties that relied solely on electronic countermeasures or terrain-following radar for protection. Today, developments in stealth technology continue the trend in aerial warfare initiated by the air battle over Namsi.

Fault for the Namsi disaster has also been attributed to lousy intelligence. I seriously doubt that was the case. On the April 12, 1951 mission, B-29s received a preview of Black Tuesday that should've taught everyone a lesson. For some reason it did not. On the other hand, it is conceivable that daylight missions would have been successful with minimum losses if they'd been properly planned to take advantage of cloud cover, electronic countermeasures, and varied tactics. If we'd been allowed to take out the MiG bases on the other side of the Yalu, something that would've taken no more than a week of heavy bombing, all resistance would have been eliminated and we probably would not be worrying about North Korea today.

Since the ceasefire was signed on July 27, 1953 there have been well in excess of 40,000 breaches to the agreement by North Korean Forces. Over 1,200 U.S. personnel have died, hundreds wounded, 87 captured and held prisoner, and there have been more than 2,300 Republic of Korea casualties.

My first mystery novel, *Immaculate in Black*, takes a detour about half way through, ostensibly to give the reader a glimpse into the protagonist's inner turmoil. The situation involves a son who was lost and never found while flying solo cross-country in the family Cessna. In various reviews, this detour became the subject of both praise and frustration. Only after the purpose of this section was questioned did I come to realize that the lost son represented friends and fellow classmates who were lost in Korea, including those on that black Tuesday in the battle-scarred skies above Namsi.

#   #   #

Appendix

Abbreviations

AAA: Antiaircraft Artillery (Triple A)
AB: Air Base
AFB: Air Force Base
ARS: Air Rescue Squadron
BG: Bombardment Group
BS: Bombardment Squadron
BW: Bombardment Wing
CAP: Combat Air Patrol
CCF: Chinese Communist Forces
CFC: Central Fire Controller
CO: Commanding Officer
COMINT: COMmunications INTelligence
CPV: (China) Chinese People's Volunteers
DFC: Distinguished Flying Cross
DM: Davis-Monthan Air Force Base, Tucson Arizona
DNIF: Duty Not Involving Flying
ECM: Electronic Countermeasures
ELINT: Electronic INTelligence
FAWS: Fighter All Weather Squadron
FBG: Fighter Bomber Group
FBS: Fighter Bomber Squadron
FEAF: Far East Air Forces (UN)
FIW: Fighter Interceptor Wing
GCA: Ground Controlled Approach
GCI: Ground Control Intercept
GI: Government Issue
GIAD: (USSR) *Gvardeyskaya Istrebitel'naya*
   Aviatsionnaya Diviziya or Guards Fighter Aviation Division
GIAP: (USSR) *Gvardeyskiy Istrebitel'niy Aviatsionniy Polk* or
   Guards Fighter Aviation Regiment
Glasnost: Russian word for "openness"
GMT: Greenwich Mean Time

GP: General Purpose (bomb)
HF: High Frequency (radio)
IA-PVO: *Istrevitelnaya Aviatsiya – Protivo Vozdushnaya Oborona*
or Fighter Aviation – Anti-Aircraft Defense
IAD: (USSR) *Istrebitel'naya Aviatsionnaya Diviziya* or Fighter
Aviation Division
IAD-PVO: (USSR) Defense Fighter Division
IAP: (USSR) *Istrebitel'niy Aviatsionniy Polk* or Fighter Aviation
Regiment
IAK: (USSR) *Istrebitel'niy Aviatsionniy Korpus* or Fighter
Aviation Corps
KIA: Killed in Action
KORWALD: Korean War Aircraft Loss Database
KPA: (N. Korea) Korean People's Army
KPAFAC: (N. Korea) Korean People's Armed Forces Air Corps
IP: Initial Point
MIA: Missing In Action
MSGT: Master Sergeant
NKA: North Korean Army
OIAE: (USSR) Independent Fighter Squadron
OIAK: (USSR) *Otdel'niy Istrebitel'niy Aviatsionniy Korpus*
or Independent Fighter Aviation Corps
OIAP: (USSR) *Otdel'niy Istrebitel'niy Aviatsionniy Polk* or
Independent Fighter Aviation Regiment (e.g. 351st)
OVA: (China & N. Korea) Unified Air Army
PCS: Permanent Change of Station.
PDI: Pilot Directional Indicator
PLAAF: (China) People's Liberation Army Air Force
POW: Prisoner of War
PVO: (USSR) Air Defense Forces
QRA: Quick Reaction Alert (Soviet)
R & R: Rest and Recuperation
RAAF: Royal Australian Air Force
ROK: (S. Korea) Republic of Korea
RPM: Revolutions Per Minute
Scanner: Left or right gunner on the B-29
SCAP: Supreme Commander, Allied Powers
SHORAN: SHOrt RAnge Navigation
SIGINT: SIGnal INTelligence
SN: Serial Number

SOP: Standard Operating Procedure
SRS: Strategic Reconnaissance Squadron
TAS: True Air Speed
TCW: Troop Carrier Wing
TDY: Temporary DutY
TRS: Tactical Reconnaissance Squadron
UAA: Sino-Korean Unified Air Army
UN: United Nations
UNC: United Nations Command
USAF: United States Air Force
USMC: United States Marine Corps
VFR: Visual Flight Rules
VHF: Very High Frequency (radio)
VVS: (USSR) *Voyenno-Vozdushniye Sily* or Air Forces
WW II: World War Two
ZI: Zone of Interior. (The 48 contiguous states)
ZULU (time): Same as GMT

B-29 Crew Rosters (Known): 307BW

Able Flight: 371st Bombardment Squadron

Able Flight Lead, Aircraft SN#44-61816

Posit.	Name-L.F. M.	Rank	S/N	Home Town
A/C	Fogler, Clarence I.	CPT	AO697409	
P	Pyfrom Stanley C.	1LT	AO558193	
B	Kourafas, Nick T.	1LT	AO2092928	
N	Meier, Frederick	1LT	AO1911500	New York NY
RO (S)	Peebles,	1LT		
FE	Dees, Ralph	MSG	AF14085361	
RE**	Hoke, Marvin L.	TSG	AF32754384	
CFC	Spivey, Fred R.	SSG	AF34827007	
LG	Miller, Rolland L.	CPL	AF17261903	
RG	Richards, Loren J.	SGT	AF17299810	
TG	De Pratter ?	SGT	AF17299810	
SHOR	DeJung, Clifton J.	CPT		
ABC	Ledbetter, Henry F.***	COL		

(S)Substitute **Radio/ECM *** Wing Director of Operations ?Data Uncertain

Able Flight #2, Aircraft SN#44-87760

Posit.	Name-L.F. M.	Rank	S/N	Home Town
A/C	Lewis, James R.	CPT	AO697409	St. Louis, MO
P?				
B?				
N?				

RO?				
FE?	Bata, L.G. "Pappy"	TSG		
R?	Brugeman, R. G.	SSG		
CFC	Fairchild, Malcolm L	TSG	AF18043050	DEQUINCY, LA
LG?				
RG?				
TG	Webb, Jerry	SSG	AF16279127	VILLA RIDGE, IL
SHOR?				

? Data Uncertain

Able Flight #3, Aircraft SN# 44-94045

Posit.	Name-L.F. M.	Rank	S/N	Home Town
A/C	Krumm, Robert M.	CPT	AO-804464	Cedar Rapids IA
P	Horner, John J.	1LT	AO-1911849	Swedesboro NJ
B	Poyner, Con F.	1LT	AO-725476	Ranger TX
N	Nutting, John M.	CPT	AO-685703	North Leeds ME
RO	Hudson, Laurence H.	1LT	AO-2092806	Brooklyn NY
FE	Johnson, Johnny M.	MSG	AF18012759	San Angelo TX
R	Marshall, Isreal, Jr	CPL	AF14353049	Jacksonville FL
CFC?	Hays, Melvin B.	SGT	AF39192109	SEATTLE WA
LG?	Osborne, Jess A, Jr	CPL	AF13351603	Lebanon VA
RG?	Gallant, James A.	SGT	AF15295553	Williamstown OH
TG	Johnson, Gerald E.	CPL	AF13337205	Arcadia PA

| SHOR? | McAdoo, Ernest R. | SSG | AF13337425 | Black Lick PA |
| ? | Newswanger, Quentin L. | TSG | AF14164294 | Quarryville, PA |

? Data Uncertain

Baker Flight: 372nd Bombardment Squadron

Baker Flight Lead, Aircraft SN# 44-86295, Crew, L-29-CO

Posit.	Name-L.F. M.	Rank	S/N	Home Town
A/C	Reeter, William F	1LT		Central IL
P	McQuaid, James R.	CPT		
B	Hardgrove, John W	1LT		
N	Edwards, Morton G	CPT	AO716392	Wichita KS
RO	Williamson, Monte C	CPT		
FE	Wilson, Edmond. L	SSG		
R?	Richards, Donald D	SSG		
CFC?	Walters, H. L	TSG		
LG?	Gretchen, John. E	SGT		Freeland PA
RG?	Turpin, Randy	CPL		
TG?	Victor, Russell B	SSG		
SHOR?	Bisson, Norvin T	SGT		
CC*	Polk, Walter H	SGT		
OBS?	Carroll , John W	L/C		

*Not listed on KORWALD   ?Data Uncertain

Baker Flight #2, Aircraft SN# 44-61940, Crew E-27-BO

Posit.	Name-L.F. M.	Rank	S/N	Home Town
A/C	Foulks, James Arch Jr	CPT	AO-2086021	Union City TN

P	Beissner, Fred L. Jr	1LT	AO 1903050	San Antonio TX
B	Mooradian, Ara	CPT	AO-932011	Fresno CA
N	Wentworth, Lloyd G	1LT	AO1911526	
RO	Black, Wayne Forrest	CPT	AO-0590031	Milton TN
FE	Botter, William Joseph	TSG	AF33570888	Dawson OK
R	Strine, John T.	SSG		
CFC	Kiser, Kenneth E	SSG	AF10601617	
LG	Jones, James	SGT		
RG?	Fuehrer, Alois Anton	SSG	AF13223572	Rosemont PA
TG?	Coffey, Arthur A.	CPL	AF11200414	Lowell, MA
SHOR?	MacClean, Gerald	SGT?		
OBS**	Cogswell, Robert W.	MAJ	11889A	Bridgeport, CT

?Data Uncertain **301st BOMB WG HQ SQ. Observer

Baker Flight #3, Aircraft SN# 44-27347

Posit.	Name-L.F. M.	Rank	S/N	Home Town
A/C (S)	Griner, William R. Jr.	MAJ		
P*	Rhodes, Chris	LT		
B	Cartwright, Oma B	1LT		
N	Odeneal, Pinkney B	1LT		
RO	Thornton, Glen S	1LT		
FE	Cummings, Archibald M	TSG		
R	Iantorno, Charles F	CPL		Chicago, IL

CFC	Slagowski, Clyde L.	TSG	AF37086506	
LG	Turner, Dewell	CPL		Conway, AR
RG	Dickerson, Paul	CPL		
TG	Whitaker, Bill	SGT		Hazard, KY
?	Laird, Deane F.	1LT		
?	Markel, Carroll B.	MAJ		

(S)Substitute *Not listed on KORWALD ?Data Uncertain

Charlie Flight: 370th Bombardment Squadron

Charlie Flight Lead, Aircraft SN# 44-70151

Posit.	Name-L.F. M.	Rank	S/N	Home Town
A/C	Shields, Thomas L.	CPT	AO-837209	Valley Stream, NY
P?	Penninger, Roger W.	1LT	AO-778935	Elsinore, CA
B?	Smith, Ted W.	CPT		
N?	Wahlgren, Edward C.	CPT	AO-695357	Valley Stream, NY
RO?	Goldbeck, Emil B.	CPT		
FE	Hamblin, Robert W.	MSG	AF12127986	Richmond Hill NY
R?	Dougherty, Joseph S.	SSG	AF13041845	Erie, PA
CFC	Gross, William A	SGT	AF6950944	
LG?	West, Carl E.	CPL	AF13346889	Ravenwood, WV
RG?	Webb, Edward A	SGT	AF18350787	Oktaha, OK
TG(S)	Stainbrook, Paul E. Jr.	CPL		
?	Vretis, James G.	1LT	AO-590680	East Moline, IL
OBS?	. O'Neal, Julius	LTC	4792A	Fairfax SC

	E.			

?Data Uncertain   (S)Substitute

Charlie Flight #2, Aircraft SN# 44-86395

Posit.	Name-L.F. M.	Rank	S/N	Home Town
A/C	Field, Donald L.	MAJ		
P	Pafe, Basil	1LT		
B	Kelly, Charles	1LT		
N(S)	Walsh, Ray	CPT		
RO	Higgins, James			
FE	Kroboth, Francis	MSG		Nazareth PA
R(S)	Moore, Edward	SGt		
CFC?	Shaw, Parker C.	SSG		
LG?	Seward, James E.	PFC		
RG?	Holt, Christopher	SSG		
TG?				
?				
OBS?				

?Data Uncertain   (S)Substitute

Charlie Flight #3, Aircraft SN# 44-61824

Posit.	Name-L.F. M.	Rank	S/N	Home Town
A/C	Dempsey, Peter	CPT		
P	James, ?			
B	Wagenhalls, John	CPT		
N	Aragima, Michael	CPT		
RO	Carter, Paul	1LT		
FE?				
R?				
CFC?				
LG?				

RG?				
TG?				

?Data Uncertain Not Placed: FE: Ammons, James

F-84: 111TH FTR BMB

Posit.	Name-L.F. M.	Rank	S/N	Home Town
P	Shewmaker, John W.	CPT	AO-956997	Harrodsburg, KY
P	Schirra, Walter			

RF-80: 15TH TAC RCN SQ

Posit.	Name-L.F. M.	Rank	S/N	Home Town
P	Duquette, Norman E.	2LT	AO-956997	Plattsburg NY
P	Powell, Raymond	2LT		

Killed or Missing in Action (27)

(Listed Alphabetically)

Black, Wayne Forrest	CPT	372BS
Botter, William Joseph	TSG	372BS (also POW)
Coffey, Arthur A.	CPL	372BS
Cogswell, Robert Whitney	MAJ	301BWHQ
Dougherty, Joseph Stephen	SSG	370BS
Edwards, Morton G	CPT	372BS
Foulks, James Arch Jr.	CPT	372BS
Fuehrer, Alois Anton	SSG	372BS
Gallant, James Alvin	SGT	371BS
Hays, Melvin Blaine	SGT	371BS

Horner, John Joseph	1LT	371BS
Hudson, Laurence Harold	1LT	371BS
Krumm, Robert Mitchell	CPT	371BS
Marshall, Isreal, Jr.	CPL	371BS
McAdoo, Ernest Robert	SSG	371BS
Mooradian,Ara	CPT	372BS
Newswanger, Quentin L.	TSG	370BS
Nutting, John Mainard	CPT	371BS
O'Neal , Julius Elliot,	LTC	370BS
Penninger, Roger William	CPT	370BS
Poyner, Con Foly	1LT	371BS
Shewmaker, John William	CPT	111FBS
Shields,Thomas Lester	CPT	370BS.
Vretis, James George	1LT	370BS
Wahlgren, Edward Charles	CPT	370BS.
Webb, Edward Arvil	SGT	370BS
West, Carl Emmons	CPL	370BS

Wounded in Action (20+)

Bisson, Norvin T.	SGT	372BS
Carroll, John W.	L/C	372BS
Beissner, Fred L. Jr.	1LT	371BS
Goldbeck, Emil B.	CPT	370BS
Gross. William A	SGT	370BS
Johnson, Gerald Emmett	CPL	371BS
Johnson, Johnny M	MSGT	371BS
Jones, James	SGT	372BS
Kiser, Kenneth	SSG	372BS
MacClean, Gerald	SGT	372BS
Menlo, Johnny	MSG	371BS
Osborne, Jess Alex, Jr.	CPL	371BS.
Reeter, William	1LT	372BS
Smith, Ted W.	CPT	370BS
Stainbrook, Paul	CPL	370BS
Strine, Jone	SSG	372BS
Victor, Russel B.	SSGT	372 BS
Walters, Herman L.	TSGT	372BS
Wentworth, Lloyd	1LT	372BS

Thornton, Glen S.	LT	372BS
Unidentified (with Reeter)		372BS
Unidentified (with Reeter)		372BS
Unidentified (with Reeter)		372BS

Prisoners of War (8)

James Jones	SGT	372BS
Johnson, Gerald Emmett	CPL	371BS
Johnson, Johnny M	MSGT	371BS
Kiser, Kenneth	SSG	372BS
MacClean, Gerald	SGT	372BS
Osborne, Jess Alex, Jr.	CPL	371BS.
Strine, Jone	SSG	372BS
Wentworth, Lloyd	1LT	372BS

Soviet Crew Rosters (Known): MiG-15bis

303rd GIAD – Strike Group (58 MiGs)
Overall Group Commander – LTC Smorchkov

18th GIAP – 20 MiG-15bis

1st Squadron (8 aircraft)
    LTC Aleksander P. Smorchkov (group leader)
    MAJ A. F. Maznev (squadron leader)
2nd Squadron (6 aircraft)
    CPT V. N. Shalev (squadron leader)
    SLT V. I. Stepanov (wingman)
    SLT Vasiliy Shabanov (wingman)
3rd Squadron (6 aircraft)
    CPT Pavel N. Antonov (squadron leader)
    SLT Lev N. Shchukin (flight leader)
    SLT I. I. Shavsha (element leader)
    SLT V. A. Kornev (wingman)

523rd IAP – 18 MiG-15bis

1st Squadron (6 aircraft)
    MAJ Dmitriy P. Os'kin (deputy CO)
    MAJ A. P. Trefilov (squadron leader)
    SLT Valentin P. Filimonov (wingman)
    SLT Dmitriy A. Samoylov (element leader)
    SLT M. A. Zykov (wingman)
    CPT Grigoriy Kh. D'yachenko (Zampolit)
    SLT A. M. Shevarev (wingman)
2nd Squadron (6 aircraft)
    MAJ Stepan A. Bakhayev (squadron leader)
    CPT Viktor P. Popov (deputy squadron leader)
    CPT N. I. Mitrofanov (Zampolit)
    SLT N. G. Kovalenko (element leader)
    SLT Rybalko (wingman)
3rd Squadron (6 aircraft)
    CPT Mazilov (squadron leader)
    SLT Vasiliy M. Khurtin (pilot)

17th IAP – 20 MiG-15bis

1st Squadron (8 aircraft)
    MAJ Boris V. Maslennikov (deputy regimental CO)
    CPT Stepan S. Artemchenko (squadron leader)
    CPT Nikolay V. Sutyagin (deputy squadron leader)
    SLT Sergey S. Bychkov (flight leader)
    SLT Vasiliy F. Shulev (Zampolit)
2nd Squadron (6 aircraft)
    CPT Mikhail S. Ponomaryev (squadron leader)
    CPT Ivan N. Morozov (flight leader)
3rd Squadron (6 aircraft)
    CPT Mikhail N. Shcherbakov (squadron leader)
    SLT Aleksey N. Nikolyaev (element leader)

324 GIAD – Covering Group (26 MiGs)
Overall Group Commander – LTC. Vishnyakov,

176th GIAP – 14 MiG-15bis

1st Squadron (8 aircraft)
    LTC Sergey F. Vishnyakov (Commander 176th GIAP
    CPT Ivan A. Suchkov (deputy regimental commander)
    CPT Petr S. Milaushkin (deputy squadron leader)
    CPT Grigoriy I. Ges' (flight leader)
3rd Squadron (6 aircraft)
    CPT Sergey M. Kramarenko (squadron leader)
    SLT Ikar Gulyy (wingman)
    CPT Ivan V. Lazutin (element leader)
    SLT Sergey A. Rodionov (wingman)

196th IAP – 12 MiG-15bis

1st Squadron (6 aircraft)
    LTC Aleksey I. Mitusov (deputy regimental CO)
    CPT Lev N. Ivanov (squadron leader)
3rd Squadron (6 aircraft)
    MAJ Nikolay K. Shelamonov (squadron leader)

Soviet Killed in Action

SLT Vasiliy M. Khurtin (KIA on return to base)

Selected Biographical Sketches of Combatants

Beissner, Fred L: Pilot on Baker Two. Separated from the Air Force in 1952 to attend the University of Texas. Became an aerospace engineer with Convair, LTV, and finally for contractors at NASA Langley until his retirement in 1994. He has a daughter, three sons, and three grandkids.

Cummings, Arch: Flight Engineer on Baker Three. Enlisted in Army Air Corps in 1943, and graduated from pilot training a year later. Three years after the end of WW II he enlisted again and wound up as a B-29 Flight Engineer. After Korean War he was recalled as a 2nd Lt. and assigned to B-25 training. Became a Maintenance Officer in F-105s. After retirement Arch worked 25 years as an instructor for United Airlines.

Dickerson, Paul: Right gunner on Baker Three. Passed away in February, 2003 and was buried at Arlington.

Fogler, Clarence I: Aircraft Commander on Able One. In 1966, while assigned to a Strategic Air Command,'s 306th Bombardment Wing at McCoy AFB, Florida, Fred Meier and "Fog" teamed up once again, this time in B-52s.

Gray, R. W: Commander, 15th TRS at Kimpo. Pilot and adjutant of the lst Strat Recon Sqdn under Erv Wursten and Ray Eakes. Later became Asst. Personnel Officer at Wing Hqtrs. Assigned to Forbes from MacDill, left there when the base closed and went to Barksdale. Flew P-38s in the Southwest Pacific in WWII, and RF-80s and RF-86s in the Korean War.

Griner, William: Aircraft Commander on Baker Three. He stayed in the Air Force untill 1974, and was one of the first to pilot the SR-71 at Beale AFB.

Kramarenko, Sergey Makarovich: MiG Commander,176th Regiment. Married Yulya Alekseyevna, and raised two children, elder son Aleksandr Sergeyevich and daughter, Nadezhda Sergeyevna. Kramarenko became aviation adviser in Iraq in the early 1970s and later in Algeria and achieved the rank of General-Major of Aviation before retiring. On the anniversary of the Korean War he was invited to the United States by veteran American pilots that he said "treated me very well . . . They were my adversaries then, but my friends now. We decided it was better to talk to each other around a table covered in vodka bottles than to take aim at each other."

Kroboth, Francis: Flight Engineer on Charlie Two. Enlisted in the Army Air Corp in 1940 and hauled coal in 1949 during the Berlin Airlift. Taught Social Studies after retiring in 1968.

McQuade, James R: Pilot on Baker Lead. With Reeter's recommendation, McQuade was upgraded to aircraft commander and given his own crew.

Meier, Frederick: Navigator on Able Lead. Flew with Fogler again in B-52s in 1966. Eighteen years after Black Tuesday, he went back (in his words) "to fight the same enemy." He became a squadron commander in the 460th Tactical Recon Wing, Tan Son Nhut AB, Vietnam, 1969-70, flew backseat in an F4 but was wounded near his quarters by a rocket burst. He returned to duty as commander of the 360th TEWS, a unit that "flew fancy Goony Birds. After retiring he received a degree in Education, began a teaching career, moved to Spokane and then went into the stock brokerage business where he stayed until 1995.

Miller, Rolland: Gunner on Able Lead. The Black Tuesday mission was his 52nd and last daylight mission. Crew flew four more night missions before being sent home and eventually stationed at Lake Charles Air Force Base. After leaving the Air Force, Miller became an investigator for the Federal Government and subsequently retired.

Moore, Edward: Substitute Radio Operator on Baker Three, commanded by Major William R. Griner, Jr. Joined the Marines when he was sixteen and served two years. Subsequently spent two years in the Air Force.

Nelson, Max: Radar Operator on 98BG mission, 24 October, 1951. Discharged after returning to states and got into photographic and computer retail sales until he retired in 1993. Since then he's been into computer programming and golf.

Pyfrom, Stanley C: Pilot on Able Lead. Entered the Army Air Corps in 1942 and served as a B-17 bombardier. Awarded a DFC for dropping a 500 lb bomb on a Nazi sub operating in the Gulf of Mexico. Entered pilot school in 1948. After his combat tour in Korean War, he served in Morocco, New Mexico, Greenland, and Japan. Retired in the Pensacola area, died from congestive heart failure on 9 April, 2000 and was buried with full military honors in Barancas National Cemetery.

Reeter, William Eldon: Aircraft Commander on Baker Lead. Awarded the Silver Star for his actions on Black Tuesday. After the Korean War, he transitioned to B-47s. Chosen in 1956 as SAC's Crew of the Year. In 1958, assigned to the first class of pilots to fly the B-58 Hustler, the world's fastest and most advanced bomber. Spent four years as a B-58 instructor at Carswell AFB in Fort Worth Texas and in late 1969 was assigned to fly the AC-119G Shadows in Vietnam. He died on September 6, 1999.

Smorchkov, Aleksandr Pavlovich: Veteran of the World War II and Commander of the 18th Aircraft Regiment & Second AE MiG-15 Flight Leader on Black Tuesday. Received "Gold Star" order for his service in the Korean War and "Hero of the Soviet Union." Retired as a Colonel. Honored as an "unsurpassed storyteller," he died on 16 November 1998.

Turner, Dewell: Substitute left gunner on Griner's aircraft. Born in 1932 in Van Buren County, Arkansas and enlisted June 6, 1950. After Namsi, he finished his tour on another crew, returned to Barksdale AFB, and was discharged in 1953. Married Shirley Russell, Ozark, Arkansas in 1957, took advantage of the GI Bill and earned a Social Sciences B. A. Worked for The Social Security Administration 35 years before retiring as Tulsa District Manager in 1992. Helped run his wife's clothing store until she retired in 1997. Three Children, one girl, two boys, five grandchildren, all boys, ages 4 to 15.

Wagenhalls, John: Spent most of 1951 assigned to the 370th Bomb Squadron. Returned to the US on the first day of 1952 after flying approximately fifty bombing missions.

Wentworth, Lloyd: Enlisted in the US Army Air Corps June 24, 1946 as a Private, Aircraft & Engine Mechanic School, Keesler Field, MS. Served as aircraft mechanic with 1252nd Air Transport Squadron, Westover Air Force Base, MA. Graduated from Navigation School October 12 1950. On 23 October 1951, as a 1Lt in the 372 Bomb Sqn., 307th Bomb Wing, Okinawa, was shot down on 49th mission in North Korea approximately 10 miles south of Chonju. Most of POW time was in Camp II, Pingchongi. Was returned to duty on the last day of the prisoner exchange in September 1953. After upgrading school, spent 10 years flying B-47s at Barksdale & Lockbourne AFB's. Flew 101 combat missions in Vietnam. Retired as a Colonel in 1970 with 24 years service. Completed college after retiring and is now the Controller for the Utility Commission in Albany, GA."

Notes

Chapter 1: The Mission

1. Author, logbook notes and personal memorabilia from Korean War, October 1951: 1.
2. Fifty-caliber ammunition crates were about the same size and shape as military-issued footlockers, and often used as such. I still have mine: 1.
3. On October 2, 1951 five other members of the crew and I were scheduled to test hop *The Outlaw* after it underwent battle damage repair. *The Outlaw's* nose art had been copied from a famous poster of Jane Russell, star of the Howard Hughes 1941 movie by the same name. Called the first "Sex Western," the movie was originally banned by US censors and not released to the American public until the late 40s. This "Outlaw" lived up to her name when number one engine failed during takeoff and the plane crashed. Although the aircraft broke in two, there were no serious injuries: 1.
4. Nick Kourafas, correspondence with Frederick Meier, 2001: 1.
5. Frederick Meier, e-mail to author, 5 May 2001: 1.
6. Spot promotions were given to bomber crews for specific duties performed under special circumstances, primarily as motivational tools. When either the duty or circumstance changed, the individual lost the spot promotion. Enlisted personnel attached to the 307th but assigned to another Bomb Group could not be promoted. (Miller, e-mail, 19 May 2001): 1.
7. Meier, e-mail to author, 23 February 2001: 2.
8. Meier, "Personal Diary for Tuesday, 22-27 October 1951": 2.
9. Rolland Miller, e-mail to author, 13 April 2001: 2.
10. Dewell Turner, e-mail to author, 14 February 2005: 2.
11. William Reeter, letter to his wife, 9 November 1951: 2.
12. "Aisle stand" was the common name for the tiny, uncomfortable aisle seat where instructors, observers, commanders, and the like rode when not performing crew duties--more accurately, an aisle *seat*: 2.
13. Fred Beissner, e-mail to author, 2006: 3.
14. Edward Moore, e-mail to author, 30 June 2006: 3.

15. Miller, e-mail, 26 April 2001: 3.

16. Archibald Cummings, e-mail to author 2007: 3.

17. Miller, e-mail, 13 April 2001: 3.

18. Although *Sit & Git* was painted as nose art on a 307BW B-29, its appearance was short-lived: 4.

19. A few accounts (including a flight simulation video game) have listed *Miss N. C.* as one of the B-29s that flew the Black Tuesday mission. This would not have been not possible. *Miss N. C.* was assigned to the 19BG and one of its crews on 23 October 1951. *Miss N. C.* did, however, fly with the 19BG on the April 12 mission described herein: 4.

20. Heavy weight takeoffs were often more dangerous than enemy opposition: 4.

21. Miller, e-mail, 13 April 2001: 4.

22. For some reason, crews in my unit (19BG, 28BS) were usually provided box lunches instead of the described rations: 4.

23. Meier, e-mail to author, 13 April 2001, et al: 4.

24. Cheju-do Information Network. "Introduction to Chejudo Island:" 5.

25. It took six years of research to uncover the identity of the ninth bomber in the Black Tuesday formation. Until members of Major Field's crew were finally located and interviewed, it had been widely accepted that only eight B-29s had attacked Namsi Airfield: 5.

26. John Duquette, *Everyman a Tiger Web Site*: 5.

27. John Duquette, e-mail, 14 April 2001: 5.

28. Diego Zampini, e-mail, 14 March 2005, et al: 5.

29. Information based on an interview with General-Major Georgiy Ageyevich Lobov published in *Aviatsiya i Kosmonavtika* magazine (November 1990): 5.

30. The instrument on the pilot's panel was called a PDI (Pilot Directional Indicator): 6.

31. Researched records show Taechon also spelled with an end *g* (Taechong): 6.

32. Alan Reeter, interview by author, 2002, et al: 6.

33. Miller, e-mail: 6.

34. Krylov: 6.

35. German Askold, and Igor' Seidov. *Red Devils on the 38th Parallel.* Trans. Stephen L. Sewell: 6-7.

36. Leonid Krylov and Yuriy Tepsurkayev. "The Black Week for Bomber Command" (*Mir Aviatsiya,* Russia, 1999): 6-7.

37. Meier, e-mail: 7.

38. Miller, e-mail: 7.

39. Paul Dickerson, e-mail to author, 2001: 7.

40. Duquette, e-mail: 7.

41. Norman Duquette, "Black Tuesday." *Everyman a Tiger Web Site*: 7.
42. John Duquette, e-mail, 14 April 2001: 7.
43. Meier, "Personal Diary": 8.

Chapter 2: The Korean Air War

1. Author, logbook notes and personal memorabilia from Korean War, October 1951: 9.
2. The material in this and following chapters contains an amalgamation of sources too numerous to list in their entirety. Moreover, a single paragraph may contain information obtained from several sources, as well as the author's personal experiences. The following authors supplied the main body of documentation for this chapter and are listed in the approximate page order in which their material is first referenced:
3. John Biewen, *The Cold War Turns Hot*. American Radioworks; American Public Media: 10.
4. James Bradley, *Flyboys: A True Story of Courage* (New York: Little Brown and Company, 2003): 10.
5. Timothy Warnock, ed. *The U.S. Air Force's First War: Korea 1950-1953 Significant Events*: 12-30.
6. Robert Dorr and Warren E. Thompson, *The Korean Air War*: 11-23.
7. John Pike, "Korean War." http://www.globalsecurity.org/military/ops/korea.htm: 12-15.
8. Robert Futrell, *The United States Air Force in Korea, 1950-1953*: 12.
9. David Mets, "The Not-So-Forgotten War, Fodder for Your Reading on the Air War in Korea a Half Century Later:" 12.
10. U. S. Senator Joe McCarthy, a Wisconsin Republican, became famous for making claims that there were Communists in the federal government, but his tactics and his inability to substantiate his claims led to his being censured by the Senate. In the American lexicon, the noun "McCarthyism" most often alludes to the use of unfair investigatory methods in order to supress opposition: 12.
11. Air Force Historical Studies Office, *Steadfast and Courageous: FEAF Bomber Command and the Air War in Korea, 1950-1953*: 14-28.
12. Dean Acheson, "Secretary of State Dean Acheson Memorandum of conversation, September 7, 1950" (*Papers of Dean Acheson* Truman Presidential Library): 14.

13. John Bruning, *The Air Battle for Korea 1950-53*: 15.

14. In World War II more than 330,000 Allied troops were evacuated from the French beaches near Dunkirk as the German army closed in around them: 16.

15. Joseph Baugher, "B-29 in Korean War:" 16.

16. Air Force Historical Studies Office, *Steadfast and Courageous: FEAF Bomber Command*: 16.

17. One of the most challenging and successful amphibious operations in military history, the Inchon invasion was conceived and executed by General Douglas MacArthur over the objections of most other commanders: 16.

18. After a number of incidents, "Close air support" was usually conducted beyond the "bomb line, " a line on the ground forward of which aircraft could expend ordnance without fear of hitting ground troops and without have to coordinate with friendly ground troops (i.e. through forward air controllers). It was usually drawn by the ground force commander at the range limit of field artillery . . . 15-20 miles north of the front lines (Duquette, e-mail, 19 May 2001): 16, 22, 23 & 25.

19. Rolland Miller recalled night combat sorties designated as "Bulldog" or "Phantom" missions, where they dropped their bombs on ground controlled targets "in the vicinity of the bomb line." Sometimes they would have to make several passes before releasing their load, and in some instances messages were sent back that they had hit the target-- an indication that friendly observers were close enough to immediately assess the damages. (Miller, e-mail, 19 May 2001): 16, 22, 23 & 25).

20. Walter Karp, "Truman vs. MacArthur." American Heritage Magazine, April/May 1984: 20.

21. Larson, George, "Final Glory of the Superfortress." *Military History*: 20.

Chapter 3: The Combatants

1. "Korean Defense Service Medal." Foxfall Medals, <http://www.foxfall.com/csm-common-kdsm.htm> (Foxfall Press, Inc. 2007): 29

2. The "Korean Defense Service Medal" was authorized and signed into law by President George W. Bush in December 2002 in recognition of the ongoing Korean conflict, 1954 to present: 29.

Secret Soviet Involvement

1. In a twenty aircraft regimental Soviet sortie the normal break would be 8-6-6 for the 1st, 2nd and 3rd Squadrons with the regimental commander or group leader flying with the 1st Squadron. Eighteen aircraft most likely equate to a 6-6-6 breakdown, 14 to an 8-6 and 12 to a 6-6 with only two squadrons each in the latter two formations (Sewell, e-mail, 16 September 2006, et al.): 29.

2. Ralph Wetterhahn, "The Russians of MiG Alley," *Retired Officer* August 2000: 29-44.

3. Aleksandr Smorchkov, "Interview to the Russian newspaper" (*Komsomolskaya Pravda*, June 1950): 29-30.

4. Sergey Kramarenko, *In the Skies of Two Wars* (Moscow 2003): 30.

5. Diego Zampini, e-mail to author, 1 October 2006: 30-31.

6. Kramarenko: 31.

7. Boris Abakumov, "The Unknown War: In the Skies of North Korea," trans. Stephen Sewell (Kursk, Russia: *Pravda*, 1997): 31-34.

8. Zampini, e-mail to author, 1 October 2006: 34.

9. Stephen Sewell, e-mail to author, 25 February 2005: 35.

10. _____, e-mail, 25 February 2005: 35.

11. Smorchkov, Interview: 36.

12. "Makhonin" was probably Bud Mahurin, the American fighter ace shot down on 13 May 1952: 37.

13. Warren Thompson and David McLaren, *MiG Alley Sabres vs. MiGs Over Korea* (Specialty Press, 2002): 37.

14. Zampini, e-mail, 24 April 2006: 37.

15. Frank Farrell, *No Sweat.* 1st Books, 2005: 38.

16. _____, e-mail to author, 26 April 2006: 38.

17. Zampini, e-mail, 11 September 2006: 38.

18. _____, e-mail, 14 March 2005: 39-40.

19. Sewell, e-mail: 18 April 2001: 40.

20. Zampini, e-mail: 24 April 2006: 42.

21. Sewell, e-mail: 18 April 2001: 42.

22. Leonid Krylov and Yuriy Tepsurkayev, "The Black Week for Bomber Command" (*Mir Aviatsiya,* Russia, 1999): 42-44.

23. "Missing in MiG Alley." Nova. PBS Television: 42-44.

24. German Askold, and Igor' Seidov, *Red Devils on the 38th Parallel.* Trans., Stephen L. Sewell: 42-44.

America's "Retreads"

1. Author, logbook notes and personal memorabilia from Korean War, October 1951: 45.

2. Frederick Meier, e-mail to author, January 7 2007, et al: 45.

3. Max Nelson, e-mail to author, 6 May 2006: 46.

4. John Bruning, *Crimson Sky: The Air Battle for Korea 1950-53* (Brassey's, 1999): 46.

5. Author, notes: 46.

6. Meier, e-mail, January 7 2007: 47.

7. Pike, John, ed., "Randolph AFB, Texas" (globalsecurity.org, 30 January 2008): 47-48.

8. Peter Bowers, *Boeing B-29 Superfortress*, Warbird Tech Series, Vol. 14 (North Branch MN: Specialty Press Publishers, 1999): 48.

9. Anthony Queeno, e-mail to author, 2006: 48.

10. Frank Farrell, telephone conversation, January 2008: 48.

11. CFCs were also referred to as "ring gunners." (Farrell): 48.

12. Author, notes: 48-49.

13. Wikipedia, free encyclopedia. ".45 ACP," (30 January 2008): 49.

14. ____, ".22 Hornet," (30 January 2008): 49-50.

15. Author, notes: 50.

16. Alan Reeter, e-mail to author, 17 February 2006, et al: 50-52.

17. Stan Kavrik, interview by the author, 11 July 2006: 52.

18. Max Nelson, e-mail, 6 May 2006, et al: 53-54.

19. The author recalls buying a case of beer for his crew: 54.

20. Author, notes: 54-55.

21. Kavrik, interview, 11 July 2006: 55.

22. Meier, e-mail, 30 April 1951: 55.

23. Glenn Garig, e-mail to author, 12 January 2006: 55.

24. Farrell, e-mail to author, 6 August 2006: 55.

25. Author, "B-29s in the Korean War Nose Art," 30 January 2008: 55-56.

26. Author, notes: 56.

27. C. J. Christ, e-mail to author, 24 January 2006: 57.

28. Author, "B-29 . . . Korean War Nose Art:" 57.

29. Garig, e-mail, 12 January 2006: 58.

30. Meier, e-mail, 10 December 2006, et al. 58.

31. Author, notes: 58-59.

32. Christ, e-mail, 24 January 2006: 59-60.

33. Author, notes: 60.

Chapter 4: The Machinery of War

1. Author, logbook notes and personal memorabilia from Korean War, October 1951: 61.
2. Yefim Gorden, *Mikoyan-Gurevich MiG-15* (Midland Publishing, 2001): 61.
3. Davis, Larry. *Air War Over Korea: A Pictorial Record* (Carrollton, TX: Squadron/Signal Publications, 1982): 61-62.
4. N. L. Volkovskiyand I. V. Petrova, eds., Stephen Sewell, trans. *The War in Korea 1950-1953* (*Izdatel'stvo Poligon*, Russia, 2000): 62.

Radio and Radar

1. Sewell, Stephen, e-mail to author, 5 February 2003: 63.
2. Cookie (Sewell) notes that Soviet documents show that they knew all eight frequencies used by B-29 formations, who were using them, and what each channel was used for. The Soviets were also able to access tactics and formations from monitoring radio and radar: 63.
3. N. L. Volkovskiy and I. V. Petrova, eds., Stephen Sewell, trans. *The War in Korea*, et al: 63-65.

SHORAN

1. Ned Scholz, "SHORAN." *Welcome to SuperNed'sWebsite*: 66-69.
2. Barker, Hal and Ted Barker, comp., "1st SHORAN Beacon Unit," *Korean War Project*: 66-69.
3. Max Nelson, e-mail to author, 25 January 2007, et al: 66.
4. Although Max could not pinpoint the location of the SHORAN stations, his computation of probable distance and azimuth placed the "L" station on Tok-Cho-Do Island, 20 miles off the Inchon Coastline in the Yellow Sea, and the "H" station just south of the 38th parallel on the east coast. Namsi would have been nearly 250 miles from that "H" station; however, Max felt that the bombers could not have had access to a second nearer station because the arcs had to intersect at "close to a 90 degree angle" to be accurate: 66.
5. Frank Farrell, *No Sweat*. Bloomington IN: 1st Books, 2005: 66-67.
6. Ray Coia, e-mail to Frank Farrell, forwarded to author, 31 January 2007: 67.
7. Nelson, e-mail: 67-68.

8. Frank "Bud" Farrell, e-mail, 7 February 2007, et al: 68.

9. Bud pointed out the likelihood of Soviet electronic intelligence using direction-finding equipment to precisely locate SHORAN stations. (In WW II the Germans were in the process of locating U.S. SHORAN stations in the winter of '44-'45). Once the stations were located the Soviets could have used this information for aerial interception as well as for positioning AAA on the ground: 68.

10. Adrian Narducci, e-mail to Frank Farrell, forwarded to author, 7 February 2007: 68.

11. Nelson, e-mail, 25 January 2007, et al: 68.

12. 98th Bombardment Wing Headquarters, *SHORAN Operator's Bombing SOP*: 68-69.

13. Farrell, e-mail, 7 February 2007: 69.

14. Author, logbook notes from Korean War, October 1951: 69.

15. Farrell, e-mail: 69.

16. Nelson, e-mail, 28 January 2007: 69.

Antiaircraft Artillery (AAA)

1. Volkovskiy, N. L. and I. V. Petrova, eds., Stephen Sewell, trans. "Chapter 12. Organization of Air Defense of Objects in the Rear and Ways to Inform Air Defense Artillery Assets," *The War in Korea 1950-1953* (Saint Petersburg, Russia 2000): 70-74.

2. Stephen Sewell, e-mail to author, 23 December 2006, et al: 70.

3. Ron Maynard, ed. *KORWALD - Korean War Aircraft Loss Database,* 2001: 71.

4. Frank " Bud" Farrell, e-mail to author, 17 April 2006: 72.

5. Bud felt (and I agree) that several B-29 losses attributed to MiGs were actually lost due to AAA--especially at night toward the end of the war: 72.

6. Ray Coia, e-mail to author, 11 February 2007: 74.

The Boeing B-29 Superfortress

1. Peter Bowers, *Boeing B-29 Superfortress*, Warbird Tech Series, Vol. 14 (Specialty Press Publishers): 74-75.

2. Anthony Pomata, "Boeing B-29 Superfortress Bomber--A Snapshot History." *HistoryLink.org*: 74-78.

3. Chester Marshall, *B-29 Superfortress*. Osceola WI: Motorbooks International, 1993: 74-78.

4. Pimlott, John. *B-29 Superfortress*, Chartwell Books Inc., 1980: 74-78.

5. Author, logbook notes and personal memorabilia from Korean War, October 1951: 75.

6. Bill Gunston, *The Encyclopedia of the World's Combat Aircraft*, Chartwell Book, Inc., 1976: 75-76.

7. Bowers, *Boeing B-29 Superfortress*: 76.

8. Author: 77-78.

9. Bombs going astray also accounted for a number of "friendly fire" incidents during close support missions: 78.

10. Rolland Miller, e-mail to author, 10 March 2001: 78

11. Wayland Mayo, "The 19th Bomb Group in Korea." *B-29's Over Korea*: 78-79.

12. Joseph Baugher, "Douglas XBLR-2/XB-19," <http://home.att.net /~jbaugher2/b19.html> (1 February 2008): 79.

13. Bowers, *Boeing B-29 Superfortress*: 79.

14. Anthony Queeno, e-mail to author, 2006: 79-80.

15. Author, notes: 80.

16. Queeno, e-mail: 81.

17. Scott Hards, "An afternoon with Saburo Sakai." *Warbird Digest*, 1998: 80-81.

18. There is considerable evidence that LBJ never completed this particular mission: 80-81.

19. Diego Zampini, e-mail to author, 14 March 2005: 81-82.

20. Bowers, Boeing B-29 Superfortress: 82.

21. Marshall, *B-29 Superfortress*: 82.

22. Stone, Charles, "RB-29 Crew Operations." *Recollections of an RB-29 Crew in Japan*: 82-83.

23. Bowers: 83.

24. Author, notes: 83.

25. Since no one on the crew ever saw one, the mischief-makers were *assumed* to have been "rats," most probably the desert variety. Given the circumstances, it is entirely possible they were, in fact, gremlins. A gremlin is defined as "an imaginary gnome like creature who causes difficulties in aircraft." Korean War era B-29s had no shortage of gremlins: 83.

26, Marshall: 83-84.

27. Author, notes: 84.

28. James Foster, e-mail to author, 18 January 2006, et al: 84-85.

Mikoyan-Gurevich MiG-15

1. Yefim Gorden, *Mikoyan-Gurevich MiG-15: The Soviet Union's Long-lived Korean War Fighter* (Midland Publishing, 2001): 85-96.
2. Gunston, Bill. *The Encyclopedia of the World's Combat Aircraft.* (New York: Chartwell Book, Inc., 1976): 86.
3. Stephen L. Sewell, e-mail to author, 2001-2007: 86.
4. Zhang, Xiaoming, *Red Wings Over the Yalu* (Texas A&M Press, 2002): 87.
5. "Missing in MiG Alley." Nova. PBS Television: 88-96.
6. Sewell, e-mail, 20 April 2001: 88-89.
7. ____, 25 January 2006: 88.
8. German Askold, and Igor' Seidov. *Red Devils on the 38th Parallel.* Trans. Stephen L. Sewell: 88-96.
9. Sewell, e-mail, 20 April 2001: 90.
10. Igor Seidov, e-mail to Diego Zampini for author, 16 September 2006: 93-94.
11. Zampini, e-mail: 91.
12. Sewell, e-mail, 5 January 2005: 94.

Chapter 5: Prelude to Disaster

1. Ron Maynard, ed. *KORWALD - Korean War Aircraft Loss Database,* 2001: 99.
2. James Foster, e-mail to author, 18 January 2006: 99.
3. Author, logbook notes and personal memorabilia from Korean War, October 1951: 99.
4. Dorr, Robert F. *B-29 Superfortress Units of the Korean War* (Osceola WI: Osprey, 2003): 100.
5. Ralph Livengood, *B29 Navigator Korean War 1951* (Bloomington IN: 1st Books, 2003): 100.
6. Rolland L Miller, postal and E-mail to author, 2001: 100.
7. Frederick Meier, e-mail to author, 24 February 2001: 100-101.
8. Meier wrote: " . . .21 degrees of right drift put us 7 miles into Manchuria:" 101.
9. ____, e-mail, 30 May 2001: 101.
10. Sergey Kramarenko, *In the Skies of Two Wars* (NPP Del'ta Publishing, Moscow 2003): 101-102.
11. Livengood, e-mail, 18 February 2004: 102.

12. Ralph Livengood put to rest once and for all the claim that Miss N. C. flew on the Black Tuesday mission. Ralph wrote, "As for Miss NC let me assure you an airplane with that nose art and tail # 6376 was in the 19th BG and I flew ten missions in it including the April 12 mission:" 102.

13. Livengood, *B29 Navigator Korean War 1951*: 102-103.

14. ____, e-mail to author, 2005: 104.

15. Vincent Scarano, "Vincent Scarano Remembers the Deadly April 12, 1951 Bombing Mission Against the Bridges Over the Yalu River." *B-29s in the Korean War*: 103-104.

16. Ron Maynard, ed. *KORWALD - Korean War Aircraft Loss Database,* 2001:104.

17. Diego Zampini, e-mail to author, 14 March 2005: 104-106.

18. Igor Seidov, e-mail to Diego Zampini for author, 11 September 2006: 106.

19. Leonid Krylov and Yuriy Tepsurkayev, "The Black Week for Bomber Command." *Mir Aviatsiya*9: 110.

20. Australian War Memorial, "Typhoon Ruth - 14-15 October 1951:" 106-109.

21. Dewell Turner, e-mail to author, 5 December 2006: 106-108.

22. Miller, e-mail to author, 13 April 2001: 108.

23. Robert Jackson, *Air War Over Korea* (New York: Charles Scribner's Sons, 1973): 109.

24. Robert Futrell, *The United States Air Force in Korea, 1950-1953*: 109.

25. John Bruning, *Crimson Sky: The Air Battle for Korea 1950-53*: 109.

26. Joseph Savko, e-mail to author, 2004-2006: (Joe provided aircraft serial numbers cited throughout this text.): 110.

27. *Steadfast and Courageous: FEAF Bomber Command and the Air War in Korea, 1950-1953.* Air Force Historical Studies Office (Pentagon, Washington, DC, 2000): 110.

28. Aleksandr Smorchkov, Interview to the Russian newspaper, *Komsomolskaya Pravda*, June 1950: 110.

29. Foster, e-mail, 18 January 2006: 111-112.

30. C. J. Christ, e-mail to author, 24 January 2006: 112.

31. ____, telephone conversations with author, 2005-2007: 112.

32. To C. J. and his navigator, the attacking MiG appeared to be firing wing guns. Since there is no evidence that MiG-15s of the era ever mounted wing guns, it is more likely that the large cannon flashes appeared to spread to the leading edges of the wings: 112.

33. Smorchkov, "Interview:" 112-113.

34. Maynard, *KORWALD*: 112-113.

Chapter 6: Target: Namsi Airfield

1. There are, however, references to "carpet bombing" at the onset of the Korean War—a practice that was apparently stopped immediately: 115.

2. Author, logbook notes and personal memorabilia from Korean War, October 1951: 115.

3. Livengood, *B29 Navigator Korean War 1951*: 115.

4. John Duquette, e-mail to author, 14 April 2001: 115.

5. Harden, E. R. "Alone, Unarmed and Unafraid." *Everyman a Tiger Web Site*: 115.

6. Leonid Krylov and Yuriy Tepsurkayev, "The Black Week for Bomber Command" (*Mir Aviatsiya*, Russia, 1999): 116.

7. James Johnson was the Wing Commander of the famed 4th Fighter Interceptor Wing flying F-86 *Sabres*. Nicknamed the "Mayor of Sabre Jet City," he was credited with ten MiG-15s destroyed, three probables, and nine damaged to become the first double jet ace wing commander. Johnson graduated from the University of Arizona in 1939 and won his wings in 1940. When the Japanese attacked Pearl Harbor, he commanded the 43rd Pursuit Squadron, flying P-40 *Warhawks,* responsible for the protection of the Panama Canal. In Europe he flew P-47s as commander of the 48th Fighter Bomb Group and by war's end had flown 92 missions and scored one victory against an Fw-190. Johnson next saw combat in Korea. When Johnson married in 1979, his best man was Barry Goldwater: 116.

7. This author believes that James Johnson's "Stupid idea" remark could be expanded to include all airfields that were under construction in North Korea. It is fairly incomprehensible that they should think they could survive a U.N. onslaught that could only get worse. Alternative thought, however, suggests that the airfields themselves might have been built as bait for an elaborate trap: 116.

8. Thompson, Warren E. and David R. McLean, *MiG Alley Sabres vs. MiGs Over Korea* (North Branch MN: Specialty Press, 2002): 117.

9. Krylov and Tepsurkayev, "The Black Week for Bomber Command:" 117-118.

10. John Bruning, *Crimson Sky: The Air Battle for Korea 1950-53* (Dulles, VA: Brassey's, 1999): 117-118.

11. N. L. Volkovskiy and I. V. Petrova, eds., Stephen Sewell, trans., " . . . Organization of Air Defense . . ." *The War in Korea 1950-1953* (Saint Petersburg, Russia, 2000): 118.

Chapter 7: Black Tuesday

1. Frederick Meier, e-mail to author, 4 May 2001, et al: 119.
2. Robert Jackson, *Air War Over Korea* (New York: Charles Scribner's Sons, 1973): 119.
3. *Historical Data Report for 307th Bomb Wing Medium Combat Echelon, Oct 1951* (US Air Force Historical Agency: Maxwell Field Ala., 1978): 119-140.
4. Robert Futrell, *The United States Air Force in Korea, 1950-1953*: 119-140.
5. John Bruning, "Death Ride to Namsi," *Crimson Sky: The Air Battle for Korea 1950-53* (Dulles, VA: Brassey's, 1999): 119-140.
6. Various accounts of the Black Tuesday mission have listed the number of B-29s as anywhere from eight to 25. Most American writers agreed on "eight," a figure that was likely derived from an entry in the above cited 307th reference, which states, " . . . the Wing lost three aircraft to enemy action and two aircraft sustained major battle damage . . . Three other aircraft, also receiving major battle damage, are being repaired locally." This entry probably led to the assumption that these eight were the only aircraft that flew the mission. In fact, Major Field, flying in the Charlie Two position returned undamaged. A later reference in the 370BS "Engineering" section makes note of the following, "On the 23rd of the month <u>four</u> (my emphasis) of our aircraft flew a combat mission and only three returned safely. Aircraft 44-70151 (Shields) was destroyed by the enemy. Aircraft 44-61824 (Dempsey) suffered major battle damage." Field commanded the third B-29. The fourth B-29 aborted and was replaced by Field. In addition to the above references, I have jpeg images of navigator's flight logs that list <u>nine</u> aircraft. Exaggeration was not limited to the Russian viewpoint. Almost all "official" reports regarding the Black Tuesday mission state that 150 MiGs attacked the B-29s. The actual count was 44: 119-140.
7. Diego Zampini, e-mail to author, 14 March 2005, et al: 120.
8. Diego wrote, "The Russian MiG-15 pilots were in cockpit alert, waiting for the order to scramble . . . they knew something important was about to happen, because the previous day (22 October) (they) detected a single "recce" aircraft taking pics of Namsi . . . (and) were sure that the next day the airbase would be 'visited':" 120.
9. Stephen Sewell, e-mail to author, 2005: 120
10. On Black Tuesday the 196th IAP 2nd Squadron was on R & R at Port Arthur: 120.

11. German Askold and Igor' Seidov. *Red Devils on the 38th Parallel.* Trans. Stephen L. Sewell (Kyiv, Ukraine: Ruslan Publishing, 1998): 120-121.

12. Zampini, e-mail, 14 March 2005: 121.

13. After tangling with the F-86 Sabres a few times during departure south of the Yalu River, the Russians climbed to 11,000 meters (36,000 feet) or higher before crossing the Yalu (Zampini): 121.

14. Zampini, e-mail, 14 March 2005, et al: 121.

15. Francis Kroboth, telephone interview by author, 2007: 121.

16. John Duquette, e-mail to author, 13 May 2001: 122.

17. N. L. Volkovskiy and I. V. Petrova, eds., Stephen Sewell, trans., "... Organization of Air Defense:" 122.

18. Rolland Miller, e-mail to author, 13, 20 April & 16 May 2001: 122.

19. Miller's piece of flak was recovered by the ground crew that repaired their airplane: 122.

20. Dewell Turner, e-mail to author & photos, 23 February 2005: 122.

21. Edward Moore, e-mail to author, 9 September 2006: 122.

22. Alan Reeter, interview by author, 2002: 123.

23. Leonid Krylov and Yuriy Tepsurkayev, "The Black Week for Bomber Command" (*Mir Aviatsiya,* Russia, 1999): 123.

24. Fred Beissner Jr., e-mail to author, 8 February 2006, et al: 123.

25. Krylov and Tepsurkayev: 123-124.

26. Askold and Seidov. *Red Devils on the 38th Parallel:* 124.

27. Anthony "Tony" Queeno, e-mail to author, 18 January 2006: 124.

28. Tony, ex B-29 gunner, estimated the effective range of the bomber's .50 caliber guns was 600 yards: 124.

29. Sewell, e-mail, 20 April 2001: 124.

30. Meier, e-mail, 19 April 2001, et al: 124.

31. Meier recalled, "The 'intelligence' people suggested it (AAA) was from German 88's, radar tracking and altitude assisted:" 124.

32. _____, 28 April 2001: 124.

33. Nick Kourafas, target photo of Namsi Airfield, 14 October 1951: 124.

34. Meier, e-mail, 4 May 2001: 125.

35. Miller, e-mail, 13 April 2001: 125.

36. Rolland wrote, " . . . You can see the cloud formations below us (in the photo) and why we used the SHORAN method for the run . . . (I need) to explain why I took the picture of '045' instead of looking for MiG's. We had just passed through an area of extremely heavy anti-aircraft fire. The bursts around us had diminished and we had not received any radio warnings about MiG's. I thought we were in the clear. I wanted to get a picture of 100 pounders being dropped so I clicked away. About a minute after that, T/Sgt. Marvin Hoke the radio operator said over the intercom that MiG's were in the vicinity. I looked up and

they were everywhere . . . One MiG made a pass on "045" and hit him. Smoke and flames were coming from the #2 engine and wing and the aircraft started an immediate decent. I started shooting at the incoming MiG's and had to look away from '045'. I did get a glimpse of it just before it went into the clouds and saw two chutes quite a distance behind the aircraft:" 125.

37. John Wagenhalls, e-mail to author, 28 December 2001: 125.

38. Moore, e-mail, 9 September 2006: 126.

39. Kroboth, telephone conversation with Edward Moore, e-mail to author, 27 August 2007: 126.

40. Zampini, e-mail, 31 August 2001: 127.

41. Bruning, *Crimson Sky: The Air Battle for Korea 1950-53*: 127.

42. Wally Schirra was the only astronaut to fly all of America's first three space programs: 127.

43. Askold and Seidov, *Red Devils on the 38th Parallel*: 127.

44. Edward Unser, email to John Duquette, forwarded to author, 14 April 2001: 127.

45. Krylov and Tepsurkayev: 127-128.

46. Askold, and Seidov: 127-128.

47. Miller, e-mail, 128.

48. Nick Kourafas, "Personal Notes From 22 October 1951 through 27 October 1951:" 128.

49. Meier, e-mail, 4 May 2001: 128.

50. Miller, e-mail, 2 February 2001: 129-130.

51. Turner, e-mail, 23 February 2005: 130.

52. Paul Dickerson, telephone interview and e-mail to author, 2002: 130.

53. Beissner, e-mail, 8 February 2006: 130-131.

54. Fred wrote, " . . . BAD FIRE . . . Mayday calls and another round of attempted damage control, then bailed out . . . I free fell until out of the undercast, and then after orienting myself (over water but in sight of the coast), I looked around and saw the other three chutes from the front above me but in plain sight. Almost immediately I saw the plane hit the water with the left wing following. We barely got out in time:" 130-131.

55. Turner, e-mail, 23 February 2005: 132.

56. Wagenhalls, e-mail, 28 December 2001, et al: 132-133.

57. Miller, e-mail, 14 April 2001: 133.

58. Miller, e-mail, 19 May 2001: 133.

59. Miller, wrote, "I can remember having fighters framed in the orange dots of the gun sight reticle ring and pushing the firing button and the guns would not fire. This occurred when we banked to the left:" 133.

60. Duquette, e-mail, 13 May 2001: 133.

61. The 1777th's claim may have been valid. It is not clear which, exactly, caused two of the bombers to catch fire, AAA or cannon fire: 133.

62. Askold and Seidov, *Red Devils on the 38th Parallel*: 133.
63. Miller, e-mail, 19 May 2001, et al: 133-134.
64. Turner, e-mail, 23 February 2005: 134.
65. Wagenhalls, e-mail, 28 December 2001, et al: 134.
66. Moore, e-mail, 9 September 2006: 134.
67. Beissner, e-mail, 8 February 2006: 134.
68. Australian War Memorial. "War at Sea: The Royal Australian Navy in Korea:" 134-135.
69. Duquette, e-mail, 16 May 2001, et al: 135.
70. _____, e-mail, 28 May 2006: 135.
71. Beissner, e-mail, 8 February 2006: 135.
72. Alan Reeter, interview by the author, 2004: 136.
73. Alan Reeter, e-mail to author, 2004-2006: 136-137.
74. Kourafas, "Personal Notes:" 136.
75. William Reeter, letter to his wife, 9 November 1951: 136.
76. Turner, e-mail, 23 February 2005, et al: 137.
77. Evans, Douglas K. *Saber Jets Over Korea: A Firsthand Account.* (Blue Ridge Summit, PA: Tab Books, Inc, 1984): 137-138.
78. Ruffin Gray, email to John Duquette, forwarded to author, 16 April 2001: 138.
79. _____ e-mail to author, 22 May 2001: 138.
80. John Masterson, e-mail to John Duquette, forwarded to author, 16 April 2001: 139.
81. Meier, e-mail, 4 May 2001,et al: 139.
82. Fred Meier remembered: "They put away the Gugenheimer (cheap whiskey) and brought out the Seagrams and CC (Canadian Club):" 139.
83. Igor Seidov, e-mail to author, trans. by Diego Zampini, 11 September 2006, et al. 139.
84. Samoylov witnessed both of O'skin's claimed B-29 kills: 139.
85. Ron Maynard, cd. *KORWALD - Korean War Aircraft Loss Database*, 2001: 139.
86. Author, notes: 139.
87. Kourafas, "Personal Notes:" 139-140.

Chapter 8: Aftermath

1. Turner, e-mail & photos to author, 14 February 2005: 141.
2. Edward Moore, e-mail to author, 30 June 2006, et al: 141.
3. Miller, e-mail to author, 12 April 2001, et al: 141.
4. John Duquette, e-mail to author, 14 April 2001, et al: 141.

5. Ernest Harden, "Alone, Unarmed and Unafraid," *cottonpickers.org*: 141-142.

6. Miller, e-mail to author, 13 April 2001, et al: 142.

7. Frederick Meier, e-mail to author, 8 April 2001, et al: 142-144.

8. Meier wrote, " We were not aware that we had a 37mm cannon shell in the #3 fuel tank until the ground crew started the repair:" 142.

9. _____, "Personal Diary for Tuesday, 22-27 October 1951:" 143.

9. Moore, e-mail, 30 June 2006, et al: 144.

10. William Reeter, letter to his wife, 9 November 1951: 144.

11. Air Force Historical Studies Office, *Steadfast and Courageous: FEAF Bomber Command and the Air War in Korea, 1950-1953*: 145.

12. Author, logbook notes and personal memorabilia from Korean War, October 1951: 145.

13. *Time Magazine.* "Air War: An Old Lesson," October 1951: 145.

14. Max Nelson, e-mail to author, 6 May 2006, et al: 145-147.

15. Pilot Flimsy, 98th Bomb Wing, Operations Order 335-51, 24 October 1951, "Jakeman Able and Jakeman Baker Flights:" 146.

16. Leonid Krylov and Yuriy Tepsurkayev, "The Black Week for Bomber Command" (*Mir Aviatsiya,* Russia, 1999): 146.

17. Stan Kavrik, interview by the author, 11 July 2006: 146.

18. Krylov and Yuriy Tepsurkayev, et al: 146.

19. Nelson, e-mail, 6 May 2006, et al: 147.

20. Diego Zampini, e-mail to author, 14 March 2005, et al. 147.

21. Kavrik, interview, 11 July 2006: 146-148.

22. Author, notes: 148-149.

23. The date Vandenberg scrubbed our mission has not been ascertained. The event itself, however, is burned in my memory. On 10-27-51 we flew a night "primer" mission, which was similar to a GCA in that we were verbally directed by radio transmission against military targets near the front lines. The daylight variety was called a "golfball" mission. After a short R&R, we flew a golfball on 11 November: 149-150.

24. Anthony Queeno, e-mail to author, 30 January 2006: 149.

25. Krylov and Yuriy Tepsurkayev, et al: 150.

26. Zampini, e-mail, 28 April 2006, et al: 150.

27. Joseph Savko, e-mail to author, 26 April 2006: 150.

26. Ron Maynard, ed. *KORWALD - Korean War Aircraft Loss Database,* 2001: 150-151.

27. Author, notes: 151.

28. Farrell, email, 17 April 2006: 151.

29. Farrell's book, *No Sweat,* covers the hazards of night bombing in great detail: 151.

30. Turner, e-mail, 23 February 2005: 151.

Chapter 9: Analysis, Conclusions . . .

1. Author, "Black Tuesday Over Namsi" (*VFW* 89, no.2, October 2001): 153.
2. John Duquette, e-mail to author, 23 May 2001, et al: 153.
3. John noted that "Futrell's Official USAF account lists no F-86s lost on 23 October 1951, but shows three F-86 pilots MIA on that date:" 153.
4. *Historical Data Report for 307th Bomb Wing Medium Combat Echelon, Oct 1951* (US Air Force Historical Agency: Maxwell Field Ala., 1978): 153.
5. Author, logbook notes and personal memorabilia from Korean War, October 1951: 153-167.
6. John Duquette, *Everyman a Tiger Web Site*, et al: 154.
7. Duquette, e-mail, 23 May 2001, et al: 154-155.
8. _____, e-mail, 28 May 2001: 156.
9. Yefim Gorden, *Mikoyan-Gurevich MiG-15* (Midland Publishing, 2001): 156.
10. Bill Gunston, *The Encyclopedia of the World's Combat Aircraft* (New York: Chartwell Book, Inc., 1976): 156.
11. Anthony Queeno, e-mail, 30 January 2006, et al: 156.
12. Scott Hards, "An afternoon with Saburo Sakai." *Warbird Digest*, 1998: 157.
13. Air Force Historical Studies Office, *Steadfast and Courageous: FEAF Bomber Command and the Air War in Korea, 1950-1953*, et al: 158.
12. Farrell, email, 15 April 2006: 158.
13. Leonid Krylov and Yuriy Tepsurkayev, "The Black Week for Bomber Command" (*Mir Aviatsiya* Russia, 1999): 158.
14. Stephen Sewell, e-mail to author, 6 December 2006: 158.
15. _____, comp., *Russian Claims from the Korean War: 1950-53*: 159-160.
16. *Pacific Stars and Stripes*. "Huge Aerial Slugfest Costs Reds 18 MIGS." October 1951, et al: 159-160.
17. Ron Maynard, ed. *KORWALD - Korean War Aircraft Loss Database,* 2001, et al: 161.
18. Author, notes, et al: 161-165.
19. It should be pointed out that although there were only nine aircraft on the Namsi mission, these nine B-29s carried 180,000 pounds of bombs, a load that would have required thirty B-17s in WW II: 165.

20. Sergey Kramarenko, I*n the Skies of Two Wars* (Moscow 2003): 165.

21. Author, notes, et al: 166-167.

BIBLIOGRAPHY

Abakumov, Boris S. "The Unknown War: In the Skies of North Korea."
Kursk, Russia: Pravda, 1997.

Acheson, Dean. "Secretary of State Dean Acheson Memorandum of
conversation, September 7, 1950." *Papers of Dean Acheson* Truman
Presidental Library, <http://www.trumanlibrary.org/hstpaper/
acheson.htm#mocf> (8 January 2008).

Alfond, Dolores Apodaca, comp,"Korea Cold War." *National Alliance of
Families For the Return of America's Missing Servicemen.*
<http://www.nationalalliance.org/ > (11 January 2008).

Australian War Memorial. "War in the Air: The Royal Australian Air
Force in Korea." *Out in the Cold, Australia's Involvement in the
Korean War.* <http://www.awm.gov.au/korea/ausinkorea/raaf/
raaf.htm > (10 January 2008).

_____. "Typhoon Ruth - 14-15 October 1951." *Korean War 1950-53.*
<http://www.anzacday.org.au/history/korea/ruth.html> (10 January
2008).

_____. "War at Sea: The Royal Australian Navy in Korea."
<http://www.awm.gov.au/korea/ausinkorea/navy/navy.htm> (10
January 2008).

Askold, German and Igor' Seidov. *Red Devils on the 38th Parallel.*
Translated by Stephen L. Sewell. Kyiv, Urkaine: Ruslan Publishing,
1998.

_____. "1st SHORAN Beacon Unit, <http://www.koreanwar.org/
html/units/usaf/1shoran.htm> (31 January 2008).

Baugher, Joseph. "B-29 in Korean War." April 17, 2000.
<http://home.att.net/~jbaugher2/b29_12.html> (10 January 2008).

_____ "Douglas XBLR-2/XB-19." October 14, 2003.
<http://home.att.net/~jbaugher2/b19.html> (1 February 2008).

Biewen, John. *The Cold War Turns Hot* American Radioworks;
American Public Media. <http://americanradioworks.publicradio
.org/features/korea/a1.html> (10 January 2008).

Bowers, Peter M. *Boeing B-29 Superfortress*. Warbird Tech Series, Vol 14. North Branch MN: Specialty Press Publishers , 1999.

Bradley, James. *Flyboys: A True Story of Courage*. New York: Little Brown and Company, 2003.

Bruning, John R. *Crimson Sky: The Air Battle for Korea 1950-53*. Dulles, VA: Brassey's, 1999.

Cheju-do Information Network. "Introduction to Chejudo island." <http://www.chejuinfo.net/intro/e_int.html> (8 January 2008).

Davis, Larry. *Air War Over Korea: A Pictorial Record*. Carrollton, TX: Squadron/Signal Publications, 1982.

Dooner, William R, "Thunderjets Over Korea," *Air Classics*, 1980.

Dorr, Robert F. *B-29 Superfortress Units of the Korean War*. Osceola WI: Osprey, 2003.

_____ and Warren E. Thompson,. *The Korean Air War*. Osceola WI: Motorbooks International, 1994.

Drogobych, 293720 Ukraina. *Small Air Forces Observer* vol. 17 no. 1 (65). January 1993.

Duquette, John N., *Everyman a Tiger Web Site*, 2000-2008. <http://www.cottonpickers.org/> (11 January 2008).

Duquette, Norman E., "Black Tuesday." *Everyman a Tiger Web Site*. 2000-2008. < http://www.cottonpickers.org/Main.htm> (10 January 2008).

Eksuzyan, Robert. "Little Fanfare for Korean war Veterans." <http://www.aeronautics.ru/nws002/korean_war_soviet_pilots_reuters.htm> (10 January 2008).

Evanhoe, Ed. "Confirmed Soviet Aces in Korea 1950-53." *The Korean War*. <http://www.korean-war.com/sovietaceskorea.html> (10 January 2008).

Evans, Douglas K. *Saber Jets Over Korea: A Firsthand Account*. Blue Ridge Summit, PA: Tab Books, Inc, 1984.

"Fact Sheet." United States of America Korean War Commemoration.

<http://korea50.army.mil/history/factsheets/air_f_fs.shtml>
(9 January 2008).

Farrell, Frank *No Sweat*. Bloomington IN: 1st Books, 2005.

Futrell, Robert F. *The United States Air Force in Korea, 1950-1953*. New York: Duell, Sloan and Pearce, 1961.

_____ and Albert Simpson. "United States Air Force Operations in the Korean Conflict 25 June - 1 November 1950," USAF Historical Study No. 71. 1952.

_____ *Tactical Employment of Strategic Air Power in Korea*.

German, Askol'd Andreyevich and Igor' Atayevich Seidov. *Red Devils Over the 38th Parallel*, First Edition. Kiev, Ukraine: OOO Ruslan 1998.

Gordelianow, Igor M. (SAFCH #1066), *Small Air Forces Observer* vol. 17 no. 1: Drogobych, Ukraina. January, 1993.

Gorden, Yefim. *Mikoyan-Gurevich MiG-15: The Soviet Union's Long-lived Korean War Fighter*. Hinkley, England: Midland Publishing, 2001.

Gunston, Bill. *The Encyclopedia of the World's Combat Aircraft*. New York: Chartwell Book, Inc., 1976.

Harden, Ernest R. "Alone, Unarmed and Unafraid." *Flying*: May 1954. <http://www.cottonpickers.org/alone,_unarmed,_unafraid.htm> (22 January 2008).

Hards, Scott "An afternoon with Saburo Sakai." *Warbird Digest*, 1998 <http://www.warbirdforum.com/sakai.htm> (11 January 2008).

Headquarters, 98th Bombardment Wing (M) (ADVON). *SHORAN Operator's Bombing SOP*. APO328: 1 February 1952.

Historical Data Report for 307th Bomb Wing Medium Combat Echelon, Oct 1951. US Air Force Historical Agency: Maxwell Field Ala., 1978.

Jackson, Robert. *Air War Over Korea*. New York: Charles Scribner's Sons, 1973.

Karp, Walter. "Truman vs. MacArthur." American Heritage Magazine. April/May 1984. <http://www.americanheritage.com/articles/ magazine/ah/1984/3/1984_3_84.shtml> (22 January 2008).

"Korean Defense Service Medal." Foxfall Medals. <http://www. foxfall.com/csm-common-kdsm.htm> Foxfall Press, Inc. 2007.

Korean War Project. Compiled by Hal and Ted Barker. <http://www.koreanwar.org/index.html> (10 January 2008).

Korobov, Anatoliy and Voyennye Znaniya. "The Special Tour To...The Secret War." *Russian Defenders - People of Honor and Duty.* 2005.

Kramarenko, Sergey Makarovich. *In the Skies of Two Wars.* NPP Del'ta Publishing, Moscow 2003.

Krylov, Leonid and Yuriy Tepsurkayev. "The Black Week for Bomber Command." *Mir Aviatsiya* (Russia), 1999.

Larson, George A "Final Glory of the Superfortress ." *Military History*, 03982, 1998.

Livengood, Ralph. *B29 Navigator Korean War 1951.* Bloomington IN: 1st Books, 2003.

Marshall, Chester. *B-29 Superfortress.* Osceola WI: Motorbooks International, 1993.

Maynard, Ron, comp. *KORWALD - Korean War Aircraft Loss Database.* 2001. <http://www.dtic.mil/dpmo/pmkor/korwald_afct.htm> (11 January 2008).

Mayo, Wayland. "The 19th Bomb Group in Korea." *B-29's Over Korea.* <http://www.b-29s-over-korea.com/19th_bombgroup/19th_Bomb _Group_Korea.html> (11 January 2008).

McGill, Earl J. "Black Tuesday Over Namsi." *VFW* 89, no.2 (October 2001): 42-45.

_____ *B-29s in the Korean War Nose Art.* <http://home.comcast.net/~ noseart/0noseart.html> (30 January 2008).

Mets, David R. "The Not-So-Forgotten War, Fodder for Your Reading on the Air War in Korea a Half Century Later." *Air & Space Power Journal* - Winter 2003.

"Missing in MiG Alley." Nova. PBS Television, 18 October, 2007. Transcript posted on <http://www.pbs.org/wgbh/nova/transcripts/3418_warplane.html>

Nelson, Max. *98th Bomb Wing Korea 1951.* <http://www.ccchemet.com/nelson/98th.html> (11 January 2008).

Pacific Stars and Stripes. "Huge Aerial Slugfest Costs Reds 18 MIGS." October 1951.

Pike, John, ed. "Korean War." *Military.* <http://www.globalsecurity.org/military/ops/korea.htm > (16 January 2008).

_____, "Randolph AFB, Texas." *Military.* <http://www.globalsecurity.org/military/facility/randolph.htm 30 January 2008).

Pimlott, John. *B-29 Superfortress.* Secaucus, NJ: Chartwell Books Inc., 1980.

Pomata, Anthony E. "Boeing B-29 Superfortress Bomber -- A Snapshot History." *HistoryLink.org.* <http://www.historylink.org/essays/printer_friendly/index.cfm?file_id=3828> (10 January 2008).

Russian Claims from the Korean War: 1950-53. Translated and Compiled by Stephen L. Sewell. <http://www.korean-war.com/sovietunion.html> (8 January 2008).

Scarano, Vincent. Vincent Scarano Remembers the Deadly April 12, 1951 Bombing Mission Against the Bridges Over the Yalu River." *B-29s in the Korean War.* < http://mywebpages.comcast.net/b29 sinthekoreanwar/Scarano1.JPG> (22 January 2008).

Sea Power Centre Australia. "HMA Ship Histories, HMAS Murchison." <http://www.navy.gov.au/spc/history/ships/murchison.html> (10 January 2008).

_____ "HMA Ship Histories: HMAS Sydney III." <http://www.navy.gov.au/spc/history/ships/sydney3.html> (10 January 2008).

Scholz, Ned. "SHORAN." *Welcome to SuperNed's Website.* <http://www.angelfire.com/ne2/nedpage/ > (8 January 2008).

Seidov, Igor'. "Shield of the Night." *Mir Aviatsi,* pp. 29-34. Translated by Stephen Sewell). Russia: January 1993.

Smorchkov, Aleksandr Pavlovich. Interview to the Russian newspaper, *Komsomolskaya Pravda,* June 1950.

Soviet Air Order of Battle - Korea 1950-53. Translated and Compiled by Stephen L. Sewell. <http://www.korean-war.com/ussrairorderofbattle.html> (11 January 2008).

Steadfast and Courageous: FEAF Bomber Command and the Air War in Korea, 1950-1953. Air Force Historical Studies Office, Pentagon, Washington,DC. 2000.

Stone, Charles S. "RB-29 Crew Operations." *Recollections of an RB-29 Crew in Japan.* < http://www.rb-29.net/index.htm> (8 January 2008).

Thompson, Warren E. and David R. McLaren, *MiG Alley Sabres vs. MiGs Over Korea.* North Branch MN: Specialty Press, 2002.

Time Magazine. "Air War: An Old Lesson," October 1951.

Turner Publishing Company. "American Ex-Prisoners of War", Paducah, KY 1988, p 176.

U. S. Department of Defense. "DoD Announces Korean . . . Medal." <http://www.defenselink.mil/releases/release.aspx?releaseid=7063> (8 January 2008).

Volkovskiy, N. L. and I. V. Petrova, eds. *The War in Korea 1950-1953. Izdatel'stvo Poligon.* Translated by Stephen L. Sewell., Saint Petersburg Russia 2000.

Warnock,, Timothy A., ed. *The U.S. Air Force's First War: Korea 1950-1953 Significant Events,* 2000. <http://afhra.maxwell.af.mil/korean_war/korean_war_chronology/kw_contents.html> (8 January 2008).

Wetterhahn, Ralph. "The Russians of MiG Alley." *Retired Officer* August 2000.

Wikipedia, the free encyclopedia. ".45 ACP," et al.

<http://en.wikipedia.org/wiki/.45_ACP> (30 January, 2008).

Wintermute, R. L. "Namsi Vets Recall Action" Lake Charles AFB Newspaper, 1952.

Yaremenko, V.A, A.N. Pochtarev, and A.V. Usikov. V. A. Zolotarev, ed. *Russia (USSR) In Local Wars and Regional Conflicts In the Second Half of the 20th Century.* Moscow: Kuchkovo Polye Publishing, 2000.

Zaloga, Steven J. "The Russians in MiG Alley, Air Force Magazine Online, February 1991 <http://www.afa.org/magazine/1991/ 0291russian.asp> (8 January 2008).

Zampini, Diego. "Russian Aces over Korea." <http://www.acepilots.com/russian/rus_aces.html> (8 January 2008).

Zhang, Xiaoming. *Red Wings Over the Yalu.* College Station: Texas A&M Press, 2002.

Index

Kangdong, 22
Karasyev, Anatoly, 42
Karatayev, (Maj.), 96
Karlin, Anatolly, 91
Kater, (Sqdn. Leader), 135
Kavrik, Stan, **52-53**, 55, 146-148
Kelly, Joe, 25, 101, 144
Khominich (Lt.), 87
Khurtin, (Lt.), 122
Kimpo AFB, 7,13, **135-139**, 141, 154
Kiser, Kenneth, 131, 135
Korea
  history, 10
  Peninsula (geography), 11
  38th parallel, 21
Kormilkin, G., 35
Korniyenkom, Nikolay, 6, 127
KORWALD, 150, 161
Kourafas, Nick, 1-2, 7, 128-130, 133, 136, 139, 143
Koyu, 73
Kozhedub, Ivan, 33, 37, 40, 42
Kramarenko, Sergey, 30-31, 35, 39, 101, 165
Kroboth, Francis, 121
Krumm, Robert, 5-7, 119, 125,
Krylov, Leonid, 21
Kumanichkin, Aleksandr, 40, 42
Kurtin, V. M., 81
Kwaksan, 26

Lamb, Reginald, 106
Lavene, Harry, 19
Ledbetter, Henry, 2, 119, 139, 143
LeMay, Curtis, 137
Lewis, James, 5, 139, 141
Litvinyuk, Sasha, 33
Livengood, Ralph, 102-
Lobov, Georgiy, 42, 90

MacArthur, Douglas , 12, 14-17, 20, 22
MacClean, Gerald, 135

Manchuria
  bases, 17, 40, 167
  everyday (Soviet) life in, **31-34**
  sanctuary, 22, 113
Mao Tse Tung, 17
Markel, (Major), 139, 141
Marshall, George, 12
Martin, Joseph, 22
Maslennikov, (Major), 121, 124
Masterson, John, 139
maximum effort mission, 100
McCarthy, Joe, 12
McQuade, James, 132
Medyantsev, (Lt. Col.), 133
Meier, Fred, 1-2, 4, 7, 45, 47, 100-101, 108, 124-125, 128, 134, 142-144
Michelson, Bill, 135
MiG Alley, 6, 20
Mikoyan-Gurevich MiG-15, 18-19, 23-24, **85-97**,
  armament, 92
  limitations, **91-95**, 161, 164
  problems, 89-90, 99
  tactics, 40-43
Miller Rolland, 2-4, 6-7, 78, 100, 122, 125, 128-130, 133-134, 141
Miss Behavin', 146, 148
Miss Minooky, 146
Miss N. C., 102
Mitchell, Ronald, 106
Mitusov Aleksey, 32, 121
mongoose, 108
monsoon season, 105
Mooradian, Ara, 131, 135
Moore, Edward, 3, 122, 126 128-129, 141, 144
morale, 105, 148, 164
Moscalenko, K., 30
M.P.I., 146
Murcheson, HMAS, 134-135

Made in the USA
Charleston, SC
27 November 2009